Becoming a World-Class Hunter
A Bow Hunter's Spiritual Journey

Sean C. McVeigh

D0807003

McVeigh Ministries, Inc.
Pennsylvania

Becoming a World-Class Hunter
A Bow Hunter's Spiritual Journey

Sean's Outdoor Adventures books may be ordered through booksellers or by contacting:
Sean's Outdoor Adventures
P.O. Box 300
Lamar, PA 16848
www.SeansOutdoorAdventures.com

Editor — Jayne McVeigh

ISBN: 978-1-937315-04-7 (paperback)
ISBN: 978-0-9841011-9-1 (eBook)

Library of Congress Control Number: 2014900308

Printed in the United States of America
January 8, 2014

Table of Contents

Introduction

In a very real sense, I started working on this book at the age of thirteen when my father first started taking me bow hunting for deer. For some reason, every time we entered the woods, I told the story in my mind of what was happening as if I was recording the events in a book for someone else to read. However, it wasn't until I was in my mid-thirties that I actually started to write those experiences down. Those writings and the many years of experiences that followed evolved into what you are now reading, *Becoming a World-Class Hunter: A Bow Hunter's Spiritual Journey!*

In the beginning of the first chapter, I recount some of my earliest hunting memories from before my dad even started taking me deer hunting. I also share some of the fundamental lessons I learned from those experiences. I hope these stories trigger some fond memories from your own childhood. I also hope you will spend some time happily thinking about those memories.

For those of you who are somewhat new to hunting, and don't have childhood hunting experiences to reminisce, I encourage you to imagine what it would have been like for you if you were in situations similar to the ones I explain.

After sharing a few of those early memories, I share the rest of my journey as a hunter into adulthood. In the process, I provide a large number of skills, lessons, and techniques I learned and developed along the way. This includes both practical hunting skills as well as a few prayerful and spiritual ideas. It is my hope that these ideas will enhance your own knowledge, understanding, and outlook on hunting. Perhaps they will even broaden your perception of what a world-class hunter truly is and how to become one yourself. Either way, I sincerely hope you will enjoy and appreciate what you are about to read! May God continue to bless and inspire you along the way!

Chapter 1 - The Beginning Stages of This Hunter

IN THE EARLY DAYS

For me, hunting began as a fun activity my older brother and I could do throughout the summer. When I was four years old, my brother and I nicknamed ourselves "The Bee Busters" as we walked around our barn with our little plastic recurve bows shooting the wasp nests off of the structure. When I think about those experiences now, it amazes me we were even able to hit such a small target back then!

In addition to "bee busting," there are two hunting stories in particular from my early childhood that make me laugh when I think about them now. The first one happened in the early fall while I was four years old. I was stalking through the tree line behind our house looking for pheasant. Halfway through the stalk I got the idea in my mind that it would be great to see a deer so that I could shoot it instead of a pheasant. Just after having this thought I looked to my left and saw a big doe and a very nice eight-point buck staring at me. They were about a hundred yards away across the field.

As soon as I saw the deer, I immediately became paralyzed with fear. In a state of panic, I backpedaled as fast as I could toward our house. Within three or four strides, I tripped and fell flat on my back. Although I was afraid to move, I knew I needed to get up and continue running in order to make it safely back to our house before the deer attacked me. As soon as I made it to my feet, I frantically looked over to see if the deer were running after me, but they were gone. Obviously, this happened before I learned that deer are timid animals that usually run away from humans as soon as possible.

On the Christmas that followed that incident, I received a small compound bow that had a ten pound pull draw weight. The simple fact that it had pulleys on the ends of the limbs enthralled me even though the bow was weaker than my recurve. At any rate, I had my next memorable hunting experience while using this compound bow. It happened the following spring.

1

The large flock of wild pheasant that lived in the overgrown field next to our house often came into our back yard near our garden to feed in the evenings. I frequently stalked through the yard after them but always had trouble getting close enough for a shot. On one particular night, as I made it to within 20 yards of the flock, I decided to try running at them as fast as I could. I then bolted at them as fast as my little legs would take me and made it to within about ten feet of the birds before pulling back and letting an arrow fly. I launched the arrow while still at full stride. To my amazement, it actually hit the bird I was looking at! However, the bow was so weak and the practice point on my arrow was so blunt that the arrow didn't even penetrate the skin. It just got lodged in the bird's feathers as it took off and flew away. I never saw that arrow again.

Although I find these stories humorous, I'm glad I never actually harvested a pheasant or shot at a deer when I was that young because I was not at the legal hunting age, and did not have a hunting license. I was just a little boy with a tenacious desire to hunt.

My dad also taught me that I should never run with a bow or arrow in my hands. Even though I didn't get hurt in either of the situations I just explained, I could have landed on an arrow if I tripped. This could have resulted in a very serious injury, so please don't run with a bow or arrow in your hands!

My experience with the pheasant also affirmed the fact that we need to always use a weapon that is strong enough to actually kill the animal we intend to hunt. We also should use the right style of tip on our hunting arrows such as a razor blade broadhead as opposed to a dull practice point.

PREPARATIONS FOR HUNTING SEASON

After growing out of that small compound bow, I switched back to using recurve bows that I either purchased at yard sales or received as hand-me-downs. The strongest one I had was made of fiberglass and had a thirty pound pull draw weight. However, the minimum draw weight required for deer hunting in Pennsylvania at that time was forty pound pull. This meant I didn't have the necessary equipment for hunting. Therefore, in the middle of the summer before I could legally hunt, my dad had me start using my mom's old compound bow. It had a forty pound pull draw weight. Unfortunately, I could barely pull it back.

To help strengthen my arms and shoulders, I sometimes exercised with bricks. I held a brick in each hand and made the same motions I would make while drawing back a bow. Initially I was only able to do this a few times before tiring out. Before long, I built my muscles up enough to be able to pull the bow back and hold it steady enough to shoot.

After using this compound for a few weeks, it became clear to me that I simply couldn't get the arrows to hit the target consistently where I was aiming. As a result, I decided to try putting sights on the bow like my dad used. I then bought the cheapest sight system they had for sale at the local hunting store.

In the evenings after my dad came home from work, he helped me get my bow sighted in. In doing this, he taught me that the sight pin moves in the direction of error. This means that if your arrow hit higher than where you were aiming, you loosen the sight pin, move it up, and then retighten it. Similarly, if the arrow hit to the left, you move the sight pin to the left, etc. You do this until the arrow hits where you were aiming on the target with the sight pin.

My father and I also attended the Pennsylvania hunting and trapping safety education course. The state required this before I could buy a hunting license.

I remember the safety education course as if it was yesterday, not because it was about hunting, but because I got to spend two whole days with my dad! It was one of the few times I got to spend that much time with him. Thinking about this and how much those two days meant to me has helped me realize just how important it is for me to spend time with my own family. Kids simply value the time their parents spend with them, and they value it more than parents often realize!

Another memorable thing I recall regarding my preparation for hunting season was when my dad gave me my first camouflage outfit. To me, that moment was sacred. We didn't have much money at that time, so the camouflage was not new. In fact, it was the old pair of army camouflage my dad wore in the early 1970s. I think he had also received the outfit as a hand-me-down. As a result, the fabric was very well worn, faded, softened, and comfortable.

Because of how special receiving that camouflage was to me, it has inspired me to create a small little ceremony for when I give my own kids their first set of camouflage for hunting. I believe this type of ceremony adds to the specialness of the hunt and the bond a child shares with his or her parent. I encourage you to do something similar if you ever have the opportunity to give a set of camouflage to someone you plan to take hunting for the first time.

FIRST BLOOD

When it was too dark outside to shoot at my target, I practiced drawing my bow in our house in order to continue building up my muscles. I'd grip the bow string tightly and slowly pull it back. I'd do this without an arrow on the string since I was indoors. After reaching full draw, I'd hold steady for a little while and then lower the string back down. I intentionally didn't release the string because I knew it could damage or ruin the bow if it was dry-fired (shot without an arrow on the string).

(Aside: I no longer practice pulling an unloaded bow because there is too much risk in damaging the bow or getting injured. Instead, I use elastic exercise bands. I encourage you to do the same if you are looking for a way to strengthen your muscles for archery.)

At any rate, on one particular night while drawing my bow in my bedroom without an arrow loaded, I reached full draw, held for a while, and then began to let down. In the process, I brought my hand that holds the bow toward me rather than just letting down with my hand that holds the string. The bow exerted a strong force on both of my hands and they sped up dramatically as they moved closer together. Suddenly, the top limb of the bow powerfully slammed into the glass light fixture directly above me in my room. Immediately after the impact, large shards of glass fell to the ground all around me. One of them struck my face. When it hit me, I felt a strong tug on my skin. In response, I quickly put my bow down on the bed. I then reached up and touched my face where I felt the hit. As I pulled my hand away, I saw that it was completely covered with blood.

Almost immediately after I looked at my hand, my dad stepped into the doorway of my room to see what the noise was. Without hesitating, he lunged at me and pinched my face to hold the wound closed and stop the blood from squirting out of my face. He then told me to follow him as he backpedaled through the hallway toward the stairs. He periodically looked over his shoulder to make sure we were not going to walk into anything.

My father and I made our way into the kitchen where my mom put a few butterfly bandages over the wound. This was done to help minimize the bleeding. We then went straight to the doctor's office where I received a set of stitches. Since the cut was above my lip on the right-hand side of my face, it almost looked as if I had half of a mustache by the time the doctor finished stitching. You can imagine the curiosity of my classmates at school the following morning!

MY FIRST FEW DEER HUNTS

Hunting created some of the happiest memories I have from that time period of my life. I was filled with intense joy every single time we stepped foot in the woods. Every aspect of each hunt seemed amplified in my senses. I can still vividly remember the smell and appearance of the goldenrod that grew alongside of the road where we parked our old, white, Chevy Nova at the public hunting ground where we hunted. I remember the many, annoying spider webs we often had to fight through in order to get to our hunting spots. I also vividly remember the smell of the freshly fallen leaves that littered the forest floor, and I loved the wonderful fragrance of the ferns that grew in various places in the forest. We even sometimes came across a box turtle or two as they slowly made their way across the ground. It always impressed me how they were able to make it around the many boulders, blown down trees, and other large obstacles they encountered on the forest floor.

As I enjoyed the sights and smells, I continued to tell the story in my mind of what my father was teaching me. The thing that makes me laugh now as I recall those memories is that I typically spent most of my mental energy thinking I was practicing the lessons better than my dad. For example, he showed me a technique for walking quietly through the woods. It involved landing the outside edge of your foot on the ground first. You then slowly lowered the rest of your foot while paying attention to what you could feel underneath it so that you didn't snap a twig.

After applying the lesson and paying close attention to the volume of both mine and my dad's walking, I thought to myself, "I'm much better at this than he is!" In the meantime, I could have walked directly past a deer without even noticing it because I was so focused on the ground in front of my feet and comparing myself to my dad. For this reason, I suggest remaining mindful of all aspects of the hunt while walking through the woods. Don't just get fixated on one or two things and lose sight of the big picture like I did.

FIRST BLOOD IN THE WOODS

The first time I drew blood while in the woods took place around the third time my father and I went hunting that season. I must have misunderstood him when he initially explained how I should get set up in my makeshift ground blind. I thought he said to start by taking the quiver off of my bow and leaning it against something near me. Afterward, I thought he said to nock an arrow on my bow string and then take another arrow out of the quiver to set in a place I could easily grab in case I needed to take a second shot. Lastly, I thought I was supposed to loosen another arrow but not take it all the way out of my quiver. Obviously, this last arrow was in case I needed to take a third shot.

About ten minutes after I got set up on this particular hunt, I decided to sit down. While diligently watching out in front of me for deer, I reached back with my right hand to feel for the ground as I began to sit. In the process, I put my hand directly on the fixed-blade broadhead attached to the end of my second arrow. The razor blade sliced right through my finger. There was no immediate physical pain, but I felt the blade going through my skin and muscle as it happened. I quickly brought my hand around in front of me to look at it. I could see almost to my bone just before blood started oozing out of the wound!

Although the cut was an awful sight, I didn't panic. I just thought quickly. Even though I didn't want to ruin the hunt, I knew I couldn't hold the cut closed for a few hours. It was bleeding way too much already! As a result, I reluctantly headed over to my dad's tree stand while holding the gash closed. As soon as I got there, I quietly called up to him saying, "Dad, I need you to come down here." He replied, "What?" I responded, "I cut my finger pretty badly. I need you to come down here." He quickly climbed down and off to the doctors we went.

Based on this accident, and the one where I shattered the glass light fixture in my bedroom with my bow, it is a good idea to maintain an awareness of your surroundings while using archery and hunting equipment! Also, *never* take an arrow out of your quiver and leave it lying around like I did in this last example! Similarly, when using a gun, never take the safety off unless you are aiming at your target and are ready to pull the trigger.

FIRST DEER SIGHTING

That hunting season ended, and I never even saw a single deer. The following season was a repeat of the first, minus the bloody accidents. After two seasons on the public hunting ground, and me not seeing a single deer, I thought we needed to find a new spot with more deer. I took it upon myself to find one.

Very often I'd ride my bike to a friend's house several miles away. As I rode up and down one particular road at night, I sometimes saw people spotlighting deer in a field. There was usually a good number of deer there with a few nice bucks in the group, so I told my dad about it. Surprisingly, he knew the man who lived next to the field, so we went and asked him for permission to hunt there. While we were standing in his driveway, a doe came out into the field and walked straight toward us. I thought this was a good sign!

We went back the following week to set up our tree stands. Mine was on the edge of the field near where the doe came out of the woods. My dad's stand was about forty yards to my left and twenty yards deeper in the woods.

This was going to be my first year hunting out of a tree stand. We couldn't afford to buy me one at that time, so we made a wooden platform using boards tightly secured to the branches with ropes. Although this worked in that situation, I would *not* recommend using this approach. An approved portable tree stand that securely straps to the tree is much better!

For a safety belt, we used three regular belts. One went around my waist, another went around the tree, and the third connected the two. Keep in mind that this took place in the mid 1980s. We were not as advanced with safety systems back then. It is now common and sometimes required for people to wear a full body harness safety system.

The morning of opening day was really exciting for me. My dad and I were in our tree stands early, and I thought for sure I was going to see my first deer while hunting. However, my hopes were slightly dampened just before daylight when two hunters came walking through the field toward me from the road. Although I kept shining my flashlight at them, they continued to walk in my direction. One of them went back into the forest. The other set up on the ground on the edge of the field about fifty yards to my left. He was also only about twenty-five yards from my dad. This really bothered me!

As it started to break daylight, it seemed as though things were turning in my favor. I say this because I heard a deer walking in my general direction from deep in the woods off to my right. Closer and closer the sounds came. Eventually it reached the edge of the field about sixty yards away to my right, but it remained inside the woods out of my sight. As I waited for the deer to step out into the open, my curiosity escalated! Was it a buck or a doe? If it was a buck, how big was he?

Five minutes passed before the deer finally stepped out into the field. It then stopped again and looked around for a brief moment. Although it was still fairly dark, I was able to see that it was a giant buck! His body and rack were silhouetted on the horizon, which enabled me to count each tine. He was a perfect ten-pointer! His rack was so symmetrical that the tines on the right side of his rack seemed to disappear behind the tines on the left side when he turned his head perfectly broadside.

The deer then started to walk again. Since there were so many branches blocking my view, I began bending and twisting in my tree stand trying to get another good look at him. After the buck went about twenty yards, he stopped and looked in my general direction. As soon as he did this, I froze still. A few moments later he spun around and gently trotted back into the woods. This greatly disappointed me! I immediately started wondering if the deer had seen me, or if he had seen or smelled the other hunter sitting on the ground to my left. Within a few minutes the other hunter got up and trudged across the field making noises of frustration and disgust. As soon as he reached the road, he turned left and walked down the hill out of sight in the direction he had originally come from.

Not long after sunrise, I heard a lot of noise coming from just inside the woods in the area where the big buck had gone. When my father and I got down out of our tree stands a few hours later, I told him about my buck sighting and the noises I heard. We immediately went over to investigate. Sure enough, there were several fresh buck rubs that had been made that morning. It seemed as though the buck hung around and made them before heading back into the forest. This excited me, and my hopes were high for the evening hunt! I thought for sure the big buck was going to come back and I was going to get a shot at him!

I remained enthusiastic and positive throughout the day while we were at home. My excitement remained elevated as I climbed into my tree stand that afternoon. I spent the first hour intensely daydreaming about the buck. However, no deer came to the field. Another hour passed, and still there were no deer. With each passing hour my emotions continued to drop a little bit more. By the time the hunt drew to a close, there were still no deer in the field. As a result, I went home feeling very depressed and disappointed.

Since hunting was not permitted on Sundays in Pennsylvania, and my dad had to work late on Monday, we didn't get back to our tree stands until Tuesday evening. Once again I started the hunt with high hopes and great expectations. However, as time went by, the feeling of disappointment began to take over again since no deer were coming to the field.

When there was just forty minutes left before dark, I heard a twig snap behind me. Without even thinking about it I turned my head around to look in that direction. To my shock and amazement, there were two doe and a buck walking broadside through the woods only twenty yards away!

There were plenty of occasions in my life where I had seen deer up close in the woods, but this was the very first time I saw one within shooting range while holding a weapon in my hand. I was completely unprepared for the way my body reacted. My heart immediately began pounding profusely. In fact, my heart was thumping so hard, and slamming so violently into my ribcage, that it seemed as if it was going to jump right out of my chest! The intense emotions I experienced at that moment were so strong that I had trouble thinking clearly. I then realized I was breathing so loudly that it sounded as if I was hyperventilating. It is a miracle the deer didn't hear me and run away! As soon as I realized how loudly I was breathing, I immediately closed my mouth and forced myself to calm down.

After calming myself a little, I thought about shooting. Largely because the belts I was wearing for a safety system were not very sturdy, and the platform I was standing on was not overly solid, I didn't feel comfortable leaning out around the side of the tree in order to draw my bow and shoot. Since the deer were headed straight toward my dad, I decided to just let them pass me.

All three deer walked directly under my dad's tree stand, and I watched as he drew back his bow. He loosed the arrow and dropped the buck dead in his tracks. Since the buck continued to shake as he lay on the ground, my dad shot him again through the vitals to quickly finish the job.

After the deer stopped moving, I called out "Nice shot," but my dad didn't hear me. I quickly and excitedly prepared to get down. As I lowered my bow, something caught my attention in my peripheral vision in the direction the deer had come from. I immediately turned my head and was surprised to see a hunter stalking through the woods in my direction. The hunter noticed me lowering my bow and came over. Once I reached the ground, the two of us went over to my dad who had just gotten down out of his tree stand. The hunter and I watched as my dad picked up the buck's head by the antlers and inspected his rack. It was a perfect eight-pointer and the nicest

buck my dad had ever harvested up to that point in time.

This was the happiest I had ever seen my dad! I loved getting to see the joy and excitement on his face as he counted each point on the buck's rack for the purpose of filling out his deer harvest tag.

Meanwhile, another hunter appeared. We didn't even know he had been set up about seventy-five yards away on the other side of my dad. The two men proceeded to tell us that they had seen this buck while spotlighting and that there were several other bucks even bigger than him in the area. The evening concluded with my father and me dragging his deer to the car!

There are multiple lessons I was able to take from this hunt. First, have a good, sturdy tree stand and a solid safety harness system so that you feel safe and secure in the stand. These pieces of equipment are necessary to be able to draw your bow back with confidence and take accurate aim at your target. Secondly, be prepared for "buck fever." Buck fever is when you experience an intense adrenaline rush when you see a game animal while hunting. You can see thousands of game animals throughout the year, but it may not be until you are actually hunting with a weapon in your hand that your spirit will feel the intensity of what is happening. Especially for those of you who have not yet experienced this type of adrenaline rush, expect it to be more intense than you imagine it could be.

Another thing I learned from this hunt is to be aware of other hunters and the deer's reaction to them. The hunter that was stalking through the woods was intentionally trying to push deer to his friend, which was actually a good idea. It would have worked but he didn't know my father and I were there. Because of our location, the deer had to pass by us before reaching his friend. If you are ever hunting in pairs, and are having trouble seeing deer, you may even want to try pushing deer toward your friend or have your friend push deer toward you.

In addition, it never occurred to me before hunting this area that deer would walk parallel to a field about twenty yards inside the woods. I always thought they would simply come from deep in the forest and walk straight out into the field like the ten-pointer did on opening morning. After studying numerous hunting areas after that day, I have found many that have had deer trails running parallel to the edge of a crop field. These trails are typically used to reach other feeding and bedding areas or as escape routes. Obviously, the deer were using this type of trail as an escape route the night my dad shot his buck. We probably would not have even seen those three deer had they not been trying to evade the other hunter.

There was one other experience I had while hunting in that location later that season that served as a teaching lesson for me. After getting into my tree stand, I was initially unable to nock an arrow on my string because the nock was filled with dirt. I eventually realized that the dirt was there because of the way I previously lowered my bow from the stand. My quiver always remains attached to my bow when being transported, and I was lowering them both down with the nock points of my arrows facing downward. When they reached the ground, the weight of my bow pushed the nocks into the ground. This filled them with dirt. To correct this problem, I began to always lower my bow with the nock points facing up toward me.

Although I began to lower my bow with the nock points facing up, I made sure to always pull my bow up into the stand with the nock points facing down. The reason for this was to make sure my arrows did not get stuck on a branch or get pulled out of my quiver as I raised the bow through the air.

A HEART BREAKING SITUATION

We never saw any more deer at that spot throughout the rest of that fall. There was simply too much hunting pressure and the deer stopped coming to the field during daylight hours. As a result, I had to wait until the following fall to hopefully get my first deer.

Although the exact spot where my dad shot his eight-pointer was not much more than a mile from our house, the closest edge of that forest was only a half mile away. I had spent many summer afternoons riding my bike through sections of that forest with my closest friends while I was growing up. Much to my sadness and dismay, some developers plowed the entire forest to the ground the following spring. In place of the forest, they built an enormous housing development.

As I write these words, it has been about twenty-five years since my dad harvested that buck. Sometimes, when I go to visit my parents and drive past that development, I often look over at the house that now sits on the spot where my dad's tree stand hung. I then say to myself, or to whoever is with me, "See that house right there? My dad shot his first eight-pointer right where they have their living room now."

I can honestly say that a large part of my spirit died when they destroyed that forest. It felt as if someone literally tore a piece of my heart out of me, and I was never the same after that. Also, keep in mind that I was only fifteen years old when this traumatizing event took place. My world-view was very small at that age. I thought this type of habitat destruction and development with houses was happening in every place throughout the entire world. Thoughts and images of forest and wilderness lands being annihilated for the sake of building houses began to plague my mind.

Before the destruction of that forest, I had always wanted to work in wildlife management when I got older. However, this experience caused me to be afraid there wouldn't be any wildlife left by the time I finished college. As a result, I began to think about working in the environmental field instead so that I could help preserve what was left of the environment.

Another outcome of that situation was that I immediately wanted to buy up all the land I could possibly obtain and have it turned into a preserve so that it could never be developed. I wanted my children and grandchildren to one day have the same joys and experiences in the woods that I had. My greatest fear was that I would not be able to save the forests before it was too late.

I was later told that the problem in my area started when the township changed the zoning regulations. They allowed for the complete annihilation of the land in order to bring in more businesses and houses. This in turn brought in more taxpayers, which meant more money for the local government.

What can you and I do about this kind of problem? We can ask that zoning regulations take into consideration the rest of the wildlife and habitat in our areas. We can help people realize that houses can still be built while maintaining a sufficient amount of wooded acreage to support the animals that live in that area.

Even if zoning offices and lawmakers do not implement these practices in their zoning regulations, we can address the investors and builders who are developing the land in our area. We can help them realize that it is possible to erect houses and make a profit without completely destroying the wildlife habitat. For example, the hundred-acre forest where my dad got his buck could have been divided into fifty, separate, two-acre lots. This would have enabled the developers to build fifty homes. In addition, they could have left half of each building lot wooded. As a result, the land would have looked much more natural and would still have been able to sustain much of the wildlife that existed there.

It is up to each one of us to make choices for the overall good of the environment. We should not make decisions based entirely on money while neglecting the animals and wildlife habitat. If we are not careful in how we manage the land, there is a chance that our children, grandchildren, and future generations will not be able to have the same kinds of joys and experiences with the outdoors that we have been able to have.

THE MOUNTAINS

As my father and I prepared for the following hunting season, my uncle Dennis brought my cousin Dennis over to our house to practice archery a few times during the summer. Since my father and I lost our hunting spot, and since my cousin was embarking on his first year of hunting, my uncle made arrangements for the four of us to go to a large tract of land in the mountains on opening day. One of his business colleagues owned the land and gave us permission to hunt there. However, since my uncle and father had very busy work schedules, they were unable to take us up to scout the area in advance. This disappointed me, but I had no choice but to accept it.

Although I wanted to be in the woods well before sunrise on opening morning, we didn't even get there until it was breaking daylight. I didn't think about it at that time, but I now realize it was probably a good idea that we arrived late since none of us knew the land very well. We would have been wandering aimlessly with no idea where to go if we got there in the dark.

Regardless, after we walked a short distance through the woods, my uncle and cousin branched off and got set up near a field. We quietly made arrangements to meet them there before going to lunch. My dad then took me back into the timber. I grumbled and complained in my mind the whole time, saying things like, "We're too late! We are never going to see anything now! This is pointless!"

After mindlessly following my dad for a while, he told me to set up next to a large tree. There was an impressive amount of deer scat on the ground in that area, but none of it looked very fresh to me, so I continued to harbor a bad attitude about the situation. I was also annoyed because we hadn't passed a single buck rub. I thought that if you didn't see any buck rubs, it wasn't worth sitting in that area.

Even though I was unhappy, I was attentive for the first fifteen minutes after getting set up. Eventually, I got bored and gave up.

Within thirty minutes, I was sitting on the ground mindlessly staring at my legs, which were stretched out in front of me.

About a half hour later, I heard a loud noise about a hundred yards away. I assumed there was a house in that direction and that the noise was just someone's front door being slammed closed. (Aside: I found out later that there were no houses in that direction, so it must have been someone shooting at a deer and missing.)

About ten minutes after I heard the noise, I randomly looked to my left. Much to my surprise, there was a young buck walking through the small clearing next to me. I couldn't believe it! I quickly rolled over onto my knees and picked up my bow.

The clearing was covered with low-growing weeds about two and a half feet high. As I started to raise my bow, the buck looked over at me. He was only fifteen yards away. In an attempt to hide myself, I slowly crouched down so that my head was below the top of the weeds. After about fifteen seconds, I got curious and impatient and tried to peek over the weeds to see what the buck was doing. He was staring right at me. He then snorted and took off running.

Almost immediately after the buck was gone, my dad jumped up out of his makeshift ground blind, which was located about forty yards away from me in the opposite direction the deer had come from. He then quickly came over and asked me where I hit the deer. Embarrassed, I told him I didn't even get a shot off.

After a short time, we followed the deer's tracks for a few hundred yards to see where he went. We did this for education purposes and in case we spotted another deer in the process. Eventually, we doubled back to meet up with my uncle and cousin for lunch.

There were several things I learned from this hunt. One was that I should not have moved at all when the deer looked in my direction. If ever a deer spots you, it is often best to freeze until the deer calms down and looks away. Also, I later learned that before a deer is even facing your direction, it helps if you hold your bow in front of your face. This breaks up the silhouette of your face and makes it harder for the deer to pick you out.

Another important lesson I learned from this hunt was to not get so negative or lose hope. Having a negative attitude often leads to misery. If I would have remained positive and alert, I may have spotted the deer sooner. This would have enabled me to be more prepared to make a shot when the deer walked into the open area.

I also learned from this hunt that there are many things to look for when scouting. Although often overlooked by some hunters, deer scat can sometimes be a very effective tool for finding areas that deer like to utilize. This includes bucks. Many hunters focus primarily on buck rubs and scrapes rather than on looking for deer scat. However, when a buck makes a rub or scrape, it is obvious he has been there at least one time, but that doesn't guarantee he will be back to that area. On the other hand, if you find a spot that has a lot of fresh *and* old deer droppings, you know that deer have been consistently visiting that area over a long period of time.

For those who may not already know, buck rubs are created when a buck rubs the bark off of a section of a tree trunk or sapling  with his antlers such as it is depicted here in this picture. Bucks do this to strengthen their neck muscles for fighting in the mating season and also to leave scent from their forehead glands on the rubbed trees. These rubbed trees serve as sign posts that the other deer can easily see from a distance and come over to inspect and smell, which is how they know what bucks are utilizing the area. (More than one buck can rub the same tree and leave his scent.)

Scrapes are made when a buck paws at the ground with his front hoofs to expose a dirt patch. He then urinates on his tarsal glands on his back legs and into the dirt patch (scrape) to leave his scent. Scrapes serve as a buck's territory markers and places where a doe can also urinate to indicate to a buck that she is coming into estrus during the mating season. When a buck checks his scrapes and finds that a doe has been there that is ready for breeding, he can follow her scent trail right to her for the purpose of mating.

THE GRUNT CALL

When I was sixteen years old my dad told me that the Pennsylvania hunting regulations did not allow anyone under the age of eighteen to hunt alone. This meant that the only time I could go hunting was when my dad was able to take me. On Tuesday during the first week of the new season, my dad and I were supposed to go hunting as soon as he got home from work. I had our gear out and ready to go and was anxiously awaited his arrival that evening. Our plan was to load up the car as soon as he got home and then go straight to the public hunting land where we hunted when I was younger.

An hour and a half before dark, the phone rang. It was my dad. He was still stuck at the office and informed me that he was not going to make it home in time to go hunting. This disappointed me, but I didn't let it stop me from at least going scouting. I quickly called my younger neighbor, Scott. He lived on a farm near my house. I asked him if he wanted to go sit in the woods across the street from his farm where we recently gained permission to hunt. Scott excitedly accepted!

After suiting up in my camouflage, I grabbed the grunt call that someone gave my dad the previous Christmas and then sprinted through the fields that separated my house from Scott's. Scott was already in his camouflage waiting for me on his front porch by the time I got there. We quickly headed through the field, crossed the street, and then went into the neighbor's woods. This small patch of woods was located in the opposite direction from where the large forest had been destroyed where my dad shot his first eight-pointer.

After Scott and I entered the woods, we went down the small hillside and crossed the creek. Scott quickly climbed a tree about thirty-five yards beyond the creek, and I headed up the adjacent hillside through a small patch of pine trees. At the top of the hill was an unplanted field that was rectangular in shape and about four acres in size.

A fence ran across the narrow side of the field from the edge of the pine trees where I was standing to another small patch of trees on the other side. I quickly tiptoed over to the only large tree along the fence row and leaned my back up against it. The small patch of pines was now about fifty yards to my left and the other patch of trees was about sixty yards on my right. Behind me was a cow pasture. In front of me was the long direction of the unplanted field. It sloped down into a valley on the other side of the field. This meant that I couldn't see to the bottom of the field. At the bottom of the slope were a tree line and another unplanted field.

As soon as I was in position, I began blowing through the grunt tube. To be honest, I didn't really know how to use a grunt call in a hunting situation. On this particular day, I simply blew into it almost without stopping. I'd grunt in one direction about nine times, stop, turn my head, and immediately being blowing into it in another direction. I kept doing this over and over again. I basically blew into it as much as a trumpet player performing in an orchestra.

Within ten minutes of when I started calling, I turned my head to look straight in front of me. As I prepared to blow through the grunt tube again, I immediately froze perfectly still and held my breath. I saw a nice set of antlers coming up over the slope in the field in front of me. He was about eighty yards away when I first saw his rack. I quickly counted twelve points! His tines were perfectly symmetrical. His antlers also had a good sized spread. The only drawback to his rack was that his tines were not very long, but that didn't bother me. Everything else about him compensated for his short tine length. Judging by his large body size, I immediately assumed he was a very old deer that was simply on his way downhill.

As I surveyed the big buck's attributes, he continued to walk directly at me with his nose in the air. He got to within twelve yards of me and slowly turned without seeing me. He then walked in a U-shaped pattern over to the pines and back down the edge of the field in the direction he had just come from. The buck was obviously looking for the deer that had been grunting.

A small prop-engine airplane started to fly overhead as the buck moved out of sight. I thought the sound from the airplane's engine would drown out any noise I might make while moving so I decided to try following the buck to see where he was going. After just a few short steps, my foot landed on a twig and snapped it. The sound it made startled the buck and sent him running down through the pine trees.

Trying as hard as I could to contain my excitement, I waited a few minutes and then tiptoed down through the pines to where Scott was up in a tree. He was still high in the tree branches when I got there. I tried to whisper, but wanted to yell, "Did you see the size of that buck?" After Scott climbed down, and we talked for a moment, we left the woods as quietly as possible. Each of us then ran to our perspective houses.

With great excitement and enthusiasm I told my dad about the buck when he got home from work. After describing the buck's rack, I boastfully said that my twelve-pointer was going to make his eight-pointer look small when I mounted him on the wall next to his!

The next day my dad and I went back to the last place I saw the buck. We set up our tree stands on the edge of the pine trees overlooking the field. I used the climbing tree stand that my parents gave me for Christmas, while my dad used his hang-on stand. He set up in a tree about seven yards to my right.

As soon as we were both in position, I began grunting just as I had the day before. My dad immediately told me to grunt less. Regardless, I expected the buck to come straight to me like he did the last time. Unfortunately, no deer came. After just twenty minutes of hunting, I started to feel embarrassed because of how confidently I had talked about getting that big buck. My dad also sacrificed a lot to get home from work in time to take me hunting that day. As light began to fade, so did my hopes. The deer never returned.

What did I learn from this experience? The most important lesson I learned was to always *read the rule book on your own*! Even though I completely hated and despised reading at that age, I should have made myself *carefully* read the regulations instead of just taking my dad's word for everything. If I would have done this, I would have learned that it was actually legal for me to hunt alone at the age of sixteen. The wording in the rule book simply indicated that I couldn't take a junior hunter with me until I was eighteen. This meant I could have brought my bow with me the evening I called in the big twelve-pointer.

Another important lesson I learned from this hunt was that you can't expect a deer to do the same thing every time you call to it. Lastly, I learned that I should not be so boastful about hunting. There are many factors that can make the outcome of a hunt uncertain. Practicing humility rather than bragging about the deer I think I'm going to get can save me from a lot of embarrassment when things don't work out the way I hoped or expected.

I KNOW NOW

By the following summer, I had finally saved up enough money to buy a new bow. It had an adjustable draw weight of fifty-five to seventy pounds. I was curious to see if I could pull it back at the peak draw weight. After getting it home and tightening it to seventy pounds, I did my best to keep the rest of my body still as I drew back the string. Simultaneously, I heard an awful tearing noise in my shoulder. After reaching full draw, I carefully lowered the string back down. My shoulder never made a noise like that before, but I didn't think much about it at that time.

To this day, I still have a lot of pain and trouble with that shoulder. This has taught me that not only is it easy to injure or damage your shoulder when trying to pull too much weight, but the negative effects can last a lifetime. As a result, I strongly recommend being careful with how much weight you try to pull back on a bow. Even though your muscles may physically be able to do it, there are still other factors such as cartilage, ligaments, and tendons that can be damaged.

After lowering the poundage on my new bow, and giving my shoulder a week to feel better, I practiced almost every day. While practicing, I often daydreamed about getting my first shot at a deer.

My neighbor Scott and I watched hunting videos almost every day throughout the summer. We also worked hard to improve our deer calling techniques. I planned to try rattling deer antlers together on opening day in an effort to attract a big buck just as I had seen the hunters do on the videos.

As the season approached, I started looking more intensely for a new hunting spot. The patch of woods I found was situated along some crop fields located behind a small office building where my classmate's dad worked. This spot was only about five miles away from where we lived. As soon as I gained permission to hunt there, my dad and I went to scout it out after he got home from work. We were only a third of the way through the soybean field when we spotted two doe feeding on the other side. We immediately stopped and stood still watching them. A moment later, a nice buck walked out into the field. He was followed by a slightly larger buck. About two minutes later, an enormous bodied buck with very dark fur and dark antlers stepped up to the edge of the woods and looked around the field. He made the other deer look small. Before he even stepped out into the field they all ran back into the woods, so we left without disturbing them any further. Needless to say, I was excited to hunt there!

As we drove home that night, I told my dad how I wanted to shoot the biggest buck that came out last. He then explained to me that the biggest bucks almost always come out of the woods last. They will wait for all of the other deer to go ahead of them to make sure the area is safe. If there is danger, the other deer will run back into the woods before the big buck even gets to the food source. In other words, if you want to shoot the biggest buck, you typically have to let all of the other deer pass by and wait for the last one to come.

My dad and I went back to that spot a few days later to hang our tree stands. Unfortunately, there were two dove hunters standing along the edge of the soybean field next to the woods when we got there. They were waiting to see if the bucks were going to come out into the field that evening. We briefly talked with them and then went to hang our stands.

When opening day of archery season arrived, I got into my stand well before daylight. As dawn broke, a group of hunters walked past me in the woods about forty yards away. One of them was clanging a metal tree stand the entire way. This intensely irritated me!

Later that morning, in an effort to salvage my hunt, I tried rattling my deer antlers. No deer responded to my call, and I felt very disappointed. Around nine in the morning, two hunters stalked through the woods toward me. Based on the direction they came from I figured it was the same people that had passed by me right at daylight. As they got closer, I could see that it was one of the dove hunters I saw the week before. This time he had his youth-aged son with him. By the looks of the kid, I'd say it was his first year hunting. Initially, I tried to wave my hands to indicate that I was there. They were oblivious to me, so I gave up. They eventually walked directly below my tree stand. I could have dropped twigs on their heads if I wanted to. As they passed under me, I felt very irritated and frustrated with them. They had completely ruined my hunt from start to finish!

No deer came to the fields that evening. It was probably because the woods had been polluted with hunters throughout the day. We went back on Monday night to try again, but I still didn't see anything. My dad on the other hand got a shot at a nice eight-pointer. When I excitedly asked him what happened, he responded, "You know the sound an arrow makes when it hits a deer?" He paused, and then jokingly said, "Oh that's right, you don't. Well anyway, I know I hit him." Obviously he said this because I had never even gotten a shot at a deer. In addition, this took place in the days before carbon arrows were used for hunting. Instead, we used aluminum arrows. Aluminum arrows made a distinct, low-sounding thud noise when they hit a deer, whereas carbon arrows often make more of a pop sound.

After my dad finished telling me what happened, we tracked his buck for a while but lost the blood trail. I didn't realize it at the time, but I think my dad felt a certain pressure to get me home because it was a school night and it was getting late. As far as I know, he looked for the buck the following morning while I was at school but didn't find him.

The night after my dad hit his buck, I abandoned my tree stand and went to the other side of the woods and sat on the ground. At one point, I was up on my knees looking out toward a field. After getting tired of kneeling, I sat back on my heels. Unfortunately, I didn't know there was a buck walking up behind me while I was doing this. As a result, he immediately spotted my movement, snorted, and retreated back into the timber. That was frustrating for me!

In those days, a Pennsylvania archery license could be used for either a buck or a doe. Although I had hoped that my first deer would be a nice buck, my standards were diminishing, and I decided to shoot the first deer that came my way. If it was a doe, I'd simply have to wait until the following year to get my first buck.

On the following evening, we went back to the same area. This time I sat on the ground in the middle of the woods about seventy yards away from my dad's stand. I decided to put some deer scent out hoping it would attract a buck.

The hunt went by slowly. However, with only seven minutes left before shooting hours were over, I heard something running through the woods. I looked intently in the direction I heard the noise. After a short time, I saw the body of a deer trotting in my direction through a dense section of saplings. As it drew closer, I was able to see that it had at least antlers on the left side of its head. I didn't see any noticeable signs of antlers on the other side but didn't look either. Instead, I focused hard on finding an opportunity to shoot. As I stared intensely at the buck's body, I raised my bow and prepared to draw. Because I felt so frustrated, annoyed, and disappointed with the way my season had been going, I never even got "buck fever." I simply remained intense, focused, and determined!

The deer continued trotting on a broadside angle about twenty-two yards in front of me. With absolute seriousness, I drew back my bow and settled my right hand into my anchor point. The deer then stopped and looked in the other direction. Within the blink of an eye, I estimated the yardage, aimed, and released the string. The aluminum arrow soared through the air and made a deep sounding thud as it penetrated the side of the buck's body. It was a hit!

My bow was so quiet that the deer never even heard the shot. It also seemed as though he didn't even know he had been hit. After a few seconds, he gently trotted in a semicircle and stopped about seventeen yards to my left. As he stood there, he looked back in the other direction again. While keeping my eyes fixated on the deer, I frantically reached behind me looking for my quiver with my hand. I scrambled to get another arrow out of my quiver for a second shot, but the buck trotted away before I was able to.

I was so excited at that moment that I wanted to yell for joy! Although it was difficult, I forced myself to keep my mouth shut. After calming myself, I sat down on the ground, leaned back against the tree, and waited until shooting hours were over. I sat there with the biggest smile on my face and constantly looked down at my watch waiting for shooting hours to end so that I could go get my dad.

When hunting hours finally closed, I got up, walked over to my scent canister, picked it up, and then eased my way down through the woods. My dad was still up in his tree stand packing up his equipment when I made it to the base of his tree. I literally couldn't wait for him to get down! With a loud whisper, I called up to him, "Hey, Dad. Remember when you asked me if I knew what it sounded like when an arrow hits a deer? Well, **I know now**!" Since he couldn't hear me, he quietly replied, "What?" I repeated my statement a little louder and again concluded with the statement, "**I know now!**" He surprisingly asked, "You got a shot?" I said, "Yeah! Didn't you hear it? It was only about ten minutes ago." He exclaimed, "No!" and then quickly climbed down.

When my dad reached the ground, he asked me to show him where I was standing and where the deer was standing at the time of the shot. I took him back to the tree I was standing next to and pointed to where the deer had been. He then walked over and looked for blood. It took him a minute, but he eventually found the spot where the blood trail started. He also picked up part of my broken arrow shaft and then tracked the deer over to where it had stopped about seventeen yards to my left. He then called me over to join him. At this point in time, it was getting dark, so we turned on our flashlights. We then followed the blood trail for another fifteen yards, but then it totally stopped.

Next to where the blood trail ended was a small pool of liquid on the ground. The forest floor was extremely dry, which made this one small patch of fluid very noticeable. Since I was the closest one to it, my dad asked, "Is that deer pee?" I said, "I don't know." I didn't know why he asked me about the liquid, nor did I understand why it would matter if it was deer pee or not.

Around this point in time, my enthusiasm and excitement began to dwindle because I thought we might not find the deer. I desperately wanted to find that deer more than anything!

After staring at the ground for a long time, my dad told me to stand on the last spot of blood. He then went in front of me about seven yards and slowly proceeded to make a clockwise circle around me looking for more blood. All I could think was, "PLEASE, GOD, LET US FIND THIS DEER!"

It was now totally dark. About five minutes after my dad began circling around me, he stopped moving about ten yards away on the other side of some bushes. He then softly called my name, "Sean." "Yeah," I responded. He excitedly replied, "Congratulations!" I yelled, "WHAT?" He repeated himself, "Congratulations!" I jumped through the bushes that separated us and saw my deer lying dead on the ground! I was so excited at that moment!

As I got closer, I counted three points sticking up on the left-hand side of his rack and thought to myself, "All right, an eight-pointer!" I then reached down and picked up his head to see that he only had two points on the other side and no brow tines. He was only a five-pointer. I was a little disappointed by that, but still happy to have finally gotten my first deer after four years of hunting!

My dad later explained to me why he wanted to know if the pool of liquid we saw at the end of the blood trail was deer urine. It was because an animal's bowls will sometimes open just as it is about to die, or just after it dies, which can cause them to excrete. He knew

that if it was the deer's urine it could mean that the buck was about to die. My dad also told me that if I ever lose a blood trail like we did in that situation, I should mark the last spot of blood. Then walk away from that spot about five yards in the direction I think the deer went. Afterward, slowly circle all the way around that spot 360 degrees at a distance of five yards. If I do not find any more blood, go ten yards away from the last spot of blood and slowly circle all the way around it again looking for more blood. Continue to increase the radius of the circles by five yards each time until finding more blood or finding the deer.

At some point after that hunt, I decided to train myself to shoot with my quiver on my bow. I got the idea to do this from watching a hunting video. The person on the video hunted with his quiver on his bow so that he could easily get a second arrow out and take another shot. I saw the value in this since I had trouble reaching around trying to find my quiver so that I could take a second shot at my buck.

A few days after I got my buck, my dad found the buck he had shot a few days earlier. It was a nice eight-pointer. It was clearly a year older than my deer. My dad's shot hit the buck in the liver, and it died about eighty yards from where we lost the blood trail. We were both sad that we didn't find the deer sooner. However, both the rack from my dad's buck and the rack from my buck had an inferior right side. This made us think that his buck might have been the older brother of mine.

PERFECT RECORD

The following year was my first year away at college. I was attending a branch campus of Penn State University about an hour away from my parents' house. I knew my chances to hunt that year would be very limited. Since I wouldn't have time to do any scouting near school, I decided to only hunt when I went home to visit my family.

The place I found for my dad and I to hunt that year was adjacent to the forest that had been destroyed and developed near our house. It seemed as though many of the deer from that forest had been pushed into this smaller patch of woods that I am referring to. Fortunately, not too many people were hunting there.

Scott and I spent many hours scouting this patch of woods throughout the summer. This was easy for us to do since it was within walking distance of our houses. I found a slight clearing near the back of the woods that had an old apple tree on the edge of it. My plan was to set up there on opening day. Since there were no trees thick enough to safely hang a tree stand, I made a ground blind using a blown down tree and some branches.

On one occasion that summer, Scott and I sat in the spots we had picked out for ourselves. Although I couldn't hang a tree stand in my area, I managed to climb up about fifteen feet in a skinny maple tree. Just a few minutes after I got into position I looked down to see a nice eight-pointer trotting right underneath the tree I was in! This made me even more excited about the spot!

Meanwhile, I started to do a lot of shooting at 3D targets on the weekends with some of my friends from school. In the process, I became discontent with the speed of my bow so I purchased a new Hoyt that had a peak weight of eighty pounds.

I anxiously looked forward to opening day of hunting season because I really wanted to get a shot at the nice buck I saw at my spot during the summer. I also wanted to see how well my new bow performed! My enthusiasm remained high that morning until I reached the clearing where my ground blind was located. As soon as I got there, I heard deer scurrying away all over the place. To make matters even worse, the clothes I wore that morning were not warm enough to compete with the unexpected chill in the air. After two hours of sitting there shivering, I decided to head back to the car to warm up.

The woods we were hunting in were extremely dense in many areas with large patches of cedar trees. In the cedar patches, there were virtually no leaves on the ground which made it easy to walk quietly. However, the forest considerably thinned out near the road. This area was dominated by hardwoods. As a result, there were more leaves and acorns on the ground. As I made it to this area of the forest, I looked diagonally toward my left and saw our car parked about a hundred yards away. I immediately turned and started walking in that direction. After taking about ten steps toward the car, I looked back over my shoulder without even thinking about what I was doing. To my utter astonishment, a doe suddenly stepped out onto the trail behind me. She was only eighteen yards away. She took about four steps in my direction but then stopped and stood still behind a thick bush.

The doe could obviously sense something was not right, but she never looked directly at me. When she wasn't looking in my direction, I pivoted my upper body a hundred and eighty degrees while keeping my feet planted in place. I didn't want to move my feet because I was afraid they'd make noise in the leaves. I then drew my bow, which created an extremely awkward and difficult position to shoot from. It was also difficult not to let the awkwardness of my stance distract me.

Although I found a small opening in the bushes that I could shoot through, I wanted to wait until the doe stepped out from behind the branches so that I could take a broadside shot. As time passed, my muscles started to tire and my arms began to shake! The fact that I had the poundage cranked up to seventy-seven pounds didn't help the situation either.

The doe began to act nervous and stepped back. It looked as if she was preparing to run, so I decided to take a shot even though she was facing straight at me. I knew this was not a preferable angle, but I loosed the arrow anyway. I then watched as the fletching on my arrow bounced against the ground as the deer turned and ran up through the woods. Almost immediately, I thought to myself, "Oh no! I missed!"

Up until that moment, I had prided myself on the fact that I had a perfect success rating. I had hit and found every single deer I ever shot at (even though it was only one). I wanted to keep my perfect record for the rest of my life, which was why I was so disappointed when I saw my arrow bounce against the ground after taking my shot.

As I walked over to where the deer had been standing, I felt very disappointed and thought about what I would say to people when they found out I missed a deer. However, all of those kinds of thoughts and feelings suddenly changed the moment I reached down to pick up my arrow shaft. Only half of it was there, and there was blood all over the end where it had been broken off! I excitedly yelled in my mind, "Yeah! I hit her!" I then sat down and leaned against a tree to give the deer the minimum 30 minute wait that is recommended for a heart or lung shot deer.

Being patient was very difficult, because I wanted to immediately start tracking her! When the grueling wait was finally over, I quickly got up and slowly started tracking. There was steady blood for the first thirty yards. I had to crawl on my hands and knees to get through the dense brush that the doe had gone through. I tracked her into a clearing about thirty-five yards from where I hit her. It was obvious she stopped there and looked around because there was a massive mound of blood bubbles on the ground about eight inches high. This was an impressive sight, and I have not seen anything like it before or since.

After looking around, I could see that the doe cut back to the left, so I followed her trail. Within twenty yards, I knelt down behind a pine tree to look for more blood. In my peripheral vision, I noticed something move on the other side of the pine tree. I looked up to see that it was the doe I had hit. She was bedded down just eight yards away from me and barely alive. I quickly and quietly nocked another arrow. I then cautiously stepped out around the edge of the pine tree and came to full draw. As I took aim, the doe's drooping head turned slightly in my direction. I then released the arrow. Since she was facing me, the shot entered her neck, went all the way through her body, and then exited out her hind quarter and kept going. She immediately jumped up and fell over. After a few seconds, she completely stopped moving. I stood still watching and waiting. Eventually, I walked past the deer to see if my arrow was in sight. It was nowhere to be found, so I headed over to get my dad. His tree stand was not far away.

As soon as I reached the tree my dad was in, I called up to him and let him know I shot a deer. He climbed down and told me about the big nine-pointer he missed an hour earlier. My head turned to see where his finger was pointing as he said this. When my head came to rest, I saw that his arrow was sticking out of a sapling. It was exciting that we both had shots at a deer that morning!

My father and I drug my doe out of the woods and tied her to the top of the trunk on his car. As we drove away, the people who lived across the street were walking out to their mailbox. The elderly woman's face looked horrified when she saw my dead deer draped over the back of our car.

What did I learn from this hunt? One thing was to always make sure to dress warmly enough! The second thing I learned was that even when you think your hunt is over, and you are walking out to the car, don't give up. Move as quietly as possible and always be ready. You never know when a deer will step out into an opening. The third thing was when transporting a deer; try to conceal the carcass if possible. There are plenty of people who oppose hunting. In many instances, they simply don't understand the importance of it. I think the best chance we have of bringing those people in touch with the reality of the life cycle and the necessity of managing the deer herd is to approach them on good terms. Seeing a dead, bloody, animal carcass on our vehicles as we drive past them is likely to upset or anger them. This in turn will make it more difficult to educate and convert them to a more realistic way of thinking.

LOOK BEHIND YOU

The following year was my sophomore year of college. I had a much better idea of what to expect while I was at school and how to manage my time. For these reasons, I planned to do a lot more hunting that year.

Throughout the first full month I was back on campus, I drove around the surrounding area looking for new hunting spots. The best place I could find that I knew I was allowed to hunt was a patch of public hunting ground about ten miles away from campus.

After trying the public hunting ground for two weeks without seeing a single deer, I went to a nearby patch of woods that bordered a cornfield. During my first time hunting this spot, I thought I would experiment with my rattle bag to see if I could call in a buck. After getting set up on the ground, I performed a series of rattles and grunts. I then intently watched the woods in front of me where I thought the deer would come from. A few minutes had passed, and I was getting tired of kneeling so I sat back on my ankles. The moment I sat back there was an eruption of noise behind me. A nice buck had been approaching without me even knowing it. However, he saw my movement when I sat back and immediately ran away.

One of the biggest lessons I learned from this hunt was that I need to be prepared for deer to come from any direction. This especially holds true when rattling. In this situation, I didn't think a deer would come from behind me, because there were only cornfields in that direction. The heavy timber was in front of me, which is where I thought all the deer would be. From that day forward, I have always kept an open mind and a readiness for the deer to surprise me from any direction, especially the area I would least expect them to come from. I also learned a few years later that deer will sometimes stay in standing corn all day long without coming out. It is very safe for them in standing corn and there is a tremendous amount of food available to them. If you are set up in the woods near a cornfield, be ready for the deer to sometimes come out of the corn and into the woods. Don't just expect them to be going from the woods into the corn. Lastly, I later learned that a buck will almost always circle to the downwind side of the area you are calling from. He does this to identify the source of the sound by using his sense of smell to prevent exposing himself to potential danger. Obviously, if he smells a human instead of a deer, he will run away.

FENCE ROW

During that same week, while I was in the dining hall on campus, a student told his friend standing near me that he shot a six-point buck that morning in a field on the northwest side of campus. His friend then said he shot a five-pointer on opening day in the woods on the southeast side of campus near the dorms. He also said that his five-pointer would have been an eight-pointer, but half of his rack except for the base had been broken off in a fight.

Since I had not been having any success on the public hunting land or the other spot I had picked out, and because I wanted to see the buck that broke the five-pointer's rack, I decided to try hunting in the area near the dorms where the student talked about. Without telling anyone, I went there after class to inspect the area.

Although I never asked, I assumed it was not permissible to hunt on the school's property even though those two students had. However, directly adjacent to the area of the school's campus where I was investigating was an enormous cornfield. Although I never verified it, I didn't think the field was part of the school's property. Directly next to the cornfield was a thick, overgrown field. The saplings in the overgrown field were littered with big buck rubs! Since there were no posted signs bordering the thick patch, and I knew the thick patch was not the school's property, I *assumed* it was okay to hunt there.

After class the following day, I drove around to the housing development on the other side of the thick patch. I parked my car and walked up into the thicket. Since there were no large trees that could be used for a tree stand, I made a ground blind along the fence row that separated the thicket from the cornfield. The fence was about four feet high and constructed of metal. The design of the fence and the position of my ground blind made it impossible for me to shoot through the fence toward the cornfield. This was unfortunate.

Since it was the third week of archery season, I decided to put some doe-in-heat scent out in front of me in hopes of luring a buck in close. Surprisingly, only fifteen minutes after getting set up, I heard loud crashing noises coming from the cornfield. As the sound drew closer, I saw the brown body of a large deer coming my way. It was a gigantic buck! His rack was so wide that the corn rows on either side of his head were literally *inside* the spread of his main beams. This is what was making the crashing noise as he trotted out of the corn.

The buck had about a twenty-seven inch inside spread. Remarkably, the base of his rack was as big around as my wrist, and he carried a tremendous amount of mass throughout his entire rack! He was an absolute perfect eight-pointer with very long tines. His brow tines were about nine inches long. The back tines, also known as the G2s, were about fourteen inches long. The next set of tines, also known as the G3s, were about twelve inches long.

The buck walked right up to the fence row and stuck his antlers in a branch that was about three inches in diameter. In one swift move of his head, he snapped the big branch completely off the tree! It was utterly amazing to watch! After making a scrape, he walked up to the fence. Without hesitating, I excitedly drew my bow and thought to myself, "He's going to smell that doe-in-heat scent and jump right over the fence!" The scent canister was only seven yards away from him on my side of the fence.

Instead of jumping the fence like I expected, the buck just stood there looking around. At that point, the draw weight on my bow was maxed out at eighty pounds, so I knew I wasn't going to be able to stay at full draw for very long.

Holding the bow back became unbearable, and my arms started shaking like crazy. I tried to create the least amount of movement possible as I eased down on the string, but the big buck saw me. Without hesitating, he spun around and ran back into the corn. Needless to say, it was *emotionally painful* for me to not get a shot at that giant buck!

Less than a minute after I frightened the buck away, I heard a man's voice over a loudspeaker coming from the direction of my parked car. The man said, "Would the hunter in the woods please come out!" The moment I heard those words, I panicked! After jumping up, I went over and grabbed my scent canister and then headed out of the woods. Half-way there, I looked down to see that one of my arrows had fallen out of my quiver. I quickly ran back to the ground blind looking for it. At that point, the voice came over the loudspeaker again and said, "Mr. McVeigh, will you please come out of the woods!" In response, I screamed in my mind, "I'm trying!" I then grabbed my arrow and moved quickly toward my car.

As I exited the thicket, I saw several cop cars parked behind my vehicle. There were troopers standing all around my car and many people lurking in the background watching. I immediately walked up to the police and asked what the problem was. They said, "Did you know you are not allowed to hunt here?" I said, "No. I didn't see any posted signs, so I thought it was okay. I'm going to school right over there and I don't know the area very well. Since I didn't see any signs, I thought it was okay to hunt here."

The head officer responded, "That's okay. They really should get some signs up, but just so you know, there is no hunting of any kind permitted in this borough." With a light laugh, I said, "It's a good thing you guys got me when you did! I just saw the biggest buck of my life! If he would have been on my side of the fence, I probably would have shot at him, ha ha ha." The head officer replied in a very friendly manner, "Yes. This is a really good area. I wish I could hunt here myself. If it ever does open up for hunting, I will be sure to let you know."

Just before I left, one of the officers handed me a piece of paper. He said, "This is just a written warning. The nosy neighbors who called this in will want to see that we at least did something about the situation. You are not in any kind of trouble." I apologized again and thanked them for being so lenient toward me.

An important lesson I learned after this hunt was that deer will almost always stop and look before jumping a fence. Sometimes they will wait several minutes before jumping. I also learned later that it is common for deer to stop before jumping over a log or crossing through a creek bed. They do this to make sure there is no danger in the area they are headed before making themselves vulnerable while crossing the obstruction. This pause before moving ahead must be accounted for when planning a shot. Ideally, you want to be positioned in a location that will allow you to make a shot *before* and not after they cross the obstruction.

I wish I could end this section right here, but I cannot. I simply couldn't get that big buck out of my mind. I wanted him so badly! In turn, I allowed my feelings of greed, pride, and vanity to influence my thoughts. Although I didn't consciously admit it to myself, my greed wanted that buck because of how big he was. My pride wanted him because I could then brag about him to everyone I knew. My vanity wanted him so that I could hear people's words of admiration for me when they saw this buck hanging on my wall.

Under the influence of these sinful inclinations, I began to have thoughts that sounded like, "Those other guys shot bucks on campus and nothing bad happened to them. Why shouldn't I be allowed to do it too? I don't think the cornfield is the school's property. It is not posted, and I'm pretty sure it is in a different borough than the thicket side of the fence. This means that the cornfield is in an area that is permissible to hunt. If anyone asks me, I will just tell them I thought it was okay to hunt there because there were no posted signs."

Unfortunately, I gave in to the thoughts and feelings I was having and hunted on the cornfield side of the fence row on Saturday morning. An hour after sunrise, a four-pointer walked up to within five yards of me. When he got that close, he smelled me and ran back a few yards before stopping and looking back in my direction. He then walked into the corn and disappeared.

That afternoon, I washed my clothes in scent elimination soap and headed back to the fence row to give it another try. I also used some fox urine to help cover up my human scent. I didn't use my doe-in-heat scent again because I was afraid the big buck would associate the smell of that particular scent canister with danger as a result of our last encounter.

As I stood along the fence that evening, I thought about the fact that the season was going to end in two weeks. In that time frame, I only had about three days that I could hunt because of my class schedule. I also thought about how I didn't want to go another year without getting a buck. As a result, although I really wanted the big buck, I decided to shoot the first buck that came by me that evening.

About an hour before dark, I blew into my grunt call a few times. Not even a minute passed, and I smelled a musty odor in the air. Simultaneously, I turned my head to the left and looked into the thicket on the other side of the fence. To my surprise, there was a little four-pointer viciously slamming his head into a tree about forty yards away. After thrashing the tree for several minutes, the buck walked down through the thicket, made a looping turn, and then started walking back up toward me. The buck's eyes were wide open as if he was in a trance. He wasn't even looking around.

The angle the buck was walking was going to give me a perfect broadside shot only twelve yards away. Since I was standing, I was able to shoot over the top of the fence at him. As soon as his head went behind a small tree, and I knew he couldn't see my movement, I quickly drew back my bow and reached my anchor point. My adrenaline peaked at that moment as my heart raced with intensity! I then took aim just beyond a tree in the direction the deer was walking.

The feeling of anticipation escalated within me at that moment! I just couldn't wait to finally shoot my second buck! Although I tried to restrain my anxious anticipation, I couldn't wait any longer and released the arrow as soon as the deer's head and neck came out from behind the tree. The arrow hit the buck somewhere around the base of the neck, and he dropped like a ton of bricks. I was amazed by the power and effectiveness of my bow! The deer dropped as if it had been hit by a bullet!

The buck lay motionless on the ground with the exception of his ribcage, which was rising and falling as he inhaled and exhaled. I thought about shooting him again just to make sure I got him, but decided not to because I didn't want to waste money by ruining another aluminum arrow and broadhead. Just then, the buck began to flail around, yet he was unable to stand. After thrashing down through the thicket for about twenty yards, he partially stood and ran out of sight.

I waited a few minutes, jumped the fence, and tiptoed over to my arrow. It had gone all the way through the deer and was covered in dark blood. After picking it up, I walked back over and leaned it against the fence to mark the spot where I was standing. I then went back to my dorm to get some classmates to help me track the deer. Three of us returned to the thicket an hour later.

Unfortunately, there were only a few specks of blood on the ground for about the first twenty yards. After that, there was nothing at all. We crawled around through the thicket for hours looking for the buck but were unable to find any sign of him.

Throughout the entire time we were tracking, I was extremely paranoid of getting caught! The more we tracked the deer, the closer we got to the houses where I had been warned by the police. I was afraid someone was going to see our flashlights moving around in the thicket and then call the cops again. After several hours of searching in the dark, we gave up and went back to the dorms.

One of my friends who helped track the deer went back the following morning while I was in class. He said he saw a four-pointer run into the corn from the thicket, but it looked totally fine and healthy. We both hoped it was the one I hit and that he was okay. Although we continued to search for a few days, we never did find any more sign of the deer.

There were two important lessons I learned from this hunt. One was to be more patient and wait until an animal's vital organs are exposed before taking a shot. More importantly, though, I realized I should only hunt in areas that I know are legal and where *I have permission*. I say this because not only did I feel paranoid while tracking, but I later realized I felt intensely anxious and afraid of getting caught the entire time I hunted in that spot. Fear of getting in trouble significantly took away from my enjoyment of hunting. As a result, I resolved to never again hunt in an area that I knew was off limits or that I did not have permission to be! I encourage you to do the same. It simply isn't worth it.

ANGLE OF THE BROADHEAD

After deciding to no longer hunt in that area, I knew that my best chance of getting a deer was to drive home to my parents' house and try some of the spots where I had permission. On the following Friday afternoon, I drove home. Our next-door neighbor frequently hunted the patch of woods where I shot my doe and my dad missed the nine-pointer on opening day the year before. He said there were three good bucks living in that patch of woods and that the nine-pointer my dad missed had been bedding down every day next to the road near the top of the property. It surprised me to hear him say that. I always imagined that big bucks would go to the deepest part of the woods away from all human activity. Then again, that is probably what most people thought, which is why the buck knew it was safe to bed near the road.

After gaining this information, I decided to go over and set up in that patch of woods about fifty yards from the road. The spot I picked was on the edge of a small clearing that had waist-high goldenrod growing in it. After building a ground blind against a pine tree, I walked back into the timber and laid out a doe-in-heat scent trail to the opening where I was set up.

Forty-five minutes before dark, I heard a deer walking about sixty yards away from me on the uphill side of the property. It was moving from the road toward the deeper timber. This made me think it was the big nine-pointer, so I quickly started grunting. To my surprise, the buck immediately trotted in my direction. He ended up stopping on the other side of some thick pine trees about ten yards away. He was so close that I could hear him breathing even though I couldn't see him through the thick pine branches.

Still being fairly inexperienced in those types of situations, I decided to try grunting again while pointing the grunt tube directly at the deer. My hope was that this would entice him to step out from behind the tree. Instead, he turned and paced back in the direction he was originally headed. As he did this, I saw the flash of an enormous, brown, deer body moving behind the pine branches. Unfortunately, I was unable to get a look at his rack.

In hindsight, I realized that because the deer was so close, the last few grunts I made must have sounded way too loud! He also would have expected to see and *smell* a deer standing directly in front of him because of the volume of the grunts. When he did not, he knew something wasn't right, which is why he left the area.

No other deer came by me throughout the rest of the hunt. About ten minutes before dark, I packed up my things. In case there were any deer within earshot, I decided to trot out of the woods making it sound as if I was a deer. To start, I hopped out of my blind and began hopping and landing my feet in the same pattern as a trotting deer. After doing this for only fifteen yards, I heard an eruption of noise behind me. When this happened, I immediately stopped and jerked my head around to see what it was. Luckily, I was standing partially behind a thick bush when this happened because an enormous buck came barreling into the clearing I just trotted out of. I assumed it was the big nine-pointer but didn't count his points to verify. I just focused on trying to get a shot!

I thought that if it was the big nine-pointer, he probably circled around to the other side of me and caught a whiff of the doe-in-heat scent trail I had put out. When he heard the sound of a trotting deer, he ran in to investigate. Regardless, immediately upon seeing the buck, I ripped an arrow out of my quiver and nocked it on my string. The buck put his head down and began sniffing the ground as he veered off to my left. He was now only eighteen yards away. This was the moment I had been waiting for. Finally, my time had come to harvest a monster buck. To do it on the ground at only eighteen yards was going to make it all the more memorable!

Without hesitating, I began to go through my normal routine of drawing my bow and aiming. As part of this, rather than grip the bow tightly with my left hand, I had been taught by some friends to keep my left hand open while pulling back on the string. As I did this, the blade of my broadhead got caught on the pointer finger of my left hand before I was able to reach full draw. This caused the arrow to pop off of the string, and it immediately fell to the ground. Just then, the big buck lifted his head and began sniffing the air. There was nothing I could do but remain frozen at full draw with my arrow lying on the ground at my feet.

When the buck finally put his head back down for a moment, I eased down on the bow string. However, the sound that my arrow had made when it hit the ground must have alerted the deer, because he started walking very heavy and stiff-legged. Deer exhibit this kind of behavior when they sense danger or are getting nervous and are preparing to leave an area.

By the time I got another arrow out of my quiver and onto the string, the buck was headed back in the direction he came from. It was now almost dark. The last chance I had to take a shot was while he walked out of the clearing. I drew back my bow but simply couldn't see my pins clearly enough to accurately shoot. I had to ease down and let him walk away. That hurt my feelings. I wanted that buck so badly, but I was not going to risk taking a bad shot. It was either going to happen the right way or not at all.

The next morning I slipped into the same patch of woods thinking I'd get another chance at the big buck. Unfortunately, I heard him running down through the woods as soon as I stepped in off of the road. No other deer came by me the rest of the morning.

On my way home after that hunt, I went through the other patch of woods where Scott and I had scouted many times in the past. It was the same patch where I called in the big twelve-pointer when I was sixteen. The moment I stepped off of the road and into that patch of woods, I could hear a few deer running in the other direction. The leaves were simply way too dry and noisy for me to walk quietly. Although I pushed the deer out of that patch that morning, I was at least happy to know there were deer hanging out in that area.

I went back to my ground blind that evening but didn't see or hear any deer. The following Saturday was the last day of the season. My plan was to drive home Thursday night and hunt all day Friday and all day Saturday. I was anxious to get back to my blind. I thought for sure I would get the buck after not pressuring him all week.

I drove home on Thursday as planned and hunted the ground blind Friday morning. Once again, I didn't see any deer. I then spent most of the day slowly stalking through the woods looking for other good spots. At one point, I spooked a deer but couldn't tell if it was a buck or doe. I also found someone else's arrow that had missed a deer. Although it rained most of the day, I never left the woods.

In the evening, I moved to a new location near a scrape I had found during the day. I laid out a doe-in-heat scent trail from the scrape to a clearing about thirty yards away where I was able to make a ground blind. About an hour before dark, I grunted a few times. I then heard a deer coming my way from the scrape. I thought it was going to work out perfectly. However, rather than come to my left along the scent trail like I needed him to, the buck circled behind me to my right. It was a small four-pointer. He came to within ten yards of me but saw me before I could draw my bow.

Since I felt I had ruined that patch of woods, I decided to try somewhere else the following morning, which was also the last day. In an effort to find out more information about some of the local hunting spots, I called my friend's dad. He told me he had not been having any luck and that there was no way I'd be able to shoot a buck on the last day of archery season. He said the deer had been way too pressured in our area and that they were not going to move during daylight hours. In response, I told him I'd call him and let him come see my buck after I shot him.

After hanging up the phone, I decided to try the spot I walked through the previous Saturday and heard the deer running out of. That patch of woods was about a hundred yards wide and a half mile long. The narrow direction of the patch sloped downward from the road to a creek. On the other side of the creek was a cow pasture to the right and a patch of pines to the left. Above the pine trees is where I grunting in the twelve-pointer when I was sixteen.

In the morning, I stepped off of the road into the patch of woods above the cow pasture, tiptoed halfway down the hillside, and set up on the ground behind a tree. Not long after daybreak, I made a spectacular series of rattles and grunts. As soon as I finished, I picked up my bow in preparation for a shot. Time passed, but no deer came. This caused my hopes to dwindle. Ten minutes later, I rattled again, but still nothing came. Eventually, I put my bow on the ground and sat on my butt facing downhill with my legs stretched out in front of me. As I looked down toward the cow pasture feeling somewhat defeated, I thought to myself, "There's no use trying. My friend's dad was right. The deer around here get so pressured all season that they are not going to move during daylight hours."

Twenty minutes passed as I sat there sulking. Although it was only about 7:40 in the morning, I began to think about packing up my things and heading home. I then turned my head to the left and saw a four-point buck standing *only **six** yards away* from me! I never even heard him coming and was completely shocked by his appearance! Fortunately, he still had no idea I was there. He just continued walking past me up the hill. I waited until his head went behind a tree then carefully rolled over onto my knees. In the same motion, I swiftly lifted my bow. He was about thirteen yards away when I began to draw. Just before I reached my anchor point, the same blade of the same broadhead hit my finger and popped the arrow off of my string again! The arrow fell into my lap, and the buck looked straight at me!

This was a frustrating, difficult situation to be in, and I was so mad at that broadhead! As the buck stared me down, I very slowly closed my eyelids to hide the whites of my eyes. The buck lowered his head, and then snapped it back up. He repeatedly did this, and I knew exactly what this behavior meant. Deer do this when they think they are being hunted by a predator. They lower their head in an effort to make the predator think they are starting to feed again. This is typically when a predator tries to advance in the stalk. The deer then snaps its head back up in an attempt to catch the predator's movement. Once the predator is noticed and identified, the deer runs away.

My arms began to wear out from holding my bow at full draw as the buck continued to stare at me. The heavy poundage I was pulling along with the buck fever that was making my arms tremble were almost too much for me to handle. Even though I knew it would ruin the hunt, I thought about just easing down on the bow string. As I was about to give up and do this, the buck calmly turned and walked away. He walked straight into some thick bushes, which allowed me to ease down on the bow string. As I did this, the arrow got pushed by the bottom part of the string and the broadhead slid up into my sight window.

To my utter dismay, the broadhead got significantly jammed in the sight! I tried to quietly slide it back out, but it was completely stuck! My anger and annoyance with that arrow escalated. Removing it quickly and quietly was made even more difficult by the fact that my hands were still shaking vigorously from the buck fever.

Eventually, I was able to wiggle the arrow loose. As soon as I got it free, I nocked it back on the string and began peeking around the tree to see where the buck had gone. He was standing in the bushes twenty-five yards away facing my direction. He still had not given up on identifying me and started taking a few steps in my direction before stopping again. When he did this, I drew back my bow with my left hand closed so as to not have the arrow pop off the string again. I then leaned in as close to the tree as I could. I did this to conceal my outline and make it more difficult for the deer to identify my human shape.

I expected the buck to step out from behind the bushes at any moment, but he never did. He just stood still at the edge of them for several minutes. My arms quickly grew tired, and I couldn't hold the string back any longer. As a result, I leaned in further behind the tree so that the deer couldn't see my movement. I then eased down on the string.

Five minutes passed before the deer decided to move again. He began to walk downhill. This offered me one more chance to shoot. In order to do this, I had to maneuver my bow between the split in the tree next to me. At that point in time, the buck was on the other side of a blown down tree. I quickly guessed that he was twenty-two yards and pulled back on the string. I placed my twenty yard pin on the upper portion of his body just in case he was a little farther than the yardage I estimated. I then released the string. The buck's back immediately bowed downward in the shape of a banana as he dropped toward the ground when he heard my bow go off. Simultaneously, I watched as my arrow flew just over the top of his back without touching a single hair. If he wouldn't have dropped, I would have taken out his spine. Instead, he ran away unscathed.

As soon as I got up, I paced off the distance to where the buck had been standing. Much to my surprise, the deer was only thirteen yards away. When I got to where he was standing, I discovered that not only was he behind the blown down tree, but he was also standing in a little ditch. These factors made the deer look smaller, which also made him *appear* to be much further away than he actually was.

Some lessons I learned from this hunt were to account for topography and objects that may make a target seem closer or father than it actually is. Also, it is a good idea to use a rangefinder or some other means of determining distances in advance so that you don't have to guess the yardage when it comes time to shoot.

That particular broadhead on my arrow cost me two chances at getting a buck that year, and I never found the arrow after missing that buck. However, it helped me realize that I need to *test every single arrow* in my quiver before taking it hunting. As a result, I now shoot all of my arrows with a broadhead on them at a target made for broadheads to make sure each arrow works correctly before taking it hunting. If I had done this with that arrow, I would have discovered in advance that it gets hung up on my finger and pulled off of the string while drawing the bow because of the angle of the blades on the broadhead.

Ever since I started testing my hunting arrows as I just described, I have found many that do not fly accurately with a fixed-blade broadhead. Sometimes it is because the threads in that arrow's insert are flawed, which cause the broadhead to be slightly angled instead of perfectly straight. You can test this by spinning the arrow on the tip of your finger. You will feel and see it wobble a little if the insert is flawed. When I discover an arrow that has a faulty insert, I only use it for practicing with field points. Please note, flight issues caused by a faulty insert may not apply or be as significant if you are hunting with mechanical (expandable) broadheads.

I have also discovered that shooting a broadhead into a target even one time can significantly dull the blades. For this reason, I never use a broadhead I have practiced with for hunting unless I have properly sharpened or replaced the blades beforehand.

Another change I made after that hunting season was to stop drawing my bow with an open left hand. This is especially important for safety reasons. If your finger is in the way of the broadhead while drawing the bow, it also has the potential of being sliced by the broadhead as the arrow leaves the bow. I now keep my fingers *gently* closed around the handle. As a result, they are no longer sticking out and getting in the way.

ATTITUDE PROBLEMS

Before the start of my third year of college, I transferred to the main campus of Penn State University. By that time in my life, my passion for bow hunting had completely consumed me. I had read every hunting book and magazine I could get my hands on. The walls of the bedroom were also littered with pictures of big game animals.

If there was one thing I wanted to do in life, it was bow hunt. In fact, my dream was to become a professional hunter and make hunting videos for a living. For this reason, I saved up my money and bought the best video camera I could afford. I then begged everyone I knew to help me fulfill my passion and desire to video my hunts and become a professional hunter.

The only person I could find who was interested in helping me with my dream was a good friend of mine from high school, John Ortlieb. My plan was to shoot a monster buck on video and then video John shooting one. If we filled our Pennsylvania buck tags early in the season, we'd buy hunting licenses in New Jersey since that was the closest state to John's hunting spot in Pennsylvania. My mind was set on shooting only big bucks. Shooting a small buck became unthinkable, and I began to look down on people who did.

To make the hunting video, I would drive three hours to John's house every weekend. We would get up around three in the morning and then drive an hour and a half to his hunting spot in the Pocono Mountains of Pennsylvania. We'd hunt all day and then drive home. Since it was illegal to hunt on Sunday in Pennsylvania, I'd simply go to church on Sunday morning and then drive back to college in the afternoon.

My seemingly good desire to make a hunting video began to mold me into an uncaring person. For example, on opening day of that year, my dad hunted by himself in the woods where I shot my five-pointer. By that point in time, they had already started plowing down trees in that forest to build another housing development. My dad set up in a corner where there were still some woods left. He had two first-year deer standing under him all morning. When it came time for him to get down, he decided to fill his doe tag and take one of them. He figured it would be okay since all of the woods in that area were going to be destroyed soon anyway. He made a perfect shot and brought the deer home. When I returned from hunting in the mountains with John, my dad excitedly shared his successful hunt by showing me the deer he shot. I immediately picked on him and made fun of his deer because it didn't measure up to my prideful standards. After I was finished being judgmental and negative, I selfishly walked away and left him there to butcher the deer by himself without offering any help.

That event has become one of the worst memories of my hunting career. It deeply bothers me that I behaved that way! I really care about my dad a lot, and when I remember the look on his face when I ridiculed him and his deer, I still feel pain inside my heart from it. He was ready to celebrate the victory of getting a deer, whereas I was so filled with pride, greed, and vanity that I didn't embrace his success or the joy of the moment.

If you or I ever find ourselves looking down on someone, or think less of them because they are not meeting our standards, we should realize that we probably need an attitude adjustment. Chances are, when we are spiritually and emotionally more mature, we will look back and regret being the way we were. This especially holds true when it comes to our parents. We are supposed to be respectful toward them and not cut them down as I did in that situation. All I can say at this point is, "Dad, I'm sorry!"

GOOD DESIRES AND BAD INFLUENCES

Some of the other guys who hunted with John broke the rules while hunting. In particular, they drove around dirt roads in the mountains looking for deer. When they saw one, they'd jump out of their trucks with their bows in hand and shoot at the deer. This was completely illegal, and I was utterly disgusted with their actions! In addition to being illegal, what they were doing was not true hunting. In my opinion, it was a terrible abuse of the sport!

While the other guys drove around being outlaws, John and I took turns videoing each other. Most of our hunts were filled with rain and no deer sightings. In fact, out of all of our hunts during the first three weekends, we only saw *one* deer. It passed us while I was videoing John, and it was too far away for John to shoot. This hunt is depicted on my *Humble Beginnings Part One* video.

Things were not working out for the hunting video as I had planned, hoped, or envisioned. I even tried videoing some people at school in an effort to get a deer harvest on video but had no success. No matter what I did, *nothing* seemed to be working out for me. As a result, I started to become impatient, restless, and compulsive!

John's friends were having some success road hunting on the weekends, and my thoughts about road hunting began to shift because of how badly I wanted to make my hunting video. On the fourth weekend, after not seeing any deer all morning from our tree stand location, I felt so frustrated and desperate that I gave in to the temptation and went road hunting with the other guys in an effort to shoot a deer on video.

(Aside: Can you see how things were happening that were *out of my control*—bad weather and no deer sightings—that caused me to feel intensely frustrated? My *feelings* of frustration, coupled with my strong *desire* to make a hunting video, along with the bad example of others, began to influence my thoughts and decisions in a negative way.)

We went road hunting that afternoon and eventually came upon a doe. Everyone quickly yelled for me to get out of the truck and shoot. I jumped out and got my bow. One of the guys brought my video camera and began videoing. I was so filled with anxiety about what we were doing that I couldn't focus or concentrate. I drew my bow but was afraid to shoot. I also couldn't tell how far the doe was. At that moment, someone started yelling, "Shoot, shoot!" Even though I wasn't prepared, and I didn't feel right about what we were doing, I released the string. The arrow soared through the air and nipped the top of the deer's back. Despite the sound of a hit she ran off looking fine.

We gave the deer some time and then tried to track her. Unfortunately, we only found one small speck of blood. Despite a long time searching, we never recovered the animal. Most likely it was because I barely nipped the top of her. Regardless, I was completely ashamed of myself for my actions!

Road hunting was an awful experience from start to finish! It didn't feel like real hunting to me. Instead, it felt like one, big, massive anxiety trip. The reason is that I knew we were doing something illegal, and I was petrified of getting caught. After that day, I promised myself I would not road hunt again, and I am happy to say I have *easily* kept my promise!

I hope you realize that I could have withheld this story as well as the one with the gigantic eight-pointer near my college campus along the fence row. Instead of hiding them, I have intentionally confessed them, exposed myself, and made myself vulnerable to you and the rest of the world. However, I want you to know that I have done this for a very specific purpose. It is to help you and other people realize that even if we have good desires and good intentions, it is still possible for us to be *influenced* in a negative way by our feelings, passions, desires, and other people.

Think back to the story I told with the big eight-pointer along the fence row near my college campus. I was initially hunting in that area because I heard the other students talking about the bucks they shot on campus. Before listening to their bad example, I never even conceived the idea of hunting there because I innately knew it was wrong.

Another major factor behind my decision to try hunting near campus was my strong *desire* to get a buck. In that sense, my good desire to get a buck motivated me to look for an easy way to fulfill that desire, and I ended up following the bad example of the other students.

After allowing these things to influence me to hunt on the edge of campus, I saw the giant eight-pointer. That buck lived in an area that could not be hunted, and I should not have continued hunting him. Unfortunately, I allowed the new influences of greed, pride, and vanity to motivate me to keep hunting there even though the *police* told me I was not allowed.

A similar thing happened concerning my road hunting experience. I deeply *desired* to make a hunting video. However, things were not working out in my favor. This made me *feel* intensely *frustrated*. The negative *feeling* of frustration coupled with my *desire* to make the video along with the *bad example* of others—the guys who were road hunting—*influenced* me to *think* about doing something I knew was wrong. I ended up giving in to those thoughts, feelings, and influences in an effort to fulfill my *desire* to make a hunting video and someday becoming a professional bow hunter.

These two situations are good examples of how even our good desires can be turned into something negative if we allow them to be influenced by the bad example of other people or our own sinful inclinations. With that in mind, can you think of a time in your own life when you were negatively influenced in a similar way? It doesn't even have to be in a hunting situation. It could be any life situation.

If a particular instance came to your mind, I encourage you to analyze that situation a little bit and identify the different factors involved. Primarily, note the *influences* you received from other people, as well as your own *thoughts*, your own *feelings*, and your own *desires*. Clearly recognizing and identifying these details can give you a new form of *power*. This awareness gives you the opportunity to *intentionally choose* to overcome those factors the next time they happen instead of simply given in to them like you might have if you were not watching out for them and making a focused effort to overcome them.

If you are interested in this type of self-improvement, I encourage you to take a few minutes right now before continuing on to the next section so that you can consider the ideas I just presented. As you consider these things, you may even want to go back and reread this section to help open your mind to more insights and ideas. As you do, I pray that God will help you gain an outstanding level of insight and awareness that will be useful and helpful for you throughout the rest of your life!

IT FINALLY HAPPENED

Although I still wanted to shoot a big buck, my desperation in wanting to simply get a deer harvest on video significantly lowered my standards. By this point in the season, I was willing to shoot the first deer that came by as long as the camera was rolling. Even if it was a small deer like the one my dad got opening day, I was going to shoot!

Reaching this mental and emotional state of desperation purged a lot of my bad attitudes. This helped me realize I should not have looked down on my dad or anyone else regarding the size of the deer they shoot.

It was now the second to the last Saturday of hunting season, and John and I went through our normal routine. I drove all the way home from college and met him at his house. We slept for about three or four hours, got up real early, and then drove all the way up to the mountains. On this particular morning, we went to a new spot where John had hung tree stands during the week. About a half hour after daylight, I made a series of rattles and grunts. Twenty minutes passed, but still no deer were moving through the area.

By seven-thirty in the morning we had been awake for four hours. I was feeling hungry so I sat down. I then took the cheese sandwich I had made out of my backpack and started eating it. Just after taking my second bite, John tapped me on the shoulder and whispered, "Deer, deer, it's a spike!" I immediately jumped up and scrambled to find a place to put the sandwich. It seemed as though there was nowhere to put it, so I quickly bent down and set it on the platform of my tree stand. I then grabbed my bow. I also pulled my grunt call out of my jacket and grunted at the buck. Within a few seconds, he turned and came straight toward the tree we were in!

The deer was approaching from the exact opposite side of the tree from me. At first, he was angled toward my left, so I carefully lifted my bow and arrow and maneuvered them around to the left-hand side of the tree. The buck then angled back to the right, so I quickly and cautiously cleared my bow and arrow around the tree to the right-hand side. However, as I did this, I shifted my feet and ac-cidently knocked the sandwich off of the platform of my tree stand. It hit the ground and made a loud thud. This caused me to panic, but fortunately the buck didn't run away. He simply kept coming toward us.

As the buck continued to approach, he turned and angled over toward the left again. In response, I quickly and carefully cleared my bow and arrow around the tree again and got ready facing left. The buck then angled back to the right, so I lifted my bow and arrow, turned my body, and got ready facing the right-hand side of the tree. To be honest, I felt as if I was dancing the two-step behind the tree!

The deer walked up to the base of tree we were in and saw the plastic bag that my sandwich had fallen out of. He then stepped toward the bag with his nose out sniffing. I completely panicked and thought, "Oh no! He is going to smell the bag and run!" Even though the buck was still on the other side of the tree from me, I quickly drew back, aimed, and shot. Much to my surprise and embarrassment I completely missed the deer! He then ran down through the woods about twenty-five yards and stopped.

(Aside: I was even more embarrassed about this miss when I watched the video footage later and saw that the buck was not even spooked at all by the bag. In fact, he even put his nose into it and lifted it up off the ground. However, I didn't see any of that while it was happening because I was so focused on the back of the deer where I was aiming for a shot.)

As I mentioned, the buck was only twenty-five yards away when he stopped running and looked back in our direction. Since he was still within shooting range, I quickly nocked another arrow. If you watch either of my early videos—*The Spirituality of Hunting* or *Humble Beginnings Part One*—you'll notice that the buck hears me make a noise while nocking the arrow. However, it was not the sound of my arrow clipping onto the string. It was actually the sound of my arrow slipping off of my metal arrow rest and hitting the riser of my bow.

Even though the deer was somewhat alerted and could run away at any second, I didn't have a clear shooting lane so I couldn't take a shot. All I needed was for him to take two steps in the direction he was facing. As soon as I thought he was going to do this, I drew back my bow and got ready. Unfortunately, instead of walking in the direction he was facing he turned and walked straight away from me. While still at full draw, I tried to bleat with my voice to get him to turn, but he did not. Eventually, I eased down on the bow string.

I thought the hunt was over. I thought I had ruined my chance of finally getting a deer harvest on video. This terribly depressed me!

Just then, John started whispering, "Grunt, grunt!" I didn't think it was going to work, but I tried it anyway.

As soon as I let out the first grunt, the deer looked back in our direction. When he tried to look away, I grunted again. In fact, every single time the buck started to look away, I grunted. It was a trick I had learned from a lecture I had once attended on calling deer. Basically, every time a deer tries to look away from you, you call to it. However, as soon as the deer looks or walks in your direction, you immediately stop calling.

While I continued to grunt at the buck every time he looked away, he began to pump his tail. This was a good sign! It indicated he was becoming aroused. He then turned and started to walk back in our direction on the downwind side of us. I estimated the trail he was on to be about twenty-two yards away. As the buck stepped into my shooting lane, he stopped to smell a spot where I had sprayed some doe-in-heat scent that morning on our way into the woods. I was already at full draw before the buck stopped moving so I focused my mind and intently aimed at the crease behind his shoulder. I then released the string. The sound of my bow went off and the arrow went into flight. I watched as the deer began to duck as my arrow drew closer, but it wasn't enough. My arrow hit its mark behind his shoulder. It was a perfect strike!

The buck ran up through the woods about thirty yards and stopped. He then turned around and stumbled back toward the spot where he was standing when I shot. Although you can't see it clearly on the video, he flipped over onto his back at the end of his run. The moment he hit the ground, I excitedly yelled, "He's down! He's down! Good boy, I got him good!" I was so intensely excited at that moment that I started to stutter and stumble over my words on the video. It took a few seconds for me to regain my composure enough to actually think and speak clearly for the camera.

To this day, every time I watch that hunt on video I begin smiling. I also think about how much *joy* it brought John and me. We worked so hard to simply get a deer harvest on video that the size didn't matter anymore. The accomplishment itself made us happy! Through that situation, I finally experienced the true joy of the hunt.

Looking back, I realize that it was through the hardships and disappointments we faced that season that purged me of my bad attitudes. From that perspective, I am very glad everything worked out the way it did. I'd rather shoot a small buck, be happy, and become a better person because of it, than shoot a monster buck, yet end up being a greedy, selfish, prideful, and inconsiderate person because of it. Don't get me wrong, I'd still like to shoot a nice buck, but not at the cost of my own integrity and character as a person. How about you? Which would you prefer? Why would you prefer that one over the other?

SECOND YEAR SECOND DEER

The following year, I drove all the way home from school to hunt with John Ortlieb on opening day. As was our usual routine, we hunted at John's spot in the Pocono Mountains. It was our second year videoing and his turn to be in front of the camera. I filmed John shooting a young deer that morning, which is the second deer harvest portrayed on my video titled *The Spirituality of Hunting*. That footage is also on my *Humble Beginnings Part One* video. By the way, both videos, as well as many others, are available on the videos page of my website, SeansOutdoorAdventures.com.

At college, I had become the president of the Penn State Archery Club. One of my new friends from the club offered to video for me a few times. On one of our first hunts together I realized after we got to the woods that I forgot one of my bags of equipment at my apartment. It contained my camouflage pants, cap, flashlight, and knife. Since we could manage to hunt without them, we simply went into the woods and set up our tree stands anyway.

Still frustrated and motivated by my inability to get very much video footage of *me* shooting deer, I was prepared to shoot the first deer that walked by us. A doe fawn was the first deer to come our way that evening, and I planned to shoot! Unfortunately, just before she stepped into my shooting lane, she took off running. I bleated with my voice in an effort to stop her, but it didn't work. Not having a chance to shoot at the deer greatly upset me, and I wondered why she ran.

That deer ended up coming back down through the woods about fifty yards away from us. She continued in the direction she originally came from and walked out of sight. A few minutes later, I heard multiple deer walking in our direction from the area where the first deer originally came from. This made me glad I didn't get a shot at the little one. My hope was that there was a nice buck in the group of deer coming our way.

Eventually, another small deer came up the hill and walked past us about ten yards away. It was probably the first time in my life I intentionally passed on a deer that was within shooting range. Eric, my cameraman, told me later that he was screaming in his mind, "Shoot! Shoot!" as the deer walked by us.

The other deer continued to walk in our direction, and I anxiously awaited their arrival. It ended up being a large doe and two more small deer. The big doe came our way slightly quartering toward me. When she was about ten yards from the base of the tree we were in, I drew back, took aim, and released the string. The arrow hit her right behind the shoulder. This made me incredibly excited, and it was a tremendous relief to finally get my second deer harvest on video!

Almost immediately after I shot, Eric whispered, "Shoot, I messed up!" Panic immediately filled my heart as I nervously exclaimed, "Did you get the hit on video?" He said, "Yeah, but I jolted right after you shot and turned off the camera. The deer was all the way up the other hill before I got it turned back on."

Keep in mind that this took place in the 1990s, which is when videos were recorded on video *tape*. It took several seconds for the camera to begin rolling the tape once you hit record, which is why Eric didn't get any additional footage until the deer was already eighty yards away running up the other hillside.

Although Eric's statement disappointed me a little, I was happy to know he at least got the hit on video. After reviewing the footage and waiting a few minutes, we climbed down.

It made me a little nervous that we didn't see very much blood around the spot where I hit the deer. We slowly packed up the tree stands and waited another half hour before tracking her. There were only a few specks of blood on the trail she ran down, which had me very concerned! About sixty yards down the trail, we found my bloody arrow on the ground. From that point on, there was no more blood at all!

Since there was no blood to follow, we slowly and quietly stalked up the adjacent hillside where we last saw the deer. It was now a little over an hour since I shot her, and I was beginning to panic!

At this point, another hunter stopped by to talk to us on his way out of the woods. We told him about the deer and showed him the video footage. He congratulated us, wished us luck, and then continued on his way.

At this point, it was getting dark fast! I thought we were going to have to leave, drive all the way back to campus to get a flashlight, and then come all the way back to the woods. Fortunately, Eric was an Eagle Scout, and he came prepared. He pulled a tiny flashlight from his pocket, and we kept looking for the deer.

The flashlight didn't give off much light, so we eventually decided to take a quick look on the ground in the direction we hadn't looked yet. If we didn't see the deer, we planned to head back to my apartment to get more supplies. I then shined the light over the bushes in the direction the deer had been running. As soon as I did this, I saw the white belly of my dead deer. Instantaneously, we erupted with shouts of joy and rejoicing!

Eric then pulled a small Swiss Army Knife from his pocket. Once again, I was happy he came prepared. Since we didn't know where any butcher shops were located, and had nowhere else to take the deer, we decided to skin and quarter the doe right there in the woods. This was the first time either of us had done something like this!

I had some rope in my backpack. We planned to hang the deer from a thick branch and then begin skinning her. Unfortunately, that didn't work. Both the rope and the branch broke when we tried hoisting the deer up. As a result, we simply skinned the side of the deer that was facing up while it was lying on the ground. We then removed the front leg as well as the back leg from that side of the deer and placed them into a clean trash bag. We then removed the loin meat and added it to the bag. Lastly, we removed all of the excess meat from the neck muscle and anything else we could find on that side of the deer's body. Afterward, we rolled the deer over and skinned that side off as well. We then did the same in removing the legs and the other meat and placed them all into a separate trash bag. Upon finishing, we carried all of the meat to my car. We then stopped at a grocery store on the way home to get some freezer paper and plastic freezer storage bags.

It became quite a memorable evening! When we got to my apartment, my roommate had a bunch of girls over. I thought they were all going to run out the door as soon as we walked in wearing camouflage and holding trash bags with deer legs sticking out of them. Much to my surprise, only one girl left. The rest stayed and asked lots of questions. My roommate's girlfriend was particularly intrigued by the anatomy of the deer. She kept bending and playing with the knee joints and watching the ligaments and tendons move. While all of that was taking place, Eric and I ordered a large pizza and slammed the whole thing down as fast as we could. We were starving!

After eating, we removed all the meat from the bones. As we did this, we cut most of it into serving sized steaks. We then wrapped them up in freezer paper and placed them into sealable plastic storage bags. They were then put into the freezer. All of the meat that was too small for steaks or roasts was cut into small cubes and placed into plastic storage bags to be used in stew. Given that this was our first time processing a deer I think we did an excellent job!

This experience enabled me to realize I am capable of processing my own deer, and I've been doing it ever since. The only difference now is that I have a meat grinder, and I grind a lot of the meat up rather than cube it for stew. I also package the meat differently now. Instead of using freezer paper, I have found that clear plastic wrap works better for me. I simply wrap the meat in the plastic wrap and push out all of the air. I then place the wrapped meat into a freezer safe plastic storage bag, push out all of the air, seal it, and then freeze it. I've had ground meet in the freezer for more than a year packaged this way without getting freezer burnt! I've also found that the deer meat tastes even better when it is slightly aged in the freezer for about six months.

Chapter 2 – Starting to Find the Spirit in Hunting

GOING INSTINCTIVE

My hopes and expectations for that hunting season remained high after getting the doe harvest on video with my friend, Eric. I thought for sure things were finally going to work out for me. Unfortunately, all of my efforts failed. I even paid my roommate to video me every single day during the late archery season while we were on Christmas break, but I was unable to get another deer harvest on video. I then graduated from Penn State in the spring and started working full time for an environmental company.

Before I go any further in my explanation of what happened next, I think I should mention that there were several life changing events that took place during my last year and a half of college that I didn't tell you about. If you are interested in learning about them, they are depicted in my book titled *I've Got to Change*. As for right now, however, I will simply say that the result of those dramatic events inspired me to develop a spiritual life and a more active relationship with God. To help facilitate this effort, I decided to try hunting instinctively the following season. I thought that doing this would help me become more in tune with the Holy Spirit through sensing the Holy Spirit while I was shooting my bow without sights.

I still had four months before the bow hunting season opener when I made the decision to start shooting instinctively so I immediately began training. When I told my bow hunting friends that I was doing this, some said, "Forget it, Sean! You can't do it! You will never hit a deer! Put your sight back on your bow, go buy a mechanical release (*I was still shooting with just my fingers at that time*), and get yourself ready for hunting season!" Their comments made it hard for me to believe in myself, which turned into a major trial for me. Thoughts of doubt and disbelief plagued my mind each and every time I drew back my bow.

While I was trying to figure out how to actually shoot instinctively, my cousin gave me a book called, *Zen in the Art of Archery*. I was hesitant to read it because I follow Jesus Christ, and I didn't want to get sidetracked by an eastern, non-Christian spirituality. However, I eventually decided to read the book hoping it would give me some clues as to how one actually shoots instinctively. I just made sure to be diligent and careful about not letting it influence my spirituality in a non-Christian way.

As I read, I looked for ways that the Holy Spirit was involved with the shot as opposed to simply accepting the ideas and terminology presented in the book. If what the author was saying was true, then the Zen Master's ability to shoot a bow instinctively and effectively impressed me. Although their ability to shoot was remarkable, elements of their philosophy bothered me. For example, they talked about emptying their mind completely. They also claimed to *not* know if they drew the bow or if the bow drew them.

The Christian life is not an act of emptying one's mind. Instead, we allow our mind to be *filled* with wisdom and knowledge from God's revelation. In addition, faith stands on reason. It is not physically possible for a bow to draw a human, which makes it clearly incorrect to teach or believe. The *reasoning* behind it is simply wrong. However, it is reasonable and possible for a human to draw a bow and learn how to release the string in an effective way so that the arrow hits where the archer intends. Similarly, it is *reasonable* to think that we need a savior because of our fallen human condition and our inability to be absolutely perfect in everything we do.

Any archer can relate to this aspect of our human imperfection after he or she takes a few shots at a target with his or her bow. Upon retrieving the arrows, he or she clearly sees his or her inability to hit an absolute perfect bull's-eye every single time. In that sense, we realize we can't rely solely on ourselves for personal perfection.

Since it seemed to me that the Zen philosophy regarding certain topics was not in harmony with my Christian philosophy, I rejected their way of thinking on those matters. For instance, instead of emptying my mind completely, I decided to look for ways that God was *with* me and working *through* me to help me sense the shot. I wanted to be *fully aware* of the reality that was taking place. I wanted to be able to tell if and when God was the one who was helping me with the shot. This aspect of learning how to *sense God's activity* is how I hoped archery would help my spiritual life. I believed this would help me be more perceptive of God's activity in other areas of my life as well.

Although I rejected a number of the concepts presented in the Zen-based archery book, there were two ideas I did take from it that I thought were helpful. One was to keep my emotions relaxed at all times. The other was to continue breathing throughout the shot. Up until that time, I had always held my breath and never tried to relax my emotions while I was shooting.

Although these two ideas were helpful, I still had no idea how to get my arrow to hit where I wanted it to every time. I also didn't know how to let God help me with the shot. At first, I tried drawing the bow and focusing on my feelings rather than on the target to see if I could just "feel the shot," but that alone didn't work. I then tried looking at the target and focusing primarily on breathing, but that by itself also didn't work.

After weeks of intense experimentation, I finally found a way of shooting instinctively that enabled me to be fairly consistent. I continued to use my feelings, remain calm, and breathe throughout the shot, but the one thing I had not yet done was *focus my eyes on one specific point* on the target. I needed to pick *one specific point* and keep my eyes *fixated* on it the entire time. Before that, I was simply looking at the whole target in general. However, *focusing* on *one specific spot* on the target made a big difference for me!

Every once in a while I was able to actually feel the Holy Spirit while I was at full draw. When it happened, I could actually sense and feel where to move my arm that holds the bow. I would then move my arm in that direction. As I moved, I continued to pay attention to my feelings. At the same time, I kept my eyes fixated on the point of aim. When I *felt* that I had reached the correct spot with my arm, I'd stop, remain calm, and then release the string. The arrow hit a perfect bull's-eye every time this occurred! It amazed me when this happened! Although I wished I could sense the Spirit and shoot a perfect bull's-eye every time, I'd say it only happened about once every fifty to a hundred shots. My other shots were pretty good, but not absolutely perfect like when I felt the Holy Spirit help me.

Before I started shooting instinctively, I thought it was going to be easy and effortless. I thought the Spirit would just take over and do the hard work for me. What I found to be true in my case was that shooting instinctively required a tremendous amount of *hard work* and practice. It demanded a great amount of body and mind training. One of the biggest challenges for me was remaining mentally focused during every single shot. I simply wasn't used to practicing that level of extreme concentration. Even still, I became pretty good at shooting instinctively. This was probably because of all the hours I practiced every day. From those hours of practice, my muscles and arms got used to the position they needed to be in to make a good shot. Some people call this muscle memory.

As hunting season approached, I started shooting from the roof of our barn to prepare myself for shooting out of a tree stand. There were plenty of people who continued to doubt me. They said I was stupid for wanting to shoot instinctively. They had no idea how proficient I had become. My hope was to prove them all wrong and prove myself capable. In fact, I wanted to prove them so wrong that I purchased seven antlerless deer licenses that year. At that time, I lived in a special regulation area of Pennsylvania that allowed hunters to buy as many antlerless deer licenses as they wanted. I chose to buy seven because seven is the Biblical number for completeness and fulfillment. In that sense, I tied my whole hunting season to a Biblical concept, which made me happy.

I knew that if I waited the entire season for a nice buck, I may never get to shoot at all. As a result, I decided to try for a big buck opening day. If I didn't get one, I'd shoot the first doe I saw during the week that followed.

My Uncle Dennis's boss recently purchased a farm about a half hour away from my parents' house. My uncle and his son, Dennis, along with my dad and I were supposed to be the only people permitted to hunt on the farm. We even needed to carry around a special card with written permission on it from the owner and leave a visible notification card in the windshield of our vehicle while we were on the property.

My father and I went over to scout the farm almost immediately after gaining permission. After intensely investigating the area and picking out tree stand locations, we headed back to our car. Unexpectedly, we came across two other hunters who were also scouting for tree stand locations. We told them they were not allowed to be there, but they told us they had hunted there for over twenty years and were not going to stop. They said they didn't care who bought the property.

This deeply bothered me! Why can't people be more respectful of other people's land? I guess these two men needed to learn their lesson just as I had learned. At some point, every single one of us must learn to respect other people's property and stay out of areas where we do not have permission to hunt. Just as the police had told me I couldn't hunt in the area where I saw the big eight-pointer along the fence row in college, we told these two men they could not hunt on this farm. However, just as I had ignored the directive of the police, these men ignored us.

How about you? What will you do if you are ever told you are not permitted to hunt in an area you really wanted to try hunting; especially one where you know a giant buck lives? Or, have you ever hunted on land you should not have? If so, what can you do to make up for doing that?

At any rate, after learning that the deep woods were going to be pressured by other hunters, I abandon my original tree stand selection. I moved toward a smaller, thin section of timber off to the side of the property. I then set up my tree stand forty yards from the edge of a cornfield.

Since no one was interested in videoing me that year, I rigged up a way to mount my video camera to the corner of my tree stand so that I could film my own hunts. Keep in mind that this took place in the 1990s before companies started manufacturing and selling video camera arms that mount to the tree next to you.

On opening morning of the hunting season, there was a buck standing near my tree when I got there in the dark. I could see his eyes glowing in the light from my flashlight. He was investigating a fake scrape I had made and left a little deer scent in. Unfortunately, he ran off before I could get a good luck at him. I went over to inspect where he was standing and could see that he actually salivated in the scrape I made. I thought this was a good sign and that it could indicate he was excited, causing him to drool.

Not long after dawn, a little button buck came in from behind me. He stayed for about twenty minutes but then headed out into the corn. An hour later, two button bucks, a large doe, and a doe fawn came out of the corn and walked directly under my stand. I was somewhat tempted to shoot the big doe when she walked through my video camera's field of view, but I restrained myself because I wanted to wait for a buck. This video footage is included on my *Humble Beginnings Part One* video at the 1:18:20 time mark.

After the morning hunt came to a close, I met with my dad, uncle, and cousin for lunch. My dad was the only other person who saw any deer. He had two fawns go past him. Although my uncle and cousin didn't see anything that morning, they were excited and happy to see the video footage I got of the deer. It gave them hope for that evening's hunt.

While I was walking back to my tree stand that afternoon, I saw another hunter. I asked him if he had permission to be there. Rather than answer yes or no, he said he had hunted there for many years. He then walked right past my tree stand through the woods. That really irritated me! Since he walked through the woods by my spot, I didn't think I was going to see a single deer that evening. Surprisingly, I had a small button buck walk into the corn just before dark.

The area was getting heavily pressured by hunters, and I didn't see another deer from that tree stand location for several days. At the end of the week, I stood on the main access road to the property and looked at the whole farm. While brainstorming as to where I should move my tree stand to, I asked myself, "Where on this farm would no one think to hunt?" I knew from all my years of hunting heavily pressured areas that you have to go where no one else thinks the deer will go. These areas become safe havens for the deer. Finding one of these is like finding a goldmine.

After spinning around looking in every direction, I observed that there was a thin patch of woods about twenty yards wide along the main road at the front of the property. Behind it were several huge cornfields separated by tree lines. Behind the cornfields was the very large patch of woods where the majority of the deer sign and hunting pressure had been. Because of the pressure, I knew that many of the deer were going to stay out of the big woods and spend most of their day in the corn where it was safe.

As I looked at the thin patch of woods in the front of the property along the main road, I thought, "No one would think to hunt so close to the road. They are all going to be in the big woods on the back of the property." I also recalled how that big nine-pointer used to bed down along the road at the one spot I used to hunt.

While looking at the thin patch of woods along the road, I noticed a little tree line that started at the thin patch of trees and ran out into the middle of the cornfield. It actually stopped right in the center of the field as opposed to running all the way across it. The moment I laid eyes on this little tree line, I smiled and excitedly said out loud, "There's my goldmine!" I knew that deer could stay in the corn all day, and that bucks could easily visit the tree line to make scrapes and rubs at any time during the day. Deer could also walk up and down the tree line to get to and from the woods along the road. I also believed no one else would think to hunt a tiny tree line in the middle of the cornfield so close to the road like that.

I immediately went over to investigate the tree line. Sure enough, there were several fresh scrapes accompanied by numerous fresh rubs and a plethora of fresh deer tracks going up and down the tree line toward the woods along the road! With intense excitement, I relocated my stand! I set it up near the middle of the cornfield about twenty yards from the end of the tree line. The largest scrape was within shooting range. Without a doubt, this was an amazing spot!

As soon as I got my stand in place, I went home in order to leave the area undisturbed for the rest of the day. The following morning I climbed into my stand an hour before sunrise. Just as legal shooting light arrived, I glanced to my left and saw three doe walking out of the corn along the edge of the tree line. They were only eighteen yards away and coming straight at me when I first saw them. They never made a single sound and silently walked through the dirt toward the thin patch of woods along the road.

Just before I stood up, I reached down and hit record on my video camera. I then quickly stood and prepared to shoot. A few seconds is all that passed before my moment of truth had arrived. Experiencing the powerful adrenaline rush made it difficult for me to focus my mind, but I did the best that I could. I then drew back my bow and intensely focused my eyes on one small spot behind the shoulder of the largest doe. My arms pivoted to follow her as she walked past the base of my tree only six yards away. I felt ready. My consistency and accuracy had been outstanding at that distance. I gave myself the okay to release the string, and I continued to focus intently on the small spot behind the deer's shoulder. In that instant, I released. Surprisingly, the lower limb of my bow bounced off of my left leg during the shot because of how steep the downward angle was that I had to aim. This caused the bow to violently jolt in my hand, and I almost dropped it! I was so distracted and startled by this happening that I didn't even see where the deer went when they took off running.

I was worried that my shot had been thrown off by the bottom limb of my bow hitting my leg. As a result, I didn't know if I hit the deer or which way it ran. All I knew was that it sounded as if my arrow hit a rock on the ground and that one of the deer ran through the corn making crashing noises.

After frantically looking down trying to locate my arrow, I finally spotted it lying flat on the ground in the first row of corn. I could clearly see the broadhead end of the arrow and there was no blood on it. With great disappointment, I thought to myself, "Oh no, I missed!" I closed my eyes and tilted my head back feeling defeated. Thoughts ran through my mind, such as, "They were right. I failed. I couldn't do it. After all that effort practicing and struggling to believe in myself, I failed. It is going to be so hard to face everyone. I can just hear their voices now 'I told you. I knew you couldn't do it. You should have listened to me. You should have put sights on your bow and used a mechanical release.'"

I no longer felt confident enough to be in the woods with a bow. I immediately thought about leaving so that I didn't risk injuring any deer. Before packing up my things, I decided to pick up the video camera and zoom in with the viewfinder to look around the area where the deer had been standing. While I was zoomed in, I passed over my arrow. To my surprise, the entire fletching end of the arrow was covered with blood! I was immediately filled with energy and intense excitement! I then realized that the reason I wasn't able to see the blood on the arrow at first was that it blended in with the red coloration at the base of the dry cornstalks.

Just as I was about to climb down to get a closer look at my arrow, two small deer came out of the corn and stood beneath me. I didn't want to spook them off, so I sat back down and videoed them.

A half hour passed as they ate the leaves from the bushes underneath me in the tree line. Eventually, they moved on to the thin patch of woods along the road.

After those two deer left the area, I climbed down and excitedly stood next to my arrow. As you may know if you watched my *Humble Beginnings Part One* video, I started documenting everything with my video camera. I filmed my bow with no sights as well as the bloody arrow. I then knelt down to see which way the deer's tracks went. The doe I hit went through the corn. As I looked up through the rows, I saw the most elaborate blood trail I had ever seen. Blood was everywhere! With tremendous ease, I followed the trail about forty yards through the corn to the deer. After rolling her over, I learned that I had made a perfect heart-shot. I then knelt down next to her praising God and feeling fulfilled and exhilarated.

This hunt enabled me to know that I could in fact harvest a deer shooting instinctively. It also reaffirmed for me that deer will sometimes bed down near roads, especially when all the hunting pressure is deeper in the woods.

SENSING BEFORE SEEING

On the following Monday morning before work, I went to a new property where I had gained permission to hunt. It was located across the street from a large piece of public hunting ground. Because it was so close to the public land, and I suspected that people snuck onto this piece of private property, I was afraid that my tree stand would get stolen if I left it there. As a result, I only left my climbing stick in place so that I didn't make a tremendous amount of noise setting it up in the dark. I would simply bring my tree stand in with me each time I hunted there and hang it on the tree when I reached the top of my climbing stick.

The first morning I hunted there, I parked my car in the landowner's driveway and then tiptoed up the road. After walking several hundred yards, I reached the intersection and turned left. The public land was now on my right and the private land was on my left. I walked along that road until I reach the area I needed to turn down into the woods to get to my spot.

By the time I reached my tree, there was only about thirty minutes left before daylight. I quickly tied my bow to the rope and began climbing the ladder stick. Just as I made it to the top of the ladder, and grabbed the very last step, I heard a deer walking in my direction from the road. I immediately froze and listened carefully. Unfortunately, the deer was coming straight toward me! This greatly bothered me because my tree stand was still strapped to my back, and my bow was still on the ground attached to the rope.

The sound of the walking deer continued to get closer until it finally stopped directly underneath me. I slowly turned my head and peered down over my right shoulder in an effort to see the deer. I immediately saw that it was a buck. I could see his white antlers glistening in the moonlight. I then yelled in my mind, "I can't believe this! Talk about bad timing!"

The buck stood there for a minute and then took off running down through the woods. Although this disappointed me, I remained hopeful and proceeded to strap my tree stand to the tree and get ready. Unfortunately, no other deer came by me the rest of the morning.

After getting down out of the tree, I headed back up to the road. As soon as I stepped onto the pavement, I had a unique experience. A thought went through my mind, and a faint sense went through my body. The thought and sense was that I needed to be ready because there was a deer bedded down along the adjacent road I needed to walk down to get to my car. The sense even indicated approximately how far down the road the deer was located. However, I didn't think about the experience or pay much attention to it because it was so faint and unfamiliar to me. I just kept walking.

After turning down the adjacent road and making it halfway to the landowner's driveway, I looked over into the woods and saw a doe bedded down about twenty yards away watching me. I didn't break stride, but simply turned my head back in the direction I was walking as if I never saw her. There was a massive tree along the road a few steps ahead of me. As soon as I stepped behind the tree, I stopped, quickly ripped an arrow out of my quiver, nocked it, and then took two steps back in the direction I had just come from. The doe was looking in the direction I was previously headed on the other side of the tree. This gave me an opportunity to draw my bow. My eyes then fixated on a patch of hair behind her shoulder. Although she saw my movement while drawing the bow, my arrow was already in flight before there was anything she could do about it.

To my surprise, the arrow did not hit the spot I was focused on. Instead, it hit the deer in the back of the neck directly behind her head. She died instantly. She never knew what happened and never felt any pain. It may have been the most effective deer harvest I had ever had. I then immediately looked up to heaven and said, "Thank You!" I knew I could not take credit for that shot. It was clearly a mercy of God that I even hit the deer let alone made an extremely effective shot. Not a single ounce of meat was damaged by the shot, which enabled me to get more meat off of the deer to donate to the homeless shelter and meals for shut-ins program I had promised it to.

The most important lesson I learned from this hunt was that the Holy Spirit can in fact speak to me through my inner senses. This helped me realize I needed to start paying closer attention to my senses in order to perceive what the Spirit was telling me. As part of this, I realized that the thought I had about the deer being bedded down near the road seemed a little different than my normal thoughts. In addition, *the way I felt* when the thought came to me was slightly different than I normally *feel* when I think about things. Realizing these differences helped me prepare myself to notice them again in the future. This also made me wonder how many times the Holy Spirit had tried to communicate with me in the past but I had totally missed the message because I wasn't paying attention to these slight variations in my senses.

I am very grateful to God for the sport of hunting because through it He obviously has taught me how to grow and mature in my spiritual life. I believe the Holy Spirit can communicate with you in the same way He did with me in this situation. If you don't already do so, I encourage you to start paying closer attention to your inner thoughts and feelings so that you don't miss the Spirit's messages. In that respect, if you ever notice that you have an idea that comes into your mind and then actually happens shortly after, please take some time to analyze the whole situation. Look for the very faint and subtle *differences* in the way you felt when the thought initially came to you. Watching and waiting for these kinds of experiences will help you be more prepared to recognize and respond to them if or when they happen again in the future.

MISSING IT

The following week I missed my first deer while shooting instinctively. I was hunting in a permanent tree stand that my neighbor Scott had built about a hundred yards from the spot where I grunted in the twelve-pointer when I was sixteen. The stand was also about sixty yards to the left of where I drew back on the little four-pointer but my broadhead hit my finger and pulled the arrow off of the string. If you will recall, I eventually got a second shot at that little buck but misjudged the distance so the arrow went over his back.

Anyway, with just twenty minutes left on this particular hunt in Scott's permanent stand, I heard a deer walking through the dry leaves on the edge of the cow pasture. It was about a hundred yards away and headed straight toward the small patch of pines where I encountered the twelve-pointer. Although I couldn't see the deer, I immediately grunted a few times in an effort to call it in my direction. To my surprise, it *ran* toward me! Before I even had a chance to think about what I wanted to do, the buck, which was only a six-pointer, was quickly walking past me just ten yards away. I drew back my bow but felt extremely unsure of myself. His rack was smaller than I wanted. While standing there at full draw, I argued with myself as to whether or not I should shoot. Before coming to a conclusion, I suddenly released the string. The arrow sailed over the buck's back, and he ran away unharmed.

The first thing I learned from this hunt was that I shouldn't even draw my bow back unless I am absolutely certain I want to harvest the animal. Secondly, if I know I want to shoot at least an eight-pointer, I should ask myself what I will do if a mediocre six-pointer walks under me near the end of a long, boring, frustrating hunt. Experiencing frustration and boredom for a long time and then suddenly experiencing an intense adrenaline rush can make it extremely difficult to think clearly. Realizing this helped me understand that in order to overcome all of my intense emotions I need to focus on my goals and *force myself* to stick to my predetermined plan!

What about you? What will you do in the future if you are in one of those types of situations? What will your plan be? I encourage you to decide in advance and then stick to it!

I QUIT

During the first four weeks of the season, I harvested five deer, missed one, unfortunately wounded two that I didn't find, and passed on several small bucks. Some of the footage from those events can be viewed on my *Humble Beginnings Part One* video.

The very last time I hunted that season, Scott was sitting with me and videoing for me. Two small deer came out of a cornfield into our clearing about an hour and a half before dark. This footage can also be viewed on *Humble Beginnings Part One*, and it starts at 1:44:20.

Both deer were standing broadside about fifteen yards away. I drew back and shot at the larger one. The shot looked perfect! Scott even whispered "Nice shot!" Although it looked as if my arrow hit the deer in the heart, it actually went slightly under the deer and stuck in the ground. The deer then ran twenty-five yards to the edge of the field and stopped. I quickly nocked another arrow and shot again. Surprisingly, the same exact thing happened.

After my second miss, I was very upset with myself. However, I looked over to see that the smaller deer was still standing in the same place looking around. In an effort to redeem myself, I quickly nocked a third arrow and drew back. Unfortunately, the arrow hit the deer directly in the guts. She ran down through the woods about seventy yards and then stopped. I was so emotionally distraught at that moment that I didn't want to shoot again. Instead, I asked Scott to go finish the deer off. He handed me the video camera, lowered his bow, and then climbed down and stalked through the woods toward the deer.

Scott got close but didn't get a shot off before she ran away. I didn't want the deer to have to suffer any more so I quickly devised a plan. I had Scott get on the upper side of the tree line she ran into. I then positioned myself on the lower side of it and got ahead of Scott by about fifty yards. My plan was to drive the deer back to Scott so that he could shoot her.

The tree line was about twenty-five yards wide and very thick. After silently stalking ahead of Scott's position, I made a tiny bit of noise. The plan worked perfectly! The deer ran straight to Scott and stopped within five yards of him! When I heard his bow go off, I breathed a huge sigh of relief because I knew the deer would not have to suffer anymore. When I made it over to Scott, he was standing still holding his arrow. The nock point was broken off, and he had a bewildered look on his face. This concerned me! He then told me he completely missed the deer. At that moment, my heart sank!

After giving the deer some time, we tracked her through the cornfield but eventually lost the blood trail. It was now getting dark, and Scott needed to go home. Before heading back to the car, I looked out toward the road and started counting the telephone poles from the intersection to the area of the field where we were standing. I also counted how many corn rows there were between us and the end of the field as we walked out. My plan was to wait at least six hours before returning. I'd then use the number of corn rows and number of telephone poles to more easily find the last place we were standing on the blood trail in the middle of the cornfield.

After I got home, I climbed into bed and sulked. I was so emotionally upset that I yelled, "That's it! I'm never hunting again!"

About two hours later, Scott's friend called me. He heard about the deer and wanted to help me find her. Even though only two hours had passed, I drug my body out of bed and met with him. We then drove back to the hunting spot.

When we got there, I counted the telephone poles as we slowly drove down the road. When we reached the correct distance, we parked the car and headed into the corn. As we walked through the corn, I quietly counted each row to myself. When we got to within a few rows of where Scott and I lost the blood trail, I had to abruptly yank my foot to the side as I stepped into the next row of corn. It took all of my balance and athleticism to keep from falling to the ground because of how abruptly I had to move my foot in order to prevent myself from stepping right on top of my dead deer!

Judging by the stiffness of the doe, it probably died before we even left the field the first time. I was extremely relieved and grateful to God that we found her so easily and that she probably did not have to suffer very long.

One thing I learned from my season of hunting instinctively was that I began to lose confidence in my shooting ability as the season progressed. Before the season started, I had practiced every single day at least two hours a day. After the season started, I stopped practicing altogether, because I was sitting in my tree stand with every spare moment I had. This last hunt helped me realize how important it is to *keep practicing throughout the season* in order to keep my archery accuracy and *mental confidence* as high as possible. The same holds true for people who shoot with sights.

Although this seemed like a valuable lesson, I didn't think very much about it at that time because I had already decided to quit hunting. However, hurting that last doe and having difficulty finding her were not the only reasons why I decided to give up hunting. Ever since I got more involved with church-related activities during my last year and a half of college, many people started telling me I should become a priest. At least at present, Roman Catholic priests do not get married. This is the religion I was raised in and believe Jesus wants me to stay in. The thought of becoming a celibate Catholic priest caused some major confusion in my life because I had always thought I wanted to be married. However, I wanted to do God's will more than anything else, even if that meant not getting married. I just didn't know how to figure out what God wanted. I didn't know if God wanted me to be a priest, be married, or simply remain single. I also didn't know what or who to listen to in order to make this very serious decision.

In an effort to find answers to these challenging questions, I joined a Catholic religious order. I basically looked and lived like a monk. The picture on the left is of me while I was in the religious order. If you have any interest in learning the full story of what I experienced while I was there—such as how we lived, what that type of life is like, what type of prayer life we followed, and how I made my decision to stay or leave—I've recorded those experiences, details, and life lessons in my book titled *What's My Vocation?* Among other places, it is available through my ministry websites McVeighMinistries.com and CatholicGuestSpeaker.com.

GOING HOME

When an individual joins a Catholic religious order, he or she is not eligible to make a lifelong commitment to stay there until after he or she has been in that community about five years. As for me, after being in my order for a year and a half, I started to really think God was trying to tell me I was supposed to leave. Surprisingly, it seemed as though He was telling me my vocation was actually to marriage. However, I was still unsure of myself or how to make the right decision. Eventually, the person in charge of our religious order told me to go home and stay with my parents for two weeks to think about it.

My dad came to pick me up and give me a ride home. We didn't speak much during the long drive. I spent most of the time intensely thinking about my life and what I should do with it. One of the biggest questions I kept asking myself was, "Now what can I do for God?"

The only thing I knew for certain was that I definitely wanted to live my life for God. As I wondered how I could possibly live my life for God in a way other than being in a religious order, a quote from Therese of Lisieux, a famous Catholic Saint, kept running through my mind. She once stated, "God does not inspire unrecognizable dreams."

With this quote in mind, I asked myself, "What are some of the dreams I have had?" I then thought, "Well, before I had my big religious turnaround in college I was passionate about making a bow hunting video." I then recalled something my own mother said to me after I gave up hunting and many other activities and hobbies in order to follow God. She sternly pointed her finger at me and said, "Sean, God gave you all these gifts, and you are just throwing them back in His face!" Her statement bothered me, because I gave those things up for God. I didn't want to think I was offending Him by giving those things up.

After recalling all of these facts, I pondered the concept of making a hunting video again. I then asked myself, "How could I do this for God?" The answer came quickly into my mind. A statistic I had read during the late 1990s while I was in the religious order indicated that the highest source of revenue in some remote towns came through the rental of pornographic videos during hunting season.

(This was back in the days when there were actual video rental stores in virtually every town.)

As I thought about this statistic, I also recalled what some of the male keynote speakers had said at some of the men's retreats I had helped out with earlier that year. Some of them talked about having to overcome an addiction to pornography. They said that this addiction can only be overcome through prayer and making good decisions. As I recalled these details, I asked myself, "Who is reaching hunters who have an attraction to pornography and teaching them how to pray? That's it! I will make a hunting video that shows people how I pray and experience God while I am in the woods hunting! This will give them ideas to help them develop their own spirituality and prayer life! Their new prayer life can then help them in areas they may struggle with in life!"

At the same time, I knew that this type of information would be useful to *everyone*, not just people who struggled with some form of addition. *Everyone* needs to develop a strong prayer life and spirituality. God's grace that comes to us through prayer powerfully helps us during our life in countless ways. What better way to develop a prayer life than while doing something we love, such as hunting?

Ideas fired through my mind as I planned out how I could accomplish my goal of making a hunting video involving prayer and spirituality. My thoughts were, "One problem is that I gave my bow away to Eric before I joined the religious order. What can I use? I know! I will make my own bow out of wood! I've always wanted to do that! That will make the whole video seem much more rustic!" As soon as I had this idea, a serious thought entered my mind that said, "No, use the Hoyt." The old Hoyt I had used to shoot my spike on video was still in the attic at my parents' house. I had forgotten all about it because I stopped using it after I replaced it with the PSE I gave Eric.

After the thought entered my mind about using the Hoyt, I sternly rejected it by saying, "No!" However, it came right back, only this time it was more serious and drawn out, "USE THE HOYT!" In a somewhat pouting, stubborn manner, I responded, "FINE! But I'm not buying arrows. You [God] are going to have to get them for me!"

When my father and I finally made it home, I greeted my mother at the door and then went into the kitchen to call Scott. As I dialed Scott's phone number, I realized how much of a positive impact I had had on his life while I was hunting with him. No one really taught him about God or brought him to church very often while he was growing up. After my spiritual awakening in college, I often talked to him about God while we practiced archery together. I even encouraged him to get baptized. Throughout the last season we hunted together, we always said a prayer together before going into the woods. I could sometimes even see tears welling up in his eyes because of how much God was touching him through the religious talks we had and prayers we prayed together. In addition, he and I were harvesting deer almost every week, while everyone else we knew were not even seeing any deer, let alone harvesting them. This made us feel very blessed by God!

As a token of his appreciation, Scott often bought me little religious pictures and prayer cards when he was out shopping. This showed me how much he appreciated and thought about our religious talks. However, as far as I knew, Scott stopped learning about God after I left to join the religious order. In that moment of dialing his phone number, I realized I had been wrong to give up archery and bow hunting. I realized I could in fact reach people through using the gifts God gave me. Who else was going to reach those people if I wasn't there to do it?

Scott answered the phone after a few rings. He was overjoyed to hear my voice. After I explained the situation, and that I was home for at least two weeks, he excitedly began asking questions.

SCOTT: So does this mean you can hunt with me this year?
ME: Well, I'd have to get arrows.
(This took place back in the days when most people still used aluminum arrows.)
SCOTT: What size do you shoot?
ME: 2317s.
SCOTT: Can you shoot 2315s?
ME: Yes. Those are the lightweight version of the arrow I shoot.
SCOTT: I've got a dozen of them here for you! Brand new, never used!

(*In a somewhat shocked and stunned tone of voice, I responded in the following way.*)

ME: But your draw length is much shorter than mine. They will be too short for me.

SCOTT: No, you don't understand. My sister bought them for me as a birthday present, but I never had them cut down to my size. They are still full length from the factory. I'm not going to use them because I switched to a different size. We could have them cut to your length, and they will be perfect for you!

(*I stood there holding the phone to my ear feeling utterly amazed. After a brief pause, I responded to his statement in the following way.*)

ME: "Uhh, umm, okay."

Within ten minutes Scott was knocking on my parents' door with twelve brand new arrows in his hand to give to me. That evening at dinner, I told my parents what happened concerning the arrows and my desire to make the hunting video for God. My dad offered to help me by videoing for me. I then told my parents I worried about getting bit by a deer tick and contracting Lyme disease. Several of the religious Brothers I lived with had contracted Lyme disease, and I didn't want to go through what they were dealing with. My mother said, "They make unscented tick spray. You can use that." She knew that it would have to be unscented because the keenest sense a deer has is its sense of smell. Although I wasn't sure if unscented tick spray would be usable in a hunting situation, I kept her idea in the back of my mind.

SECOND CHANCE

A number of things happened while I was at home that influenced me to go back to the religious order. Once again, those details are recorded in *What's My Vocation?* However, for the purposes of this hunting book, I'll simply say that I went back and continued to struggle with my decision. In an effort to help me find a sense of peace about the situation, the head of my religious order told me to pick three older Brothers in our community and ask them what they thought I should do.

About a week later, I was traveling to Binghamton, New York, with one of the older Brothers from the household I lived in. We were going to a retreat center in the woods to spend three days in silence. While we traveled, I told the Brother about my struggles and that I didn't know if I should stay or leave the religious life. He said, "As soon as you get to your hermitage, ask God to communicate to you whatever He wants to during this retreat. Be open to whatever He has to say. Allow God to speak to you wherever He wants. It could be in the chapel while you are praying or on the trail while you are walking through the woods." (Aside: A "hermitage" is typically a small, one-person shack located in a secluded place. It is intended for a person to be able to stay there and pray in silence without any distractions.)

After we arrived at the retreat facility and finished dinner with the people that lived there, we were driven out through the woods to our respective hermitages, which were located approximately a hundred yards apart from each other. As I got out of the truck, the older Brother said to me, "Brother Sean, make your prayer intention and then BE OPEN!" I nodded my head, turned, and walked to the door of my hermitage.

Upon entering, I took a close look at what was inside. There was a cot and a wood-burning stove in the main room. There was a small kitchenette with a sink connected to the main room but there was no running water. Lastly, there was a tiny room for prayer located next to the kitchenette that could barely seat one person. It was about the size of a closet. I immediately went into the prayer room to pray.

With all of my focus and attention, I asked God to reveal Himself to me in whatever way He wanted. I then prayed Evening Prayer from the Liturgy of the Hours. This typically includes two Psalms from the Old Testament of the Bible, two Canticles from the New Testament, a Scripture reading, intercession prayers, the Lord's Prayer, and a closing prayer. Admittedly, I prayed these prayers rather quickly because I was anxious to take a walk through the woods before it got dark. I had been living in New York City throughout my time with the religious order so I almost never had opportunities to be in the woods anymore.

Upon finishing my prayers, I hastily headed out of the hermitage to take my walk. As I thrust the door open, I nearly slammed into the older Brother from my community as he approached my hermitage. Instinctively, I stumbled to the side in an effort to avoid crashing into him. Once we both regained our balance, he looked at me with a reluctant and sorrowful facial expression. He then said, "I'm so sorry to break the silence, Brother Sean. I appear to have lost my watch, and the clock in my hermitage is not set. Would you mind telling me the time? I don't want to miss Mass in the morning?" I said, "That's no problem at all, Brother!" I looked down at my watch and announced the time. However, I felt very curious, so I asked him the following question.

ME: Brother, do you mind if I ask you a quick question?
BROTHER: No, not at all.
ME: What were you doing all that time?
  (*It had been about twenty minutes since we were dropped off.*)
BROTHER: Well, I went up to the water spigot to get some water. Oh yeah, and while I was there I saw a whole flock of turkeys!
  (*This greatly excited me! In an energetic way, I questioned,*)
ME: Really? Did they run away as soon as they saw you?
BROTHER: No. They just stood there.
  (*His response shocked me! With a surprised tone of voice, I responded,*)
ME: REALLY? That is not like wild turkeys at all! They have the most amazing eyesight and are very wary! They usually run away if they see even the slightest thing move that looks out of the ordinary! I found this out through firsthand experience! Did I ever tell you about the time I went turkey hunting?
  (*He quickly and excitedly responded.*)
BROTHER: No!
  (*The intense look on his face and sound of curiosity in his voice indicated to me that he wanted to hear my story, so I asked,*)
ME: Do you mind if I tell you what happened real quick?
  (*He excitedly responded,*)
BROTHER: Not at all! Please do!
ME: When I was in high school, my friend's dad took me fall turkey hunting at their cabin in Tioga County, Pennsylvania. I had never been turkey hunting before and I didn't even know the first thing

about turkeys. The guys at the cabin told me that the most important thing to remember when turkey hunting is to *be still!* Turkeys have amazing eyesight! If you move even the slightest bit, they will see you and run away. One of the men said that turkeys can even see you blink from thirty yards away.

This is why I asked you if the turkeys ran away as soon as you saw them today at the water spigot. At any rate, the first weekend I went turkey hunting with my friend's dad I didn't see or hear a single turkey. The second weekend was actually going to be our last chance to go, so there was a lot of pressure on me to get one. I set up in the morning behind a small dirt pile on the side of a mountain. As daylight came, I pulled a wooden, push-button, turkey call from my pocket and began calling. After about five minutes, a turkey actually called back to me from way down in the valley to my right! With great excitement, I began to imitate the sound the turkey was making. Back and forth we talked. I would make a call with my wooden box, and it would respond. My heart began to race with excitement!

The turkey continued to respond to my calls for about ten minutes. I imagined it would start coming closer at any second. I also thought I was sure to get a shot! Instead, its responses began to taper off. It even sounded more distant as time passed. I then started to feel disappointed and thought about giving up. After sitting there for a few minutes looking at the ground, I decided to try calling one more time. As I did, a volcanic eruption of noise broke out on the adjacent hillside across the valley to my left! It sounded as if there was a massive stampede of animals running down the mountainside.

Before I fully realized what was happening, a turkey popped out of the weeds at the bottom of the hill in front of me. It was about a hundred yards away. I was thrilled to see it! All I needed to do was lean over onto the rifle, aim, and pull the trigger. The gun was already resting on the dirt pile in front of me, so I didn't have far to move in order to get into position. As I lowered my head about two inches, the turkey saw me and ran away, **and you don't get a second chance with these animals!**

(*The moment I said those last few words, "And you don't get a second chance with these animals," I received a profound inner realization. In fact, it stunned me so significantly that it seemed to have come from God and felt as if He had just given me a surprise,*

spiritual slap in the face to get my attention! Even though the mes-
sage radically impacted my thoughts and emotions, I tried to main-
tain an unaltered disposition as I continued telling my story in the
following way.)
ME: After the turkey ran away, I sat motionless. At the same time, I
began mentally beating myself up by thinking, "I blew it! I blew it!
The guys are never going to let me live this one down! I can't believe I blew it!"

A few minutes later, I calmed down and decided to try calling
again. I pushed the button on the turkey call several times and hoped
to hear a response, but didn't. I slumped down feeling a little disappointed but hit the button on the call a few more times. Three or four
minutes passed, and I was dramatically losing hope. My disappointment turned into depression, and I thought to myself, "It's over. I
ruined it. I missed my chance. It's not coming back."

Just before giving up on the hunt, I made one last haphazard call
with the box. Within two seconds, a loud uproar of shuffling leaves
and chirping sounds erupted again on the adjacent hillside. I excitedly thought to myself, "More turkeys!" This time, I got into position
before they even came out into the open.

Peering through the scope, I looked into the weeds at the bottom
of the hill and spotted a turkey! As I continued to survey the thicket,
I saw another turkey, and another one, and another one. I thought to
myself, "WOW! It's loaded with turkeys. There are at least ten of
them standing in there." I then thought, "Okay, the first one that
comes out is getting it." I said this because in Pennsylvania you can
shoot either a male or female turkey in the fall.

Before long, a female turkey walked at a steady pace out of the
weeds into the open woods. It was moving too fast for me to follow
her and make a shot, so I picked a spot on the other side of a tree in
the direction she was walking. I took aim, and thought, "Okay, as
soon as it walks into the crosshairs of the scope, I'll pull the trigger."
Three seconds later the bird entered my scope and then walked into
the crosshairs. This is when I pulled the trigger. The bird dropped
like a sack of bricks, and I jumped up yelling with victorious joy! I
immediately ran down the hill to inspect the bird and yelled with ju-
bilation the whole way!

(At this point in the story, the Bother and I rejoiced together. Even though I was smiling and laughing, my mind was still fixated on the message I had just received when I said the words, "And you don't get a second chance with these animals." The moment those words left my mouth the Holy Spirit struck me with a profound reali-

*zation regarding the fact that I **did get a second chance**! After a brief pause, I inquisitively and spontaneously asked the Brother,)*

ME: Do you know why I was even turkey hunting?

BROTHER: No.

ME: Do you mind if I tell you real quick?

BROTHER: Please do!

ME: The spring before I got the turkey, I was on a wilderness fishing trip in northern Quebec, Canada. We had been flown to that lake on a float plane and were left there to stay in a rustic cabin for a week.

(There is a picture of me on this trip in the beginning of my book, "I've Got To Change," in case you have a copy of that book and want to reference it. My story continued in the following way.)

ME: Several weeks before we even went on that trip, one of the guys started talking about hunting for a black bear while we were in Canada. In fact, he talked about it so much that it really started to annoy me and the other two guys going on the trip! He continued to talk about it the whole way to Canada and throughout every day for the first few days we were at the lake.

On the fourth day of the trip, a bear had noticeably eaten the fish carcasses we had dumped in the woods behind our cabin. This meant it was time to hunt, especially since baiting black bear is permitted in Canada. However, the guy who had annoyed us with his relentless talk of bear hunting surprisingly changed his mind and refused to go. My friend's dad had already gotten a bear in the past and didn't want another one. This left me and one other guy as possible candidates. The other guy was not much of an outdoorsman to begin with, so he ruled himself out immediately. The next thing I knew everyone was looking at me. I looked back at the three of them and yelled, "WHAT?"

My friend's dad then handed me a 270 caliber rifle, and said, "Looks like you are shooting the bear!" I stood there for a moment stuttering, "Me? Uh, um, but I, um." He went on to say, "We will all go out fishing until it gets dark. That way we won't disturb the bear if it comes into camp. You just sit on the roof of the cabin. When the bear comes, shoot!"

Holding the rifle, I continued to stutter, "Um, but um, I." They all turned and walked away leaving me standing there alone with the gun. I didn't know what to think about the situation. I had never shot a rifle before. My dad raised me to be a bow hunter. I wasn't even allowed to own a gun while I was growing up. I knew basically how they worked, and I had shot bb guns on many occasions, but I had never shot a full-fledged rifle before.

I knew there would not be a bullet in the chamber as long as I didn't close the bolt, so I left it open. I then looked up at the roof of the cabin in a bewildered state of mind. Next, I went into the cabin and put on a head-net to keep the mosquitoes from eating me alive. I then went outside and reluctantly climbed onto the metal roof of the cabin and sat down. As I sat there, I repeatedly asked myself, "What in the world am I doing here? Why am I doing this? I have no desire to shoot a bear. I'm strictly a deer hunter. Why am I doing this?" I never came up with an answer to my question. I just kept asking myself over and over, "Why am I doing this?"

Forty-five minutes passed before I glanced up to see a black bear walking out of the woods in front of me. Since I wasn't very interested in hunting bear at that time, I didn't even get an adrenaline rush. Instead, I just began talking myself through the process of closing the bolt in order to put a bullet in the chamber. I thought, "Okay, just take your time and slide it closed nice and slow. You have plenty of time to shoot."

I applied pressure to the lever, and the bolt began to slide closed. As it got to the halfway point, a bullet jumped up from the clip into the chamber and fell halfway out to the side because of the angle I was holding the gun. The sound of the clanging metal alerted the bear, and it snapped its head up and looked around. As it surveyed the landscape searching for the source of the noise, I sat motionless and anxiously repeated in my mind, "Please put your head back down! Please put your head back down! Please put your head back down!"

After a short time, the bear put its head back down and continued sniffing around looking for more fish carcasses. This gave me a sense of relief! I finished closing the bolt and then began talking myself through the next phase of the hunt. "Okay, now just slowly raise the gun to your shoulder. Take your time. There is no need to rush."

As I began to raise the gun toward my shoulder, a large branch fell out of the tree above me and slammed down onto the metal roof next to me. It made a loud crashing noise when it hit which startled both me and the bear! The bear snapped its head back up and looked around. Very distraught by the branch falling, I screamed in my mind, "I CAN'T BELIEVE THAT! WHAT BAD TIMING!" I then began to mentally repeat over and over, "Please put your head back down! Please put your head back down! Please put your head back down!"

It seemed as if a few minutes passed before the bear put its head back down to sniff around for fish. This enabled me to breathe a sigh of relief, and I proceeded to raise the gun to my shoulder. As the butt of the gun reached my shoulder, I looked through the scope at the bear and then reached my thumb for the safety button. All I needed to do was push the safety off and pull the trigger. Just as I started to apply pressure to the safety button, the bear suddenly vanished from the scope. I frantically looked up and yelled, "WHAT HAPPENED? I CAN'T BELIEVE THAT!" The bear was completely gone. In a total state of disbelief, I said, "I blew it! I can't believe I blew it! The guys are going to kill me for this! They are never going to let me live this one down! I can't believe I blew it!"

(*The whole time I was telling the Brother about the bear hunt, I was thinking about the words, "And you don't get a second chance with these animals." When I reached this point in my story regarding the bear, I had another profound realization that was directly connected to what had happened with the turkey. I continued in the following way.*)

ME: As I sat there on the roof of the cabin mentally beating myself up, I heard a boat coming, so I immediately climbed down and went to the boat dock to see who it was. It was the one guy from our group who wasn't much of an outdoorsman. He had decided to come back early since he wasn't catching any fish.

We both went into the cabin and sat down by the back window which was open. Meanwhile, I kept saying, "I can't believe I saw the bear and blew my chance!" We then proceeded to talk about hunting for around forty-five minutes until I abruptly perked up and asked, "Did you hear that?" He responded, "No. What?" I paused, listened intently toward the window, and then exclaimed, "That right there! Did you hear it?" He retorted, "No!" I immediately stood up and said, "I hear something! I am going out there!"

I took the gun off the wall and proceeded to walk out of the front door of the cabin. I quickly walked around to the back and listened. As I stood there, I could hear loud crashing and banging noises coming from the woods. The noises grew louder and louder until finally a black bear lumbered out of the forest in front of me. I was so mad at myself for messing up my first chance that I fiercely thought in my mind, "*I'm not messing up this time!*"

The bear was only thirty-five yards away and walking straight at me. I had a powerfully strong desire to avenge myself! My motions were swift and my thoughts were clear. I was mad! I raised the gun to my shoulder with utter seriousness. The butt of the gun hit my shoulder, and my eye peered intently through the scope. The bear then turned on an angle, and I quickly pushed off the safety button. With extreme focus and determination, I pulled the trigger. BOOM! The sound of a gunshot thundered through the forest and echoed across the lake as my body jolted from the recoil.

My disposition then dramatically changed from absolute seriousness to utter surprise. I yelled out, "I got him!" The guy in the cabin was watching from the back window the whole time. He immediately responded, "You got him!" I yelled back, "I got him!" He yelled again, "You got him!" After going back and forth like this for a few seconds, I heard a loud noise and looked back over to where the bear had fallen. It was gone! I quickly yanked up and back on the bolt action and then rammed it forward to put another bullet into the chamber in case the bear came after me!

Within seconds, I heard a boat headed our way. I could see that it was the rest of the guys from our camp, so I immediately turned around and headed down toward the lake to meet them. As soon as they reached the dock and got out of the boat, I excitedly told them I just shot the bear. At first, they didn't believe me. It took a little convincing them, but we eventually walked over to the spot I had last seen the bear. As soon as we got there, we could see that the bear had rolled down to the bottom of the embankment it had been standing on when I shot. At that moment, we all celebrated the fact that I had successfully harvested a black bear!

(Aside: Throughout the entire time I was telling the Brother this story, my mind was completely preoccupied with the startling realization that I got the bear *on my second chance* too!)

I concluded my whole story by saying to the Brother, "In the fall after I got this bear, I harvested my first deer with a bow (*the five-pointer depicted near the beginning of this book*). After getting that deer, my friend's dad said, 'Sean, you have to get a turkey now. You have the chance to get the Triple Crown. There are people who hunt their entire lives and never get a Triple Crown. You have the chance of getting it at the age of seventeen.' 'What's the Triple Crown?' I asked. He replied, 'It is when you get a deer, bear, and turkey all in

the same year.' So that is the whole reason why I went turkey hunting in the first place."

(Aside: Traditionally, the "Triple Crown" was a title given to a hunter who harvested these three big game species in the state of Pennsylvania. Since my bear was from Canada, it didn't technically count as a "Triple Crown," but it was still an exciting accomplishment for me at such a young age!)

The Brother I had been sharing all of this with was completely edified and amazed by my exciting story. He perceived it to be something special and wandered back to his hermitage pondering deeply. There was a strong feeling of astonishment that filled my soul as well. I then turned and started walking up through the woods.

As I went, I intently pondered what God had just communicated to me about a second chance and the manner in which He chose to communicate this message to me!

After I walked a few hundred yards up the trail, I stopped to watch some deer feeding in a grassy field. I didn't stay long, because it was starting to get dark. I was on a mission to reach the utility shed near the main retreat house. The Brothers that ran the retreat center told me during dinner that there were some old fishing rods in the shed that I could use if I wanted to try catching some fish.

It had been a long time since I had gone fishing, so I decided to take one of the rods back to my hermitage so that I could go fishing at the crack of dawn. On my way back to the hermitage after getting a rod, I made a few casts in one of the small ponds with a plastic minnow. I managed to catch two very nice-sized largemouth bass. It was a delightful ending to an interesting day.

The following morning I rose before dawn and headed to the largest pond on the property. It was about a hundred yards in diameter. There was a little flat-bottomed boat on the edge, so I got into it, pushed off of the bank, and drifted out into the thick mist that covered the entire pond. The cool, damp air soothed my face as I calmly took in a deep breath of air. I felt so at peace at that moment!

Time passed and the mist slowly began to dissipate after the sun appeared on the horizon. I then hooked into my fifth bass. As I reeled in the small fish, I looked up to see an entire fleet of hot air balloons rising from behind the large mountain in front of me. It was a beautiful scene, which inspired me to lift my eyes to heaven and joyfully yell, "Thank You, God!" A large statue of Jesus also stood at the side of the pond which kept me mindful that God was with me, and I continued to frequently thank Him for the special, memorable morning.

The sun's rays began to more intensely pound down on me over the next hour. Because of how hot it was getting, I knew my time on the pond was coming to an end. All of the bass I had caught that morning were very small, ranging from seven to ten inches in length. I then hooked into my thirteenth one. As I reeled it in, I said in a very frustrated manner, "Come on! Let me catch a real fish!"

I continued to reel in the small bass as fast as I could, so that I could quickly take it off and keep casting for a bigger one before I had to leave. The fish skimmed along the surface of the water because of how fast I was reeling. I then watched as an enormous bass came up from the deepest area of the pond. It stealthily swam behind the little bass that I was reeling in. My jaw dropped in amazement at the sight of the massive fish! It may very well have been the biggest bass I had ever seen with my own eyes. My mind went numb at that moment. Before I even realized what I was doing, I reeled the small bass completely out of the water. The big bass simultaneously disappeared back down into the deep.

I stood there looking at the little fish flapping in the air on the end of my line and slowly began to come out of my dazed state of mind. As I began to refocus, I vigorously shook my head and yelled, "WHAT AM I DOING?" I then quickly cast the little bass back off the side of the boat about fifteen feet away and began to beg, "Please circle back around! Please circle back around! Please circle back around!"

Within seconds, the monster bass reappeared. It swam straight up to my little bass and engulfed it in one bite. The only thing sticking out of the giant bass's mouth was the mouth of my little bass and the lure. My eyes opened wide with astonishment as I witnessed this incredible event!

As soon as the big fish took my little bass into its mouth, I thought back to the 1980s when I was twelve years old. My uncle would take me bass fishing with rubber worms whenever we visited him in Florida. When we'd use weedless hooks, he taught me to open the bale on my reel and let the fish run with the worm in its mouth for five seconds before closing the bail and setting the hook. Although this is no longer a popular technique, I instantly chose to use this approach in my current situation. As a result, I immediately opened the bale on the fishing reel so that the line could run off the spool. I knew I needed to give the big bass time to get the rest of the small bass and my lure into its mouth.

The big bass swam down and disappeared into the deep water of the pond, and I patiently watched the line peel off of the spool. A few seconds later the line stopped moving. After five seconds had passed, I turned to Jesus in my mind and said, "Okay, Lord, I'm going for it." I then closed the bale, tightened up the line, and pulled up firmly on the rod to set the hook. The rod drastically bent, but the line didn't move. I then disappointingly thought to myself, "Aw, man! Did it swim under a log and get my line hung up or something?" Then suddenly, the giant bass began to pull! "OH MAN! I GOT HIM!" I exclaimed. The fish tugged, and I held on!

I hoped with all my heart that I would not lose this fish. So many times in my life I had gotten a fish halfway in only to have it get off before I could land it. In this situation, the fish actually started to lighten up on the fight before too long. This helped to ease my nerves a little. However, as I got it alongside the boat, it began to get nervous and pulled harder when I reached down toward the water. Although the fish flapped around, I managed to grab its lower jaw before it got off.

I hoisted the large bass into the boat and simultaneously praised and thanked God for the gift! After taking the treble hooks out, I held the big fish's mouth by my knee. Its tail hung all the way down past the bottom of my foot! As I looked at the fish, I almost cried tears of gratitude and amazement. I had fished for bass my entire life and never caught one even close to this size!

While I sat there welling up with tears of joy, I felt Jesus crouch down next to me and softly whisper into my left ear, "You got him on your second chance."

I was utterly and completely dumbfounded by what Jesus said to me and what just happened! In a state of astonishment, I reached over the side of the boat and gently released the bass into the pond to let it live for another day. I then sat back in the boat feeling amazed! I tried to absorb what just happened and what God said.

Although this experience was profound, I was left wondering what exactly the "second chance" was, and what exactly God meant by it. Did He mean we all get a second chance when we ask for forgiveness from our sins? This is possible, but I felt as though there was more to the message than just that for me. Unfortunately, I simply wasn't sure what it was.

DO THE VIDEO

Receiving the message about a second chance was one of the neatest things that had ever happened to me. It amazed me that God would speak to me through my hunting and fishing experiences. The way I viewed my relationship with God and how I would listen for Him to speak to me was forever changed by the events that had taken place so far during this retreat. However, it didn't end there! Later that same day after catching the big bass, I was sitting in the woods enjoying the soothing breeze on my face and the peace that it made me feel. Without realizing it, I fell asleep. As I woke, I never opened my eyes, but clearly heard a voice say to me, "Do the video." The moment I heard those words, I opened my eyes in shock. Did God still want me to make a hunting video?

After I returned to New York City where I was living with the religious order, I continued to have a nagging feeling inside of me that I was supposed to make a hunting video. I tried to run from the idea and avoid it. At one point, I even yelled at God saying, "I can't! I'm a Franciscan! Can't You just leave me alone about it?" (For those who may not be familiar, "Franciscan" is the general name for the religious order I was with.)

Although making the hunting video for God in order to reach hunters with concepts of prayer and spirituality sounded like a nice idea, I didn't want to deal with all the potential persecution it would bring upon me since I was in a religious order. I knew there would be plenty of people who would not accept it and would look negatively at me for being involved with hunting. This especially held true since Saint Francis, the founder of our order, was known as a peaceful man who had a tremendous love for animals.

Regardless, on one particular weeknight, I received a phone call from my college friend Eric. He told me he had originally sold the bow I gave him to a classmate. However, the guy never gave him the money for the bow. Since that guy wasn't using it anymore, he gave it back to Eric. Eric then said, "So I have your bow here ready for you to pick up whenever you are ready for it. I even have some arrows for you!" This amazed me, and I thanked him for it. The fact that he had arrows was important too, because I gave the other ones back to Scott. I gave them back because I renounced the idea of hunting and making the video when I initially decided to return to the religious order.

Another interesting thing happened during this time period. I went into a storage closet in our religious house looking for batteries. After I bent down and put my head between the shelves, I looked to the right trying to locate some batteries. I then turned my head to the left. There, inches from my face, was a bag of disposable hand warmers and a can of unscented tick repellent. The moment I saw them I thought back to the conversation I had with my mom when I explained my idea of making a hunting video for God. In the process, I shared my concern of getting bit by a deer tick and contracting Lyme disease. My mom suggested using unscented tick repellent. Immediately after recalling this, I thought back to the times when I used to hunt in the winter. I always used disposable hand warmers. These details gave me the impression that maybe this was God's way of nudging me to do the hunting video project for Him. Perhaps He was showing me that He was giving me everything I needed to complete the project.

The idea of doing the video continued to nag at me for days until I finally gave in and said to God, "Fine, I will tell the head of the religious order everything that has happened. I will then surrender myself to obedience. I can rest with a good conscience then."

I made an appointment with the head of our order, met with him, and explained the second chance message and how it happened. I also explained the message I received to do the video. I told him how my old bow had come back to me and how I found the tick repellent and hand warmers in the closet. He told me to just write the story of the second chance. He said maybe that was all I was supposed to do about it. As for the hand warmers and tick repellent, he told me to put them in my cell (bedroom) and hold onto them. I did exactly as he directed and was glad I didn't have to make the video.

Unfortunately, thoughts of the video often came to me while I was praying. Two weeks passed, and I kept ignoring them. One day, I was alone at the friary doing my normal chores. (Friary is the term we used for the house we lived in.) I went into the mail room and saw something completely out of the ordinary. On the desk, there was an outdoor magazine opened to the centerfold picture of a bow hunter at full draw. He was aiming at an enormous whitetail buck. I yelled, "How in the world did this get here? Who ever heard of a hunting magazine in a Franciscan friary?" I then wondered how it ended up on the desk opened to that particular picture. I felt as though it was another one of God's reminders that He wanted me to make the hunting video. I yelled out in an annoyed tone of voice, "FINE, I WILL ASK HIM AGAIN!"

I made another appointment with the head of our order, drove to his location, and then told him the whole story of the picture. I also told him a few other interesting details that had recently developed concerning the topic. I was scheduled to go to a conference only twenty minutes away from my parents' house in Pennsylvania. The conference happened to take place on the same weekend as opening day of bow hunting season in PA. It would be easy for my dad to pick me up from the conference and take me hunting for a few hours. After hearing all of this, the head of the order quickly gave me permission to try it. This surprised me!

(Aside: I was later told that the head of my order admitted to someone else that he felt "the chills" when I explained how God was asking me to make the hunting video. He also said it felt as though the hairs were standing up on the back of his neck when he listened to me recount what God was saying to me. I believe this tingly feeling he was experiencing possibly indicated the powerful presence of the Holy Spirit. If you ever experience anything like that, I encourage you to pay attention to what is going on around you in case the Holy Spirit is trying to give you a message of some sort.)

ARCHERY AND THE SPIRITUAL LIFE

Although I was living in Yonkers, New York at that time, I managed to get to Pennsylvania for a brief time to get a hunting license. While in PA, I also picked up my old bow from Eric. He invited me to hunt on his farm, so we scouted for an hour while I was there. We chose a spot for me and my dad to try on opening day, but I didn't have enough time to set up the tree stands. Eric was gracious enough to hang two stands together for me so that my dad could video me.

Since I only had a couple weeks to prepare, and I hadn't even shot a bow in almost two years, I didn't want to try hunting instinctively. Out of respect for the animal, I chose to use sights because I knew it would enable me to be more effective and consistent with such a short time to practice and prepare. After putting sights on the bow and making all the necessary adjustments so that I could use it again, I asked myself, "Where can I possibly practice?"

There was a storage room in the back of the basement of the religious house I lived in. It was filled with old beds, desks, and chairs. This was by far the best possible location for me to make a little shooting range. All four of the walls were cement block. I could lock the door once inside the room. I believed this would be important for safety reasons, to make sure no one came in while I was shooting. The length of the room also enabled me to shoot up to eighteen yards away from the target.

After making this decision, I went to look at the room. The amount of clutter and debris in the room was worse than I remembered, and I knew that clearing a shooting lane down the middle was going to be difficult! Surprisingly, a few minutes after I started moving some of the stuff around, one of the Brothers who lived in that friary with me appeared and asked me what I was doing. I didn't want to tell him exactly what I was up to, so I just said I was clearing a lane down the middle of the room. He said, "Don't bother. Father (the priest in charge of that house) just gave instructions for us to completely clear all this junk out of here and get rid of it." I couldn't believe my ears. The priest who made this decision had no idea what I was up to. In a way, I felt as though it was God's way of providentially helping me prepare for hunting season. (Please note that the priest in charge of this friary was not the one in charge of the entire order. The one in charge of the order lived several miles away in a different friary.)

Allow me to digress for a moment and say that after I started struggling with my decision to stay or leave the religious order, I began to notice that the muscles in my neck would always tense up each time I felt anxious about my decision. I dealt with it by consciously calming those muscles back down every time I felt them tensing up.

Now let me return to the present situation. The first day I drew my bow back, I realized something I had never fully noticed before in my twenty years of shooting bows and arrows. It came as a direct result of my growing awareness of the muscles tensing up in my neck when I felt stressed about my decision to stay or leave the religious order. As soon as I reached full draw, I realized that many of the muscles in my body tensed up when I drew a bow. I also realized that I didn't need to use most of those muscles to stay at full draw. I also realized that those tensed up muscles had contributed to some of the inaccuracies in my shooting in the past. After realizing these things, I began to *train myself* to notice every muscle in my body after I reached full draw. I then willfully relaxed each muscle I didn't *need* to use while at full draw.

Please note that this type of relaxation is different from the emotional relaxation I began to practice when shooting instinctively. This new awareness helped me realize I needed to intentionally relax *both* my physical muscles as well as my emotions.

The result of this type of training while practicing archery began to dramatically improve my overall level of self-awareness, which positively helped the growth of my spiritual life. It helped me learn how to *listen within* more keenly *throughout the entire day*. It helped me realize how my tensing muscles indicated things to me about my feelings and emotions that I previously had been unaware of. I was also learning how to consciously control my muscles despite the way I felt. I was able to relax them even when I felt angry, frustrated, anxious, or afraid. This helped me remain calm and think more maturely through some of the difficult situations I had been facing in life. Much to my surprise, archery quickly became one of the greatest training tools I had in my pursuit of spiritual and personal growth.

If you have never noticed any of these details regarding your muscles or feelings while shooting a compound bow, I encourage you to put this book down for a few minutes and go shoot one if you can. Pay close attention to all of the muscles in your body and take note of the ones you can intentionally relax after reaching full draw. Also, notice if you feel anxious the moment before you release your shot. Try to learn how to calm both your muscles and your feelings before releasing. Afterward, take this type of awareness, training, and muscle control with you into everyday situations. Begin to recognize how and when your muscles tense up during the day. This tensing of your muscles can indicate various spiritual and emotional influences that previously went undetected by you. You can then relax your muscles, calm your emotions, and focus on making wise decisions regardless of how you feel or are being influenced by others in that particular situation. (If you like these ideas, consider reading my book *Sin and the Spirituality of Archery* where I elaborate on ways to improve archery accuracy as well as certain spiritual components of archery.)

HUNTING WITH MY DAD

My dad picked me up from the conference the night before opening day of bow hunting season. I stayed at their house, and then we went to Eric's farm in the morning. I was looking forward to what God had in store for us. I expected God to give me a monster buck on video in order to catch the attention of all the people He wanted me to reach with my message of prayer and spirituality. I thought it was all going to be easy and work out well since I was doing it all for God. However, I was wrong!

My dad and I never even saw a single buck. We only saw a group of doe cutting through the woods in the distance. I went back to the friary in New York feeling somewhat embarrassed and confused. Why had all of that happened? Why did it seem as though I was supposed to make a hunting video? Why did I have to go through the struggle of telling the head of my religious order what I thought God wanted me to do only to come back with nothing to show for it?

After thinking and praying about the whole situation, I decided to ask for permission to try hunting *one more time*. Surprisingly, I was given permission to go the following weekend. Although I didn't think about it back then, I now realize that this was my *second chance* at getting a deer with my dad for the hunting video.

Throughout the week leading up to the hunt, I brainstormed as to where the deer might be the following weekend. I knew my friend's farm was going to be hunted by several people during the week. Most of the hunting pressure was going to take place on the upper side of the farm where my dad and I had sat on opening day. I then sketched a map of the farm and stared at it as I asked myself, "Where will no one think to hunt the deer this week?" The answer was obvious. It was along a creek bed on the bottom side of the farm. I then contacted Eric and told him where I was planning to hunt. He said, "That will be a great place. People have hunted there in the past with good success, but no one is hunting in that spot this year." Eric also said, "My dad shot a buck a few hundred yards away from that spot the other day." His comment made me feel even better about the spot I had picked. Now I just had to wait to be able to try it out.

The following Friday afternoon I met with my dad, and we went to Eric's farm. We set up our stands along the creek just as I had envisioned. As my dad climbed up the tree, I walked about fifteen yards away and sprayed a little of Eric's deer scent on the ground. I then thought to myself, "This is it. This is my last chance. If we don't get one tonight or tomorrow morning, it is over."

To be perfectly honest, I wasn't even sure how to pray while I was hunting. I thought, "Should I make a prayer of faith and just *believe* God will give me a deer?" After thinking about it, I answered myself by saying "I guess so." I then devoted myself to praying that way. Throughout the hunt, I fervently asked God to bring in a buck and let us get it on video. In addition, I relentlessly repeated in my mind that I *believed* it would come true. Lastly, I periodically praised and thanked God in advance for the gift He was going to give us.

For several hours, I *pounded* these kinds of prayers and praises through my mind. However, after a few hours of this, I was mentally and emotionally exhausted! There was still an hour left in the hunt, and I had no more energy to do anything. As the end of the hunt approached, I began to doubt everything I had just done. It greatly disappointed me to think I would not get a buck that night.

With only about fifteen minutes left, my dad tapped me on the arm and said, "Here comes a buck!" I looked back over my shoulder to see a buck walking straight in our direction. I stood up and got ready. The deer came to within ten yards of us and stopped directly behind a tree. This left me with no shot. The deer stood there for a long time, and light was fading fast.

I had given my video camera away before joining the religious order, so we were using my dad's camera in this situation. His was very cheap and produced a very low quality video. Even in good light his camera sometimes had trouble focusing. Thinking that he was not able to focus the camera on the deer because there wasn't enough light, I whispered, "Can you see him? Is it in focus?" Without looking over at me, my dad continued to look through the viewfinder and intensely whispered, "Shoot! Shoot!"

After what seemed like ten minutes, the deer began to act as if he knew something was not right. He then turned around and took a few steps back in the direction he had come from but then stopped. My dad continued to whisper "Shoot," so I drew back on the bowstring. The deer started walking again. Unfortunately, the tree was still partly in my way. I had to lean back as far as I could to be able to shoot around it. Because of the buck's body position, I had a very steep quartering away shot. I took aim, calmed my muscles, focused hard, and released the string. The arrow hit an inch to the left of where I was aiming and took out the spine of the buck. This dropped him in his tracks. The buck immediately began to squirm and moan loudly. Hearing the deer moan intensely upset me, which is something that had never happened to me before while hunting!

The deer was in some thick bushes, so I couldn't get a second shot into him to finish the job. As the buck moaned, he drug himself about six feet over to the left, but I still couldn't get a shot. Without hesitating, I quickly lowered my bow and climbed down. As soon as I reached the deer, I put a second shot into his vitals and then walked back over to the tree where my dad was.

We proceeded to take the stands down as the deer expired. The whole experience made me incredibly sad. I wasn't sure how to handle that feeling. In the past, I had always just gotten excited when I got a deer. I didn't even know it was possible to feel sad after harvesting an animal. Although I was intensely struggling with my feelings in that situation, my dad was utterly excited for me!

When we got to within fifty yards of the field, I could see that Eric was already standing there waiting for us. As we drug the buck toward him, but before he could clearly see it, I called out, "How long do their spikes have to be to be legal?" He replied, "I think it is three or four inches. Why, did you get one?" I called out, "Yeah, seven of them." (As in, seven total points.)

By the time we got the seven-pointer into the field, Eric and my dad were already celebrating with intense joy and excitement. Although I was still feeling sad, their excitement forged a powerfully bonding moment for all of us. As the evening drew to a close, I thanked God for the gift of the deer and for the gift of closeness that it created between me, my father, Eric, and Eric's father.

I'm on the left in the picture and my dad is on the right. The shirt I was wearing was actually the top half of one of the robes (habits) we normally wore. Obviously, I couldn't wear the full robe and climb a tree, which is why I used the half version in this hunting situation.

(Aside: I found out many years later that the spot where we got this deer on Eric's farm became known as "The Hail Mary Tree." It is still referred to by this name to this very day, nearly fifteen years later.)

Unfortunately, the video footage did not come out very clearly so I didn't end up using it to make a hunting video. In fact, I don't even know what happened to that footage. Regardless, I couldn't understand why everything happened the way it did. Why did it seem as if God wanted me to make a hunting video, yet it didn't work out the way I expected? Why didn't He just let me shoot a monster buck with plenty of daylight so that it came out clearly on video? What was the point of it all?

STAY FOCUSED

The following April I was sent to London, England to one of our mission houses. My assignment was to help run a soup kitchen and homeless shelter. While I was there, I still thought God wanted me to make a hunting video. As a result, I asked for permission to come back to the United States during hunting season for a week or two in order to work on the project. My request was denied by the local servant (person in charge of that friary), which is what I expected him to say. He was never a hunter, didn't understand hunting, and didn't see the importance of the video project I felt called to make.

A few months later, I finally realized through a series of dramatic events that God truly had a different plan for my life. In fact, I realized He had been leading me in a different direction all along. I just hadn't fully recognized or embraced His way of communicating with me before. One of the reasons was that I was always so concerned about what other people thought I should do with my life that I never figured out how to listen within and discern what *I* personally *felt called* by God to do.

Since I still had a year and a half left in the religious order before I was even eligible to make a lifelong commitment, I simply let them know I had concluded my discernment and was not going to stay. In turn, they sent me back to the United States, and I was able to leave and begin a new path in life. It was around early December in the year 2001 at this point in time.

Not long after I returned home I went to a friend's house to split some wood for her parents. In a discussion I had with her parents a few days later on the phone, they told me they had been seeing a lot of deer on their property. Since the late archery season in PA was going to begin soon, the day after Christmas, I asked them for permission to hunt on their property. They joyfully gave approval. As a result, I immediately went over and scouted their property looking for a good tree stand location.

Meanwhile, my friend, Scott, had given me a climbing tree stand that he was no longer using. I used this climbing stand to get set up on the top part of the property where I had permission to hunt when the season reopened. My goal was to sit until eleven in the morning, which I knew was going to be challenging because of the freezing temperatures.

Although it was difficult to sit in the cold, it was nice because the ground was covered with snow. This made the deer very easy to see when they moved. In fact, I saw eleven within the first hour and a half of the hunt! Unfortunately, they were all a hundred yards away on the adjacent property.

Around eight in the morning, I decided to try grunting a few times. To my surprise, a group of deer immediately came from across the dirt road and ran up the hill toward me. They stopped and stood still at the crest of the hill about fifty-five yards away. There were three bucks and three doe. The smallest buck had a ten inch spread with seven points. The two largest bucks began to softly spar. They both had about eighteen inch spreads. The smaller of the two had five points, and the larger one had eight points. I loudly prayed in my mind, "God, PLEASE, send them my way!"

The bucks continued to gently spar and push each other for close to an hour, and I continued to beg God to send them toward me. It surprised me that they were sparing that late in the year and that they were doing it for such a long period of time.

Eventually, a doe left the group and slowly walked down through the woods past me. The bucks then stopped pushing each other around, and several of the deer began eating the buds off of the trees as they headed toward me. Before long the five-pointer was just seven yards from the base of the tree I was in. The problem with this was that he was looking up in the air as he nibbled on the buds. I thought that if I moved even the slightest bit he was going to see me and take off running. Keep in mind that I was in a climbing tree stand on a tree with no leaves! This means I had no cover and really stood out!

A few minutes later, the big eight-pointer turned and headed in my direction. I immediately started telling the story in my mind to my friends and family of how I shot this huge buck. Fortunately, the five-pointer looked the other direction as the eight-pointer got to within fifteen yards of my stand. This gave me a chance to draw. The confident thoughts that went through my mind were, "This is a chip-shot. I can make this with my eyes closed!" Just then, I re-leased, and the arrow went flying. To my surprise, the broadhead barely sliced a little hair and skin near the top of the big buck's back.

All of the deer took off running, including the big buck. As he ran, I could see that the arrow never even penetrated his body. It on-ly slightly cut his skin. The buck then stopped running and stood be-hind a tree about thirty-five yards away. As he stood there looking around, I nocked another arrow and hoped he would step out into the open. Unfortunately, he never did. He just took off running again.

This would have been the biggest buck I had ever harvested up to that point in time, and I was very disappointed to have messed up my opportunity! I then replayed everything in my mind. This helped me realize what went wrong. My adrenaline had been pumping for so long that I wasn't mentally *focused* the way I normally am. Also, I was so overly confident in my accuracy at that distance that I didn't think I needed to focus hard on the shot. Because of these two factors, I simply released when I saw that my sight pins were behind the shoulder on the body of the deer. If I would have been paying closer attention, I would have noticed that my twenty yard pin was quite high on the deer's back.

To verify that I had not gotten any penetration into the deer with my arrow, I quickly climbed down and went over to where the buck had been standing. After picking up my arrow, it was easy to see that it had not gone through the deer. Instead, only the bottom blade on my broadhead had sliced a little hair and skin off of him. I climbed back up into the tree and called my dad on the cell phone to tell him the sad story. He told me to hang in there and stay in the stand until eleven as I had planned.

Aside from the freezing temperatures, I was still shaking profusely from the prolonged adrenaline rush I had experienced while watching the bucks for almost an hour. It seemed as though my body temperature dropped dramatically after I got back up in the tree, and I began to shiver almost uncontrollably! Even though a large part of me wanted to give up and leave, I kept repeating in my mind, "Hang in there. Hang in there."

After what seemed like an eternity, I looked down at my watch to see if it was time to leave. To my surprise, it was not even ten o'clock in the morning. I then thought to myself, "Over an hour left! I don't think I'm going to make it!"

As I shivered in the tree and looked around, I became very bothered by the fact that my foot prints were in the snow where I had walked over to check my arrow. This could cost me a deer if any came from that direction and saw my tracks before I could get a shot. I knew that deer sometimes spook from seeing human tracks in the snow.

Although it was agonizingly difficult, and I was freezing, I forced myself to sit in the stand until eleven. As that time approached, I started planning my departure. With only *one minute left* before it was time for me to get down, I happened to look down through the woods. My eyes immediately caught a glimpse of a doe trotting on a slant pattern headed in a different direction. She was only about ninety yards away. Much to my surprise, I then saw that there was a buck chasing her! For a moment, I wondered what I could possibly do to get them to head my way. A split second later the doe suddenly turned and ran straight toward me for some reason. I couldn't believe it!

The doe eventually ran past me. The buck then turned and followed the same trail the doe had traveled. I then thought to myself, "If he continues on that trail, he will pass by me at twenty yards." The buck continued to run on the same trail the doe had. As he approached, I viciously repeated one word in my mind, "Focus, focus, focus!" I drew my bow and remained determined. With all of my energy, I *focused* my mind on keeping my twenty yard pin perfectly placed on the deer. I refused to let myself miss again due to a lack of concentration at the moment of the shot.

The buck was running too fast, so I picked a spot in front of him, held still, and released the arrow just as he ran into my sight. It was an extremely difficult shot. While the arrow was in flight, I realized he was running a little faster than I anticipated. It looked as though my arrow entered him a little far back around the liver or the guts. Although the entry point looked a little farther back than I prefer, I chose to remain positive because he was quartering away from me. This gave me the hope that my arrow had angled up into the vital organs on the other side. I also consoled myself by acknowledging the fact that there was plenty of snow on the ground, which would make it much easier to track the deer.

I called my dad to tell him the good news. Afterword, I packed up my things and went straight home to eat lunch. Since it was a potential gut shot, I waited for four hours before going back to look for the deer.

When I returned to start tracking, even though I had seen where the buck ran down the hill and crossed the road, I decided to start tracking at the top of the hill where I shot the deer. The blood trail was a little harder to follow than I anticipated because the snow had partially melted during the day. In some areas, I couldn't even see the blood anymore due to the snowmelt. This forced me to focus on the buck's tracks.

Immediately after I crossed the road the blood trail vanished. In addition, there were so many deer tracks in the snow on that side of the road that I wasn't sure which ones to follow anymore. I immediately began to panic, and my emotions started to flare up in a negative way! It also seemed as though my intestines began to twist into a knot as I thought of potentially not finding this buck.

After walking about fifteen more yards into the woods, I breathed a huge sigh of relief, because I saw my buck lying dead on the ground. The arrow had gone through his liver and the lung on the opposite side. He died about a hundred and thirty yards from the spot where I shot him. Even though it was only a six-pointer, I was happy to fill my deer tag and be back on the hunting scene! This was also the first buck I had ever taken in the late archery season which made it all the more satisfying.

There were a few important lessons I took from this hunt. The first was to always remain *focused* when it is time to shoot. As part of this, I need to be aware of how an adrenaline rush can impact my ability to think clearly. This especially holds true in situations like this one where I was in freezing temperatures, and my heart was intensely pounding for a prolonged period of time.

Another thing I learned was that I need to be prepared to fight off the thought of bragging to people about how big my deer is and how I got it. Thinking about these kinds of things can become a major distraction, which is what happened in my situation. Instead, it is essential to *remain focused* on making a good shot!

The last important idea I took from this hunt was to always be disciplined and stick to my commitments to the very end. As part of this, don't lose hope. In a certain sense, I felt as though God used this whole situation to teach me this lesson. Never give up! Even with one minute left, don't give up. Simply remain hopeful, stick to your commitments, and see them through to the very end.

I can honestly say that there have been many (yet not all) hunts since this one where a similar thing has happened and I ended up getting a deer. I start by setting a time I will sit until during a morning hunt. I then remain committed to that time and *stay focused* when a shot presented itself. A perfect example of this took place in my 2012 hunting video titled *How to Hunt Whitetail Deer* at the 24:56 time mark. In that situation, I was hunting in New York, and I was freezing! I told myself I would sit until 10:30, but was struggling to do so. However, I *forced myself* to remain despite wanting to leave early. Just minutes before my designated departure time arrived, three antlerless deer appeared on the scene, and I harvested the largest one. In fact, it was probably the oldest doe I had ever harvested up until that point in time!

Therefore, I encourage you to stick to your commitments! Hang in there no matter how hard it gets. Also, I encourage you to apply this same mentality to your everyday life. Stick to your commitments to the bitter end no matter how hard it gets. This even applies to married couples who are struggling. Even when the conditions seem bleak, if you hang in there until the end and don't give up, you may just be surprised by what will come your way!

SHOULD I KEEP WORKING ON IT?

The following summer I accepted a job teaching high school religion at a Catholic high school located in Altoona, PA, which was about four hours away from my parents' house. I ended up renting a trailer on a dairy farm located about thirty-five minutes away from the school where I taught. The farmer I was renting from gave me permission to hunt on his property, but he said that a buck had to have at least eight points and the spread had to be out past the tips of its ears in order to be shot on his land. His wife also told me that I was the only one who had permission to hunt on the farm during archery season.

I had purchased a new bow that summer but was having trouble shooting it accurately with my fingers. Out of respect for the deer, and because my bow hunting friends were urging me to do so, I decided to try using a mechanical release for the first time. I had always resisted doing so because I wanted to keep an aspect of my archery traditional. I was also afraid I'd end up forgetting the mechanical release at home, which in turn would ruin my hunt.

Since I didn't have a video camera, and couldn't afford to buy one, an older lady I knew from church gave me some money to get a cheap camera so that I could keep working on the hunting video project. Unfortunately, I could not find a single person to video for me. Eventually, the lady who gave me the money to buy the camera volunteered to help. She was about the same age as my parents. At first, I declined her offer because I thought her age would be a factor. However, I later decided to let her try it since no one else was willing to help me.

Opening day of archery season presented me with several painful lessons. The first was that the screw-in tree steps I had set up were too far apart for the woman, and she couldn't get up into the tree. Quietly redoing every single step in the dark was not easy! I began sweating profusely from the rigorous workout involved with adjusting the steps, which made me feel very distraught. I always hated using screw in steps anyway, because I didn't like hurting the trees. This situation motivated me to find something else to use in the future for setting up tree stands.

Regardless, after that issue was resolved, we got into the stands. As soon as I finished hoisting my bow up, I discovered that I forgot the mechanical release. It was sitting on top of the washing machine in my trailer. At that moment, I regretted switching from shooting with my fingers that year!

As I sat there in the dark feeling exhausted and defeated, I leaned over and told my friend that the release was next to the door on the washing machine in my trailer. She excitedly said, "I'll go get it!" Before I realized what was happening, she was already on her way down the tree.

After she returned, she said she heard a bunch of deer running through the cornfield on her way back to the stand. I told her I had heard them too. They were only forty yards away from me when it happened. I couldn't help but think they would not have been spooked away had I not forgotten my release.

After the commotion of us getting set up finally settled, two flashlights came our way through the field. Even though I was shining my light at them to indicate we were there, they continued to come directly at us. They ended up setting up on either side of our location. One guy set up sixty yards behind us in a climbing tree stand. The other set up on the ground to our right about seventy yards away. This infuriated me! I ardently thought to myself, "Why can't people be respectful?"

Rather than let everything that happened bother me, I focused on praying and trusting God. I spent the entire morning begging God for a deer. I used the prayer of faith technique that I had used when I got the seven-pointer with my dad. I asked for what I wanted and then simply believed I would receive it. In addition, I praised and thanked God in advance for the deer I believed He was going to give me. After two hours of intensely praying this way, I was completely exhausted both mentally and emotionally.

A half hour before we planned to get down, I looked over to see a nice six-pointer running toward us. It was painful for me to see him and not be able to shoot him on video. He simply didn't meet the minimum size requirement. Part of me wanted to shoot him anyway and just not tell the farmer, but I knew that wasn't right, so I restrained myself.

A minute after the buck was out of sight, I spotted the hunter who was set up on the ground. He was walking in our direction. I called him over and asked him where they got permission to hunt on the farm. He said, "The farmer," but I didn't believe him because he didn't provide a name. He then walked away through the woods toward his friend.

In addition to being angry that the other hunters messed up my spot, I questioned why God hadn't answered my prayers. Had I done something wrong? Or was it just because of the inconsiderate behavior of the other hunters who crowded around me that I didn't get my deer?

My friend and I got down and left the woods. Just before she got into her car to leave, she said, "One day you will have children of your own. They won't be able to do all the things you do. They won't be able to climb trees the way you can. The next time someone is hunting with you, space the steps as if you were doing it for your twelve-year-old son." This made very good sense, and I thanked her for the insight.

The last thing she said was, "I really want to help you with your video, but I just can't. I was so scared up in that tree that I couldn't even turn the camera on and point it in a direction. I was too busy holding on for dear life!"

Even though she was wearing a safety belt, I guess she was still afraid of the height. I thanked her for trying, and then she left. Her statement helped me realize that I can't simply ask or let just anyone help me with the project. It needed to be someone who was not afraid of heights and who knew what to look for in the woods. He or she also needed to know how to basically run a video camera!

Since my bow had fallen off of the washing machine right before we had left to go to the tree stands that morning, I decided to go take a few shots to make sure everything was still in tune. It was a good thing I did, because my arrows were hitting an entire foot to the left! The arrow rest had gotten pushed over when the bow hit the floor, which I had not previously realized. This helped me understand why God had not given me a deer. If He had brought one close to me, I would have either missed it or injured it as a result of my arrows hitting an entire foot to the left.

Chapter 3 – Taking My Skills to the Next Level!

PLAY THE WIND

I didn't go back to my tree stand that night because of the other hunters. However, in a conversation I had a few days later with one of the neighbors, I learned that the hunter who had set up right behind me in a climbing tree stand had shot a big eight-pointer the evening of opening day. It was one of the big ones I had seen during my preseason scouting. This disappointed and angered me, but I didn't dwell on it or give up. Instead, I just kept trying new spots on other areas of the farm where I didn't think anyone else was hunting.

On days that I didn't have time to hunt, I'd just go out and practice archery after work before it got dark. The place where I practiced was next to a crop field. The field ran from the bottom of the hill next to my target all the way up to the top of the hill, a distance of about two hundred and fifty yards. To the right of the field was a large patch of woods. The woods also ran from the valley behind my target up to the top of the hill, but the woods kept going down the other side of the hill and behind the field.

As I practiced, I noticed that the deer always came into the field at two precise spots. When the wind was blowing from the top of the hill/field down toward the bottom, the deer entered the field about halfway up the hillside. When the wind was blowing from the bottom of the field up to the top, the deer always came out at the very top of the field. For the first time in my life, I actually got to observe how the deer were using the wind in their approach to a food source. This dramatically changed the way I approached hunting.

I tried hunting along the edge of that field over the following week when the wind direction was right. I even tried videoing myself, but was quickly frustrated with it. Very often I missed shot opportunities because I was busy moving the video camera around. After feeling stressed and frustrated with my lack of success videoing myself, and after giving it a lot of thought, I decided to put the video camera away until God sent someone to help me with the project. I figured that if He truly wanted me to make a video, He would provide the people and resources I needed when the time was right. Until then, I decided to focus all of my efforts on just improving my skills as a hunter.

The very next hunt I went on was at the top of the crop field next to my practice range since the wind was blowing toward the top. As I expected, the deer began to filter toward me on their way to the field. Among the first few deer was a three-legged doe. My heart immediately felt sad for her as she limped past me. As a result, I opted to take her instead of waiting for one of the big bucks I had been seeing coming out into that field in the evenings. I just felt as though shooting her was the ethical thing to do. I then drew my bow and made a perfect shot. However, there was a sudden downpour of rain just fifteen minutes later, which was not in the forecast. To my surprise and disappointment, I never found any blood at all after I got down and looked. As I searched for the doe in the dark with my flashlight, a giant buck let me walk within forty yards of him. This took place just sixty yards from where I shot the doe.

I looked for the doe for two days before giving up. It deeply bothered me that I could not find her! It also upset the farmer, which made me feel even worse!

This was my first time using a mechanical (expandable-blade) broadhead. It was also the last time I used that brand of broadhead. Their blades just didn't seem sharp enough. Before hunting again, I went to a sporting goods store and got new broadheads with a larger cutting diameter and sharper blades!

The evening after getting the new broadheads I tried a new spot on the other side of the farm since I felt as though I had ruined the patch of woods where I had been searching for the doe. This new spot was the only place that would work because of the way the wind was blowing that evening. To my surprise and delight, a big six-pointer went past me just twenty minutes before dark. Four minutes later a perfect eight-pointer came my way on the same trail, so I stood up and got ready to shoot.

I still had not shot an eight-pointer at that point in my hunting career but really wanted one. As I looked closely at the buck, I could see that his spread came out to almost the tips of his ears, but definitely not *past* them as the farmer required. This meant I had to let the buck go, which was painfully difficult for me to do!

After the buck passed me, he stopped and slightly turned broadside. I wanted to shoot him so badly! I then drew back my bow and took aim. He was right there offering me an easy, eighteen-yard shot. My pin was dead on his heart. All I needed to do was squeeze the release trigger! At that moment, the voice of my conscience said, "What are you going to do when the farmer sees this buck?" Although it was difficult, I chose to slowly ease down on my bow and let the buck walk away. I only hoped God would bless me with an even bigger buck for making the right decision and respecting the farmer's rules.

Unfortunately, that never happened. In fact, I didn't have any bucks come close to me throughout the rest of the season. In addition, after many more years of experiences like this one, I have come to learn that we can't expect to always be blessed with what we want in this world just because we did the right thing. Instead, we must do the right thing for the sake of being righteous, and that is it. Sometimes our reward will not come until *after* this life is over. See 2 Corinthians 5:10.

THE FOX SIGHTING

Allow me to digress for a moment and tell you about when I made the decision to leave the religious order and come home for good. If you will recall, I was living in London, England at that time helping to run a soup kitchen and homeless shelter. On the day I was getting picked up from the friary to be taken to the airport to come home for good, I saw a fox run past the gate. This surprised me since we were living in the city. It was very uncommon to see a fox running through the city in the middle of the day. However, the moment it happened, I heard a Scripture passage whisper through my mind. "Foxes have dens and birds of the sky have nests, but the Son of Man has nowhere to rest His head" (Luke 9:58). This gave me the impression that God was telling me I would be moved around a lot in service of Him. In a sense, I would not have a place to call home for a while.

With that in mind, when I went out for my next hunt on the farm the following Saturday morning after passing on that eight-pointer, I set up over a fresh scrape I had recently found. Early in the hunt, I had a beautiful gray fox come and sit next to the scrape. It was the first time I had ever seen a gray fox in the wild, and I was happy to see it. As I sat there watching, the same Scripture passage drifted through my mind again, "Foxes have dens and birds of the sky have nests, but the Son of Man has nowhere to rest His head" (Luke 9:58).

Three days later I was driving in my car at night to a prayer group meeting when I nearly hit a fox that ran out in front of me on the highway. Was it a sign? I'd say so. To my shock and surprise, I ended up moving the following week! I had unexpectedly been offered a new place to stay just minutes from where I worked and for half the cost of rent. Because of how little I was getting paid as a teacher in a Catholic school, I needed to take the offer in order to save money on gas and rent.

After moving, I could no longer hunt on the farm, so I went to the public hunting land near the farm where I had previously scouted. I was fortunate enough to harvest a doe while I was there. I was grateful for this because it fed me through the winter!

The following spring, I went out scouting for turkey season and had another fox sighting. Almost immediately afterward, I was offered a job as the Director of Youth Ministry for a Catholic church in State College, PA. The church was located about an hour northeast of where I had been living and working as a teacher. I accepted the position which meant I'd have to find a new place to live and also a new area to hunt in the fall.

I shared these fox stories with you to reaffirm the fact that God truly can speak to us through using nature, just as He had done regarding the "second chance" message He gave me while I was in the religious order. Keep these stories in mind while you are out there in nature. If you haven't received a message like any of these already, you may one day be positively surprised by what God might say to you through nature! The key is to pay attention and listen.

TOO WINDY

In addition to moving, I decided to switch back to shooting with just my fingers instead of a release for the upcoming hunting season. I practiced as often as possible throughout the summer to prepare. In addition, the Pennsylvania Game Commission made a regulation change that year which required a buck to have at least three points on one side of its rack in order for him to be legal to shoot. There were even some areas on the western side of the state that required a minimum of four points on one side. (This rule for western PA has since been modified to just three points on the main beam on one side of the rack. This compensates for the mature bucks that simply didn't have brow tines.)

The primary area I tried hunting that fall was the public hunting land located just outside of town where I was working and living. At first, I had trouble finding any deer there. Eventually, one of the janitors from the church where I worked told me about a good spot to try on the other side of the public land from where I had been hunting.

The wind was blowing at forty to sixty miles-per-hour gusts the evening I decided to try hunting this new spot. I didn't realize just how difficult it was going to be to hunt in such strong winds, because I had never tried to do it before. It was simply not common for the wind to blow that vigorously in central Pennsylvania.

There was a thicket under a power line that ran straight up the hillside at the place where I was trying that evening. The guy who told me about the spot said that the deer normally come out of the thicket and into the woods in the evening. If the deer behaved like the ones I had watched coming out into the farmer's fields when I lived on the dairy farm, then I knew they would come out of the thicket at the very top of the hill that evening since the wind was blowing from the bottom up to the top.

As I hiked up the hill, I came across several tremendously well used deer trails located about halfway up the hillside. In fact, they were so well used that I just couldn't resist abandoning my original plan and sitting near them. I quickly found a straight tree and got up into it with my climbing tree stand. After putting my safety strap on, and pulling up my bow, the wind started blowing even harder. I tried pulling my bow back to see if I would be able to hold steady enough to take a shot, but the tree was swaying way too much, and I couldn't keep my balance. Needless to say, I immediately climbed back down!

My plan was to just stand at the base of the tree for the remainder of the evening. With about a half hour left in the hunt, I looked down the hill and saw a black bear trotting by. It was only thirty yards away but never knew I was there because the wind was blowing straight up the hill from him to me. It was at that moment that I realized I should have gone all the way to the top of the hill to hunt that evening. The trails I had been hunting were probably the ones the deer used when the wind was blowing down the hill. I then turned around and looked up toward the top of the hill as far as I could see. Sure enough, I saw a deer come out of the thicket right at that moment. When it got directly above me, which was also directly downwind of me, it smelled me and took off running. Who knows how many other deer did the same thing earlier in the hunt while I was looking in the opposite direction.

What did I learn from this hunt? Aside from affirming how I should play the wind in those types of situations, I also learned that I should not plan to hunt out of a tree stand when the wind is blowing that vigorously. It is unsafe. In a certain sense, I think it could even be considered unethical to bow hunt in those types of circumstances. I say this because in addition to the wind making it difficult to hold my arms steady for a good shot, the wind could also dramatically alter the trajectory of the arrow. These factors greatly reduce the potential efficiency of a shot, which is why I think it is more ethical and respectful to wait for better weather before hunting.

DON'T BE STINGY

The end of the regular archery season was fast approaching. Although I managed to shoot two doe the week after I started hunting the spot I just told you about, I was getting nervous because I hadn't seen a legal buck yet that year.

Later that week, I talked with my college friend, Eric, to see how they were doing on his farm. He said there was a really hot scrape where I had sat on opening day with my dad the year I hunted there. Several bucks had been seen near the scrape during the week. He also said no one was hunting there on Saturday and that I'd be more than welcome to come try it out. This sounded way better than the spot I was hunting, so I excitedly accepted his offer.

It was a long drive, so I went down the night before and stayed at my parents' house. As soon as I got to my parents', I climbed up onto their barn and took a few practices shots. For some reason, my arrows were all hitting a few inches low and to the left. Since it was almost dark, I didn't want to start changing things on my bow. Instead, I planned to aim a little high and to the right if I got a shot the following morning. If I didn't get a shot, I would just go to my parents' at lunchtime to fix my bow before going back out in the afternoon.

I arrived at Eric's farm the following morning an hour and a half before daylight. Although I had a general idea of how the woods were laid out, I had not been there in several years. This made it challenging for me to find the exact spot he was talking about in the dark. Eventually, I found the scrape, hung a canister with doe-in-heat scent above it, and then got up into the tree Eric told me about.

An hour after daylight, a group of five doe fawns went under me. They walked right past the scrape and down through the woods. They didn't even notice the deer scent I put out.

Not long after the young group of deer passed, the cold air started to get to me, and I began shivering. My goal was to sit until eleven o'clock. It was now only seven, which made me think I wasn't going to make it. My hope was that the sun would begin to warm me up when it rose, which would enable me to withstand the icy temperature.

Unfortunately, the sun came up on the opposite side of the tree from where I was sitting. Since I knew that bucks typically approach a scrape from the downwind side, I turned my body to face downwind and then leaned out around the tree in an effort to let the sunlight shine on me at the same time.

An hour passed, and then a spike buck suddenly appeared. He remained true to my anticipation and walked up to the scrape from the downwind direction. I was anxious to see how he'd react to the doe-in-heat scent I left at the scrape. To my surprise, he completely ignored it and just continued down through the woods.

Another hour passed, and it became harder for me to control my shivering. Then suddenly, a fox popped out of the thicket and trotted past me. (There was no inner message associated with this sighting.) After looking down at my watch, I noticed that an animal had passed me at every single hour on the hour. I used this fact as motivation to stay there for another hour despite the cold.

After a while, I looked down at my watch and saw that only forty-five minutes had elapsed since the fox passed by. I thought for sure it had been longer than that. In an effort to encourage myself to hang in there, I thought, "Fifteen more minutes until my next sighting!" I must have looked down at my watch a dozen times after that, waiting for it to turn ten o'clock. Then finally, the minute hand reached the hour, and I raised my head wondering where the deer was at.

All of the deer and even the fox had come from behind me on the left. I looked over to that area but didn't see anything. It seemed as though no deer were going to show up, so I relaxed and looked straight ahead toward the scrape. For some reason, my head then turned to the right, and I looked behind me. I didn't intend to do this. It just happened. To my surprise, however, a nice buck was coming! It was not huge, but I knew I would shoot him if he gave me a chance!

As soon as I saw the buck, I immediately stood up, turned around, and moved myself into position for a shot. The buck was about seventy yards away when I initially spotted him and angling toward the downwind side of the scrape. The direction he was walking would cause him to pass me just fourteen yards away.

As the buck got closer, I thought to myself, "Finally! I'm going to get an eight-pointer!" His rack had perfect symmetry at first glance, which made me all the more excited.

Just before the buck was perfectly broadside, I drew my bow and took aim. Remembering how my arrows were hitting the night before, I placed my pin a little high and an inch to the right. I then released the string and watched the arrow fly. Since the deer was only fourteen yards away, the arrow hit him before he had a chance to move much. My arrow took out his spine and knocked him off his feet. It surprised me that my shot went basically where I was aiming instead of a few inches lower. At any rate, because it was a spine shot, the back half of the buck's body was paralyzed, but he was still alive. This meant I needed to shoot him again. I immediately nocked another arrow and drew back. The buck was now facing directly away from me and trying to stand up. His front legs were still functioning, and he was propped up on them.

Since my first shot went where I aimed, I placed my pin exactly where I wanted the second shot to hit. The spot I picked was through the spine down into the heart. Unfortunately, I missed the spine by an inch to the right and only took out the top and bottom of the right lung.

For the simple fact that I didn't want to shoot again and ruin another arrow and broadhead, I decided to climb down and take my stand out to the car. I figured that would give the buck enough time to bleed out and die since it would take me at least a half hour to get back to him.

Just as I made it to my car and put my tree stand and equipment on the ground, Eric's dad walked out of the cow barn. Upon seeing me, he quickly came over and asked, "How'd you do?" I happily responded, "I just shot a buck!" He said, "Oh great! Hop in the truck! I will give you a ride out to get him!" His offer was generous, but I was worried we'd get back before the buck expired. Hesitantly, I picked up my bow and got into the truck with him. We then drove out through the fields to the woods.

The buck's head was up and looking at us as we approached. This deeply bothered me! In addition, when I saw him for the first time straight on, I thought, "Oh no, he's missing a brow tine. He's only a seven-pointer." Eric's dad then said, "Looks like you'll have to hit him again. Go ahead and nock an arrow." At that moment, I realized I accidently left my shooting tab sitting on my tree stand, which was on the ground behind my car. This meant I'd have to shoot with my bare fingers, which distracted me a little.

While I prepared to shoot, Eric's dad went over and petted the deer on the head. He also started talking to the buck saying, "There you go, old boy. It's okay. It will all be over soon." He then stepped back away from the buck so that I could take my shot. I then looked at the buck's face. It had a somber look of death on it. In my soul, I felt a great sadness. Standing six yards away, I drew and released. My arrow then struck the buck directly in the heart.

The buck let out a push of air and a noise that sounded as if it had just been punched in the guts. Eric's dad then went back over and continued to hold the buck's rack and pet his head. As the deer died, Eric's dad gently laid its head on the ground. Since he raised cows for a living, he must have been used to watching animals die

up close. I, on the other hand, was not used to such things, and it bothered me a lot!

After it was over, I felt bad for initially walking out of the woods and leaving the buck there. It was because I was being so *stingy* that I didn't immediately use a third arrow to quickly put the buck out of his misery. However, this was not the first time money had influenced my decision in this way. It also happened when I shot the four-pointer at college, which I told you about in the section titled, "Fence Row." If you will recall, my first shot was a little premature. Although it did not hit any vital organs, it stunned the deer so much that he fell to the ground and lay there motionless with the exception of his breathing. At that point, I should have shot him again in the vitals to quickly finish the job.

In both of those situations, rather than care about the animals as my top priority, I decided to not shoot again because of money. I didn't want to spend money on more arrows and broadheads. If I hadn't been so stingy, I could have easily hit both of those bucks in the vitals with an additional shot. In this way, neither of them would have had to suffer unnecessarily.

After the experience I just shared regarding the seven-pointer on Eric's farm, I promised myself I would not let money motivate my decision again in this way. Instead, I vowed to intentionally care about the animals as my priority, making sure that their death was as quick and painless as possible. If this meant I couldn't hunt for the rest of the season because I couldn't afford to buy more arrows and broadheads, then that is how it was going to be!

This hunt also showed me that even if you hit an animal in a vital area, it may not bleed much if it does not intensely run immediately after being shot. Running causes the blood to pump fast out of the animal and fill up the lungs if that is where you hit it. If the animal is not running, and it has not been hit directly in the heart, you can expect the dying process to take longer. Keep this in mind when deciding when to start tracking your animal after a shot. If it only walks away and doesn't run after being shot, you may need to give it more time to bleed out and die than you would if it ran away at a fast pace.

Another thing I realized later was the reason my arrows were hitting the wrong spot the night before while practicing from the roof of the barn. It was because I was not bending at the waist. I was simply afraid to bend toward the edge of the roof with no safety harness on to keep me from falling. Not bending at the waist can cause aiming variances and alterations in the pressure points on your fingers when shooting with just your fingers as opposed to a mechanical release. Therefore, it is important to bend at the waist when shooting from high elevation in order to create the proper aiming angles as well as pressure points on your fingers if you are a finger shooter.

Now that I have shared a few things I learned from this hunt, I want to explain a few things that interested me about it. It intrigued me that I saw animals at every hour on the hour. It also interested me that this was the second buck I shot on Eric's farm. Both bucks died in a similar way. Neither of my first shots were intended to be spine shots, yet both were. This required me to get down and finish them off up close with another shot. I was also left feeling terribly sad each time. In addition, both bucks were seven-pointers. As I said before, the number seven is significant to me because it is the Biblical number that stands for completion and fulfillment. I kept all of these details in my mind in case God was eventually going to give me some kind of spiritual message through them just as He had done with the "second chance" message using the deer, bear, turkey, and largemouth bass I told you about earlier.

MOVING TO LAMAR

A large number of events took place that caused me to move to a place called Lamar, Pennsylvania. If you are interested in learning how it all happened, it is depicted in my book titled *Will You Spread My Word For Me?* which is also available through my ministry websites McVeighMinistries.com and CatholicGuestSpeaker.com.

Among other reasons, I moved to that area because I wanted to live near a less humanly populated area. Since I couldn't afford to own much land, I figured I'd move to an area that provided access to a lot of public hunting land. The house I ended up buying was near more than twelve thousand acres of public hunting ground.

In my preseason scouting, I saw two nice bucks and many doe. This made me very excited, especially for my dad. He hadn't done much hunting since I moved out after college. We made plans for him to come up to my place to hunt on opening day, and I hoped he'd get one of the nice bucks I saw.

One thing I didn't account for when originally planning the hunt with my dad was the steepness of the mountains. He had a very difficult time climbing the terrain behind my house. In addition, I also didn't anticipate the hunting pressure. For example, the spot where I was planning to sit was behind my neighbor's farm. He owned some woods that butted up against the public land. After climbing uphill for nearly twenty minutes to get to my spot, a four-wheeler came up through the woods and parked thirty yards in front of my tree stand. There was also a hunter sitting on every fender of the four-wheeler. Immediately after parking, the five of them proceeded to spread out all around me. This deeply distressed me, but there was nothing I could do about it.

The only deer I saw that morning was a small six-pointer that took off running when he saw the four-wheeler parked in front of me. When my dad and I went to my house for lunch, he told me he had hunters all around him as well. One of them even laid a blanket on the ground forty yards away from him and then sat down on it.

Although I went into the hunting season with high hopes, they were quickly dashed by the amount of hunting pressure. It seemed as though everywhere I went I encountered more hunters. This was very frustrating. In addition to needing to find a new spot without other people, I also needed to find a place where my dad wouldn't have to hike up a huge, steep mountain.

While trying a new area the following week that I thought I might be able to take my dad to, I surprisingly saw three doe moving through the woods an hour before dark. They circled around and came straight to me. The first doe stepped out in front of me just ten yards away. Although she was facing me, I thought I could take a shot and still do an efficient job by hitting her down through the spine and into the lungs. I drew back, aimed, and loosed the arrow. To my surprise, the arrow hit the ground to the left of where the doe was standing, and all three of them took off running. They then stopped about forty yards away and started snorting. The woods were so thick that there was no way I could take a second shot. All three doe walked in circles snorting at me for the rest of the night. It was a complete disaster!

As the deer walked in circles snorting, I sat in the tree replaying the shot in my mind. As I did this, I realized two things. The first was that I didn't *focus* at the time of the shot. Adrenaline had been pumping in my veins and because of how close the deer was I didn't take the shot as seriously as I should have. It was the same mistake I made in the past with the big eight-pointer in the late season just after I came home from the religious order. As a result, I planned to more frequently remind myself of that lesson so that it wouldn't happen again!

The other thing I noticed was that I never closed my left eye because of the excitement. Since I am left-eye dominant, but shoot right handed, my left eye takes over when aiming if I forget to close it. When this happens, my arrow hits almost a foot to the left of where I want it to go. Upon realizing this, I thought back to the spike I shot on video while I was in college. For the first time since that experience, I realized that I had missed that buck on my first shot for the same exact reason. I never closed my left eye. In addition, I suddenly realized that I got the spike on my *second chance*!

TAKE BETTER SHOTS

Unfortunately, my first hunting season in Lamar was rather unsuccessful. In preparation for the following hunting season, I studied the landscape more diligently and pondered long and hard about where the deer might go after being pressured by all the other hunters. This proved to be much more difficult to predict in the deep woods than it was in scattered patches of woods among large crop fields and housing developments like the area where I grew up hunting. There were literally miles of forest behind my house in Lamar, which gave the deer *many* options. Most of those options were difficult to reach by foot let alone drag a dead deer out from!

In August, I started a new job. The hours and days I had to work left me with very little time to hunt. Around the fourth week of the season, I had two hours to try hunting in the morning before leaving for work. For this reason, I decided to stay pretty close to my house. After being in my tree stand for a while, my boredom and lack of confidence in that location motivated me to bleat with my voice. A few minutes later, I looked over my shoulder to see a doe coming my way. This surprised me, and I got ready to shoot.

The deer walked on an angle up the hill in my direction. When she reached an area near where I had walked up the hill, she stopped for a moment, looked over at where I had stepped, and then went over and put her nose on the ground. She smelled exactly where I had placed my foot. I thought deer were not supposed to be able to smell where you walked if you wore rubber boots. She taught me otherwise.

The next thing she did baffled me. After smelling the ground for a minute, she picked up her head and looked at a sapling about ten feet away from her. It was the sapling I had grabbed hold of to keep my balance while I was scaling up the steep slope. She then walked straight over to that sapling and put her nose on the exact spot I had placed my hand. "Unbelievable!" I thought to myself. Even though I was wearing gloves that I had washed in scent eliminating soap, she still smelled where I touched.

The doe then tracked my steps toward the tree I was in. Since I didn't think she was going to offer me a broadside shot, I decided to shoot while she was still quartering toward me on an angle. I figured I could make the shot count since she was only six yards away from the tree I was in.

I drew my bow, took aim, and released the string. The arrow hit right where I was aiming and clearly went through at least one lung. Since I still had to get to work that morning, I barely waited thirty minutes before climbing down and tracking her. I followed the blood trail all the way up and over the mountain, which greatly surprised me. The deer then went down the other mountainside, and I eventually lost her trail in the valley before she headed up the second mountain. Since I was in charge of opening the store where I worked, I had no choice but to leave the trail. I then *ran* home as fast as I could.

Running up and down the steep mountain slope was far more exhausting than I was in the mood to deal with! By the time I made it home, I was in complete agony and out of breath. My muscles were throbbing and my hands were shaking from the exertion of the run. I took a very quick shower and headed to work.

Not finding the deer really bothered me. I thought about it throughout the day. I also thought about how incredible deer are at detecting human scent. This did not just pertain to my shoes, but even the trees I touched. As a result, I decided to train myself to keep my balance while hiking up the steep terrain near my house without touching anything as I climbed.

Hunting in Lamar was far more difficult than I imagined it was going to be. The level of awareness and wariness of the deer seemed to exceed the suburban deer I grew up hunting. Their ability to detect predators forced me to dramatically improve as a hunter.

LISTEN WITHIN

The day after I hit that doe, my friend John Thomas came to visit me for fall turkey season. He and I originally met just after I came home from the religious order. One of the first jobs I took at that time was in the fishing department of an outdoor store where John was already working. A few months after that, I accepted the teaching job I mentioned earlier and then moved four hours away. However, John and I kept in touch over the years, and this was his first time visiting me in Lamar.

Not long after John arrived we hiked up the mountain behind my house in an effort to find the deer I hit the day before. When we reached the top of the hill, we sat down to catch our breath. As I looked down the other hillside, John asked, "Do you get many deer ticks out this way?" I happily responded, "Actually no! I have not found a single one on me in the two years I've lived here, which really surprised me." As I finished saying this, I looked down at my hand to see a deer tick crawling across it. This amazed me!

Because of my experiences with God and prayer, I believed the Holy Spirit was at work in this situation. As a result, I immediately said to John, "I want you to look within yourself. Think back and observe the faint thoughts and feelings you had just before you asked me that question." After a brief pause, I continued, "Look here at my hand. This is the first deer tick I have ever found on me since I moved here. This is very unexpected. At times, I sense things, and I think you just *sensed* the tick without consciously realizing it. This prompted you to ask the question. Learn how to refine your ability to detect when you sense things in this way. Then bring what you sense into your conscious mind so that you can think about it more clearly. You will then be able to discern and follow God's influences more often in your life. As you develop your ability to do this, be mindful that it should always be used to help people and not for any form of selfish gain."

To be honest, it was a little hard for me to tell John this secret I had discovered after my many years of struggling and searching within myself and experimenting with what I noticed. The reason it was hard for me to tell him was that I still wasn't an expert at detecting these things and I wanted to be the first person I knew to master this spiritual awareness. I didn't want him to quickly become better at it than me. When I realized this immature motivation, I knew I needed to tell him my insights in order to overcome my own pride and negative motivations. Now I have not only given him the secret, but everyone who reads this book as well!

Look within yourself. As I asked you to do earlier in the book when I sensed the doe bedded down along the road the year I shot instinctively, take notice of all the times you have a thought that goes through your mind and then moments later comes true. Also pay attention to instances where you think of someone and then he or she suddenly calls you on the phone or sends you a message.

These types of spiritual things happen all the time, but many people miss them, because they are not paying attention to what is going on within and around them. They also don't take the time to notice that these types of thoughts have a distinct, faint feeling associated with them. It is this faint feeling that helps to make them noticeable and discernible.

At any rate, a month after I taught John this lesson, he called me on the phone. With intense excitement in his voice, he said, "You are not going to believe this! You know how you told me to train myself to listen within and notice when I feel a spiritual inspiration come to me? Well it worked! I was driving my friend home the other day, and I had the same sense within me that I had when I asked you about the deer tick. I suddenly knew what he was thinking, so I said, 'I know this is going to sound crazy, but are you thinking about going to buy some lumber at the hardware store right now?' He was totally shocked, and yelled, 'How'd you know that?' You should have seen the look on his face! It was so funny! Ha, ha, ha."

If you are interested in learning more about this approach to discernment and the spiritual life, I encourage you to read my book *Self-Knowledge Self-Awareness: A Master Key to the Spiritual Life* which is also available through my ministry websites.

DON'T LIE

Several of the concepts regarding prayer and spirituality that I present in *Self-Knowledge Self-Awareness: A Master Key to the Spiritual Life* I learned and developed through hunting experiences. This next situation is a perfect example of that.

Although I had off from work on this particular morning, I needed to drive in to pick up my paycheck. I strongly wanted to go hunting since the season was almost over, so I decided to get to the store just before daylight, pick up my check, and then immediately drive to the closest public hunting land. Since I had never hunted there before, I planned to walk in just at first daylight so that I could see where I was going.

This particular public hunting area was just off of Shiloh Road, along a class A Trophy Trout Stream known as Spring Creek near State College, PA. Men and women literally flocked to this stream from all around the country throughout the entire year!

Since it had just broken daylight when I arrived at this spot, multiple fishermen were already heading to the stream from the parking area. I walked alongside one of them as we crossed over the bridge to the other side of the stream. I explained to him that it was my first time hunting there. After I learned that he frequented the area for fishing, I asked him if the forest on the other side of the stream, the side we had just come from, was part of the public hunting ground. He said he wasn't sure, but thought it was because there were no "No Hunting" signs posted on that side of the stream. I asked him this because I really wanted to follow the rules and not risk getting in trouble. I also asked him this because I knew that other hunters would be less likely to wade through the stream. This could result in less hunting pressure and more deer movement on the other side.

After walking downstream a good distance, I crossed at a shallow spot and then scaling the steep hillside. Afterward, I climbed into a tree along a well used deer trail located about fifty yards from the stream. As soon as I positioned myself, I began to pray fervently for God to give me a big buck. I prayed with faith, and believed that God was going to answer my prayer. I said, "God, please give me a big buck this morning! One with at least eight points but preferably twelve! I praise and thank You in advance for the gift of the big buck, and I take in *faith* that You will answer my prayer. Amen." I fervently said my prayer over and over in my mind throughout the morning. There were many times that I amplified my praises, and tried to simply *believe* I would receive what I asked for. After praying like this for a while, I became mentally and emotionally exhausted just as I had in the past when I tried using this approach to prayer. Making the situation even more challenging was the fact that it was very windy and cold.

After a few hours, I became so cold that I just couldn't stay out there any longer and decided to leave. As I prepared to get down, I thought about how much it disappointed me that I didn't get a deer. Why hadn't God answered my prayers? I thought I did everything right. I made my intention and then *believed* in faith that I would receive what I asked for, a big buck. So why didn't it work?

As I started to leave the woods, I noticed that there were many more fishermen in the stream. I didn't want to ruin their fishing by walking through the water and spooking the fish, so I stayed on my side of the stream and battled through the thick bushes to get to the parking lot. It was much more difficult for me to make it to the parking area by staying on this side of the stream, but I did it in order to be respectful toward the fishermen.

When I finally made it out of the woods, a fisherman ran over to me, looked me in the eyes, and quickly asked, "Hey, did you know you are not allowed to hunt over there? That land is owned by the prison!" I immediately replied, "I wasn't hunting here! I was just walking through the woods on this side of the stream in order to get to my car!" Obviously, without even thinking about what I was doing, I blatantly lied to him. Why did I do that?

This experience taught me a lot about myself. It showed me that even though I try very hard to live the right way and be a good person, I am still capable of sinning without even intending to. This also helped me better understand how incredibly hard it is to be totally righteous in this life. It takes a lot of deliberate work, effort, and grace from God.

From this experience, I also realized I'd have to spend a lot of time and energy deliberately training myself to *not react* in situations like this one. It seemed to me that if it is this difficult for someone who is making a serious effort to live righteously, what does that say about people who do not even make any effort at all?

As I previously alluded to, this hunt also helped me realize something very important about prayer. While I was sitting in the tree hunting, I relentlessly prayed that I would get a big buck. I focused on *believing* that it would happen, and I *claimed* in *faith* that I would receive what I asked for. I did this because I had listened to people on Christian TV shows and radio shows say you should pray this way. However, I was grateful that God did *not* answer the prayer I made in *faith*! If He had, I could have gotten fined and lost my hunting license for hunting in an area that was off limits and actually owned by the local prison! Since I was already financially struggling, being fined would have added to my financial strain! The authorities would also have confiscated my deer, and I would not have gotten the food I needed to help offset the cost of groceries.

Thinking about other similar experiences I've had, I remembered the time I hunted on the dairy farm and had my older woman friend videoing me. I prayed fervently in the same way to get a deer throughout the whole morning of that hunt. It bothered me that I didn't get what I asked for even though I prayed with *faith* and *believed* that it would happen. However, after the situation was over, I was glad I didn't get a shot at a buck because I learned that my arrow rest had been moved without me even knowing it. If I would have gotten a shot, I would have missed or wounded the animal.

I praise and thank God for the sport of hunting and giving me experiences like these, because they have enabled me to clearly see that this approach to prayer is incorrect and ineffective. One of the reasons is that it does not account for many of the unseen and unknown factors in a given situation. Very often, God simply cannot answer prayers made using this style and approach, because it would not be in our best interest, other people's best interest, the animal's best interest, and/or the environment's best interest. After realizing all of these things, I began to search for a more effective way to pray in hunting and in everyday life situations. I wanted to find an approach that actually worked and helped me grow closer to God.

PICK A SAFE TREE IN ADVANCE

The following week also happened to be the last week of archery season. I planned to hunt on the mountain behind my house a few hundred yards uphill from where I shot the doe that I couldn't find the previous week.

The wind was blowing uphill when I entered the woods that morning, so I had to hunt even higher on the hill than I originally anticipated. It was my first time trying this particular area, so I didn't have a good tree picked out in advance for my climbing tree stand. Finding a usable tree in the dark proved to be much more difficult than I anticipated. After a long time searching in the dark using my flashlight, I saw a tree uphill from me that looked usable. It was not until I hiked up next to the tree that I realized it significantly slanted downhill. I decided to try it anyway, and just faced my tree stand in the opposite direction of the slant. It wasn't until I was completely set up and tried to draw my bow that I realized how difficult it was for me to keep my balance without the platform rocking on the tree as a result of the slant. Since daylight was quickly approaching, I decided to just stay there rather than climb down and look for another tree.

Thirty minutes after dawn, I watched a huge raccoon walk across a blown down tree to my right. As I watched it, a deer walked up behind the raccoon! I quickly stood and prepared myself to shoot. The deer was coming toward me on a trail that passed about eight yards on the downhill side of the tree I was in. Because of how wobbly my stand was, I knew I was going to have to let the deer pass behind me in hopes of getting a quartering-away shot.

Things were working out well until the deer walked behind me and put her nose on the leaves where I had walked. I couldn't believe it. She did it too! I had heavily sprayed my boots with scent elimination spray before going to bed the night before and again before walking into the woods that morning, yet the deer still detected me.

All I needed was for the doe to take four more steps in the direction she was headed so that I could take a shot. Instead, she walked straight up to the tree I was in and put her nose against the base of it. She never looked up at me, but began to act nervous and quickly spun around. Without hesitating, she started walking straight away very rapidly. In response, I quickly drew back and took aim. The angle she was headed offered me a steep quartering away shot. I released the string, but unfortunately didn't lead the deer far enough. My arrow hit her directly in the guts. She jumped in the air and ran off.

The deer ran down the hill, and I carefully watched her travel route as far as I was able to see. Once she was out of sight, I made mental notes regarding the way she ran and then I sat back down to relax. Since it looked like a gut shot, I planned to sit there without moving for at least three or four hours before tracking.

Thirty minutes later, I heard a bunch of noise coming from the direction the deer had gone. Suddenly, I saw something black. Was it a black bear? Did it get my dear? No, it was a flock of turkeys! I quickly stood and nocked another arrow since fall turkey season was open. The turkeys were headed straight up the hill about sixty yards away, so I said, "God, please let them come my way!" To my amazement, the birds suddenly turned and started walking straight toward me as soon as I finished this prayer!

I used the upper limb of my bow to help camouflage my face from the birds and I remained as still as a statue. Things were definitely working in my favor. The angle they were headed would put them behind a thick pine tree just twelve yards in front of me. I could draw my bow while they were behind that tree and then shoot the first one that stepped out on the other side of it.

To my dismay, one of the birds strayed from the rest of the flock and walked down behind me. Although I remained totally motionless, it saw my silhouette on the side of the tree as it circled. The bird immediately started chirping and ran back toward the other turkeys. The whole flock then turned around and started running away.

The feeling of disappointment began to settle in my soul. However, the very last bird stopped just before jumping over a blown down tree about thirty-two yards away. I quickly drew, aimed, and released. The arrow soared through the air. It looked as though I had estimated the distance perfectly! I began to get excited as the arrow approached its target. Then it suddenly stuck into the tree less than an inch to the left of the bird. "Ugh," I thought to myself. The turkey then hopped over the log and ran away with the rest of the flock. Although I wished I would have hit the bird, I didn't let it bother me. I simply sat back down and continued waiting.

An hour later, a spike buck walked the same path the doe had traveled. He also sniffed my trail. This educated me, but it also bothered me. Although rubber boots hold in human odor, it seemed clear to me that the deer in my area smelled the rubber, and they clearly didn't like it!

I purchased those boots through the Internet right before the season started and they naturally had a strong rubber smell to them. To my surprise, that strong smell had not faded very much even though I had been using them throughout the season. From that day forward, I concluded that I would sniff the bottom of a pair of boots with my own nose before buying them. If the rubber had a very strong odor, I would not buy them! If I had trouble smelling the rubber even when they were brand new, then I'd buy them. I'd also be sure to get them early in the summer and wear them around the yard so that the smell of the new material could wear off before the season started. Even still, I hoped that a manufacturer would create a footwear product that had absolutely *no smell* at all.

One thing was for certain, the deer in Lamar were pushing me to improve my skills as well as my knowledge of the hunting products I used. I also realized I needed to find ways to approach my hunting spots from an angle that the deer would not cross before I had a chance to shoot. This also meant I could not visit the same stand very often because the deer would easily detect the scent I left behind while walking in and out of that area. I also learned that whenever possible I needed to have a specific tree picked out before I tried setting up in the dark. In addition, significantly slanted trees are not safe and should not be used with a climbing tree stand!

A NEW SPIRITUAL DIMENSION

After four hours had passed, I climbed down and began to slowly track the doe I hit. I followed her all the way down the hill. She went into a thicket and actually laid down *inside* a half-hollowed-out-tree trunk. She then got up and started circling in the thicket. This twisted me into knots while I tracked her. After she finished doing that, she left that thicket and went into another one. She then proceeded to do the same thing in that one. This deer amazed me but also frustrated me at the same time!

There were several times I lost the trail or wasn't sure which blood spots were going into the thicket and which ones were coming back out. It was one of the most difficult tracks I had ever experienced. Fortunately, I eventually figured out that she completely left that area and headed toward the stream.

Allow me to digress for a moment and tell you that a group of workers had set up and started cutting trees along the road about an hour after I shot this deer. Judging by the direction the blood trail was headed, I started to worry that the deer had crossed the road before the workers got there and then their noise pushed her deeper into the forest on the other side.

Regardless, not long after I tracked the deer out of the thicket, the drops of blood became less frequent and harder to see. I ended up on my hands and knees crawling looking for blood. The very last drop of blood I found was next to a track that angled toward the road where the workers were cutting. Judging by the angle she was coming from in relation to this last track, it seemed clear to me that she went out and crossed the road. This caused me to think, "She must have made it across before they arrived and started working."

Just as my dad had taught me, I marked the last spot of blood and slowly made a complete circle around that spot looking for more blood, only, I did it crawling on the ground! I expected to find my next bit of blood in the direction of the road. However, despite my intense effort I could not find any. The feeling of strain and failure began to intensify within me. I had to consciously calm my emotions and stay focused and determined. I decided to begin crawling toward the road in the direction the last deer track was headed.

At this point, I began to call on Saint Anthony. He was a Catholic Franciscan priest who died in 1231. He was famous for his preaching when he was alive, but now has become known as the patron saint of lost things. There were many times in my life when I prayed the Saint Anthony prayer and either found my lost item immediately or within a very short period of time.

The wording of the Saint Anthony prayer is, "Dear Saint Anthony, please come around. Something is lost, and cannot be found." In this situation, I replaced the second part of the sentence with the words, "My deer is lost, and cannot be found." As soon as I made this prayer, a thought very softly whispered through my mind. "Your deer is in the other direction." Simultaneously, I had an inner sense of where the deer was located along the edge of the stream. This sense felt much like the one I had regarding the doe I shot while walking down the road the year I hunted instinctively.

In this situation, I didn't immediately follow the thought and feeling I received after I made that prayer. Instead, I continued to crawl along the path I was already headed. Within five minutes, I became so frustrated and restless with the lack of deer sign that I decided to stand up and turn completely around. I then started slowly walking toward the stream in the direction I had sensed the deer was located. As I walked in this new direction, I intently studied the ground looking for tracks or a speck of blood but I wasn't seeing any.

Although I was *not* feeling very confident, I kept walking slowly in the direction I had sensed the deer. After traversing about thirty yards, I randomly looked down at the ground. To my amazement, there was a speck of blood on a leaf. This excited me, and I immediately bent down to look for more sign. Although I didn't see any more blood right away, I began to move as quietly as possible toward the stream. After a while, I found another speck of blood in the direction I had been heading. It seemed as though the prayer response and inner sense I received were leading me in the right direction!

After traveling another forty yards, I crouched down on my hands and knees. I stared at the ground for a while looking for blood but then caught movement out of the corner of my eye. I immediately turned my head in that direction. To my surprise, I saw the deer bedded down about twenty-three yards away. She was still alive, and I could see my arrow sticking out of her.

Because of the position of the deer in relation to where I was located, I needed to stalk down a small embankment and around a patch of trees in order to get a shot into her vitals. I knew it would be extremely difficult to get there without being seen. In order to give myself a chance, I slowly took off my fluorescent orange hat and vest, which are required while moving during the overlap between archery and fall turkey season in Pennsylvania. After safely making it five steps down the embankment, I prepared to maneuver around the tree. This would leave me very exposed to the deer's sight and my chances of being seen were very high. Just then, the doe partially stood and readjusted herself before lying back down. This made me extremely nervous, and I almost panicked. Thankfully, she still had no idea I was there and she was not facing me.

The deer's breathing was labored, and I felt bad for her. Although I wanted to hurry up and finish her off, so that she would not have to suffer anymore, I knew I couldn't rush it. By that time, her blood had already clotted. I knew that if I frightened her off before getting a second shot there would most likely be no blood trail to follow.

Three yards separated me from the spot I needed to get to in order to make a perfect shot. I decided to wait for an airplane to go overhead to disguise the sound of my movement. Just then, a thought went through my mind that sounded like a female's voice. I hope you don't think I am crazy, and I know there is a chance you won't even believe me, but honestly, I somehow knew it was Mary's voice, as in, Mary the mother of Jesus. Although it was faint in volume, she sternly said, "No! You need to shoot now!"

This thought surprised me, but I actually ignored it at first. It was easy for me to dismiss because of how faint and subtle it was. However, within a few seconds, I caught movement out of the corner of my eye. The stream that the deer was bedded next to was also a class A Trophy Trout Stream. At that exact moment, a fisherman was wading through the water, casting, and walking in my direction. It wouldn't be long before the deer heard his noise over the sound of the flowing stream and took off running.

The voice I heard was right. I needed to shoot, and I needed to do it NOW! The deer looked partially in the other direction, so I quickly and carefully stood, stepped to the side, and drew my bow all in one motion. There was a small opening in the bushes, but I still needed to move a few inches to the side in order to get a clear shot into the vitals. I then leaned to my left, held steady, and loosed the arrow. It was a perfect strike. The deer jumped up and ran into the stream. She proceeded to lunge through the water to the other side. Both arrows were now sticking out of her, which reawakened the bad feeling I had about the situation.

As the deer ran across the stream, the elderly fisherman kept yelling, "Hey! Your deer ran across the stream! Hey you! Hunter! Your deer ran across the stream!" Over and over he yelled this, and I began to get annoyed. When the deer made it across the stream, it fell onto the rocks. This snapped both of my carbon arrows in half, but I didn't care about them. I only cared about the animal and ending any suffering she may be feeling. The deer then tried to stand back up but fell over again. I reached for another arrow and tried to figure out what to do. She then slid into the water and began to drown. Meanwhile, the man kept yelling at me, "Hey you! Your deer ran across the stream!" Feeling very annoyed, I thought to myself, "I know. Be quiet! It would be helpful if you were not yelling! You're going to spook the deer even more!"

At this point in time, I quickly ran back over to my fluorescent orange, put it on, and then quickly made my way over to the stream. The man was now on my side of the bank. Since the deer was too far for a safe shot, I hastily surveyed the area to determine how I could quickly get over to her in case I needed to shoot again. As I looked down to the bridge, I said to the fisherman, "I'm going to run down, cross the bridge, and circle around to the deer." He offered to stay there and watch her for me.

I moved as fast I could safely travel with my equipment in hand. After crossing the bridge and running up the road, I unknowingly passed the spot where the deer was lying. Once I figured this out, I turned around and headed back in the correct direction. As I did this, the fisherman stepped out onto the road. He had already drug the deer up from the stream. I quickly went to meet him and thanked him repeatedly. He said the deer was already dead by the time I started jogging toward the bridge so he just crossed the stream and brought her up for me.

This experience added a new spiritual dimension to my hunting. It also shocked and amazed me every time I thought about it for the rest of the day! The fact that it actually happened also gave me a new confidence in finding hit animals. I believed that if I just stayed calm, prayed, and listened carefully within, I would have much more success in tracking animals in the future because of the help I was receiving from my heavenly family members.

HUNTING GUIDE

I didn't want to bore you with the details, but I had been working in sales since I moved to Lamar, and I absolutely hated it. My heart's desire since the end of my college days was to start a full time guest speaking ministry for churches, schools, and organizations. I wanted to go around to these places giving talks focused on inspiring people to grow in their relationship with God. However, this dream had not yet materialized, which forced me to continue working in jobs I didn't like.

My inner restlessness with these jobs eventually reached a point where I just couldn't take it anymore. As a result, I started to think about what type of job I could possibly do that I would actually like. Since bow hunting was my favorite thing to do outside of being a guest speaker, and I originally had a dream of becoming a professional bow hunter when I was growing up, I started to look for a way to apply myself to this desire and still make money. My conclusion was to start contacting hunting outfitters in the Midwest to see if any were looking for a hunting guide for the upcoming fall. Much to my surprise, I had a job offer in Illinois the very next day. It was a four week position during archery season. The outfitter even said I could hunt while I was there! This was not a difficult decision for me to make. I accepted the position immediately! Although I had to turn down multiple other offers, I did accept one other position with an outfitter in Ohio. They needed a guide for one week during shotgun season in December.

I was happy that the Illinois position only lasted for four weeks because I was getting married during the summer. I simply didn't want to be away from my wife for too long just after getting married.

LEARNING TO SCORE

The areas where I grew up hunting, and the public hunting land near my house in Lamar, did not support a large number of big-racked bucks. For example, I talked to one very old man who had been hunting on the public land behind my house for over thirty years. He was very picky about the bucks he shot and only harvested the largest ones he saw every year. He had taken a total of thirteen bucks off of the mountain behind my house over the years. The largest one barely scored 120 according to the Pope and Young measuring standards. This isn't even big enough to make it into the Pope and Young record book. The net score for a typical whitetail buck must be at least 125, and a non-typical buck must have a net score of at least 155 in order for it to be recorded in the record book.

At any rate, since I never hunted in areas with a lot of large bucks, I never bothered to learn how to score them using the Pope and Young measuring standards. However, since I was now going out to Illinois to work as a guide, I knew I needed to change that FAST! I started by downloading the official Pope and Young scoring sheets and reading the directions on how to score a buck. I then watched as many hunting videos as possible throughout the summer. I tried to spot score every single buck I saw. It was especially helpful when the hunting video included the score of the buck after they harvested it. This enabled me to compare my guess with the actual score.

I became very proficient at spot scoring as time went on. I even began to impress myself. There were times when I'd watch thirty hunts in a row on a video and guess nearly every buck's score correctly to within three inches. Still, I knew I wasn't perfect. There were instances when I was *way off*, but for the most part, I was definitely getting the hang of it.

The other main thing I worked on that summer was my long distance shooting. As I mentioned before, I had switched back to shooting with my fingers instead of a mechanical release. However, I started to realize that despite my hours of practice each week, I still wasn't able to shoot my bow with the accuracy and consistency I wanted to at longer distances. Out of respect for the animals I hunted, I decided to switch back to using a mechanical release. I simply wanted to make sure I performed my task of shooting as efficiently and effectively as possible when hunting an animal. In addition, my wife had bought me a brand new, top-of-the-line Hoyt as a wedding gift. The technology of bows had become so advanced that I felt I could best utilize my new bow's capabilities by using a mechanical release. However, even though my focus was changing in my shooting style for hunting, I took the sights off of my old compound and started using it for shooting instinctively with my fingers at my practice range just for fun.

STATE RECORD

In Illinois, I was supposed to have a week to scout and hang tree stands before my hunters arrived. After guiding for three weeks, I would then be allowed to hunt a piece of property a few miles away for a week. However, after just two days of scouting, my boss said, "We have a few lady hunters coming in this week, and I'm putting Deborah Knoff with you. It shouldn't be too hard. She has a spot she really likes, so you can just set her up there the first morning. I also have to tell you that she holds the Illinois Department of Natural Re-

sources Big Buck Recognition State Archery record for women. The buck had 14 points and gross scored a little over 191!" (*Deb is pictured here with her record breaking buck. Just looking at her hand enables you to see how massive the base of the rack was!*)

Needless to say, I was a little intimidated at first by my boss's statement. After all, I was just some guy from Pennsylvania who probably never even saw a buck in the woods that scored over 150. Regardless, I knew the deer in my area of Pennsylvania were among some of the toughest in the country to harvest, which had significantly helped me develop my scouting and hunting skills to a more proficient level. Thinking about this gave me a sense of confidence which replaced my feeling of intimidation.

Throughout the first day and a half of Deb's hunt, I bounced her around between some of the best stands I had hung. She shot three doe, but had not seen any good bucks. While she hunted, I continued to scout hard and began to hone in on a nice ten-pointer. There is a glimpse of him on my *Humble Beginnings Part Two* video at the 18:40 time mark.

The first time I watched this buck he was chasing a group of doe back and forth through a river bottom. At one point, he was up on a hillside and made a strange noise. I thought to myself, "What in the world was that?" I then turned my head to the side and saw a four-pointer standing near the tree I was in. It suddenly dawned on me that the buck had just wheezed. I hadn't recognized it at first because I didn't hear the two short snorts that typically are made before the wheeze. It also sounded a little different than the snort wheezes I had heard people do on hunting videos. The buck's wheeze sounded more like the moan someone would make after getting punched in the guts. This guttural effect was missing when people tried to imitate the sound using a plastic deer call.

As I traveled back to the lodge that morning, I practiced mimicking the sound the buck had made. While making the long, drawn-out wheeze sound with my mouth, I also used my diaphragm to make the deep guttural sound. It didn't take long for me to master the technique, and I was excited!

The following morning I watched that same ten-pointer in a nearby field. At midday, I hung a stand along the top of a ridge where I thought he was bedding down. I then told Deb that I had a nice buck figured out. She agreed to try the stand, and I offered to video the hunt. This excited her, and we headed to the spot. As I parked my vehicle, the rain began to come down a little harder. I turned to her and said, "I hope you don't mind, but I'd rather not take the video camera out in this rain. However, I'd still like to sit with you and watch the hunt." She didn't mind at all, so we headed up through the woods. By the time we made it to the stands, the rain had stopped. This made me wish I had brought the video camera anyway, but I was not going to go all the way back to my vehicle to get it at that point.

Five minutes after getting in the stand I asked Deb if she was ready. She said, "Yes," so I bleated twice. Not even a minute later, I looked to my left, and my eyes opened wide with astonishment. "HERE HE COMES!" I yelled in my mind. Immediately, I reached around the tree, tapped her on the shoulder, and said, "Good buck. Good buck. He's a shooter!" She glanced over and saw him coming. Without even standing up, she shrugged her shoulders, made a disinterested facial expression, and said, "Too small." In my mind, I yelled, "Ugh! Why can't I be the one shooting? He is perfect!" After a brief pause, I thought, "Oh well. I guess I can understand. After all, she is the state record holder for females."

It hurt me to watch such an awesome buck walk past me at eighteen yards, broadside, just slightly quartering away. Rather than focus on my negative feelings, I studied the buck's rack. This was the closest I had been to him yet. However, after looking more closely at him, it may not have been the same buck. Although his tine length and symmetry were about the same, the spread on this buck's rack seemed wider. He also seemed to have a little more mass than the one I had seen before.

The buck walked past me and was now about thirty yards away. The angle he was moving was taking him off of the ridge and down into the river bottom. Suddenly, I heard Deb say, "Wait a minute! He's not too small!" The next thing I knew, I saw her bow from the corner of my eye. Almost immediately, I heard a shot go off. I then watched as her arrow soared through the air and went *barely* under the buck's vitals. He immediately took off running.

After running for about a hundred and fifty yards, the buck stopped and looked back in our direction. In my mind, I disappointingly thought, "Oh man! I can't believe that!" Deb then said, "Try to call him back!" I hesitantly said, "Okay," but thought it wouldn't work. If anything, I thought we'd just be educating him against hunters, which would make it more difficult to harvest him. Regardless, I gave it a try just in case it worked. The buck looked toward us after I called but didn't move. Deb said, "Try calling again!" I did, but the buck turned and trotted away.

I could understand Deb's reason for wanting to try calling the buck back. She only had one day left and there was nothing for her to lose by trying everything possible to get him to come back. However, the buck got spooked by our efforts, and no other hunters saw him for the rest of that year. This is something to keep in mind if you ever go to hunt with an outfitter. The later in the season you go, the more the deer may have had experiences like this one, which can make it harder for you to harvest them.

TRACKING

While I was guiding in Illinois, if one of our hunters shot a deer in the heart or lungs during the morning, we usually tracked it within an hour after the guides arrived on site. Deer that were hit in the liver during the morning were given at least forty-five minutes if it was raining hard, but usually a few hours if it was not raining.

When our hunters shot a deer in the evening, we usually picked them up and took them back to the lodge for dinner. From there, we'd get the details of the shot. If it sounded like a good hit, we'd go looking for the deer about an hour after dinner. If it did not sound like a good hit, we'd wait even longer. If it was a gut shot, we typically waited until the following day if the weather and temperatures permitted it. Deer that were shot in the liver in the evening were at least given a few hours, but often were left overnight before tracking. Even if the hunter thought he or she hit the deer in the heart or lungs, we'd leave and come back the following morning if we had trouble tracking it for the first fifty to one-hundred yards.

After tracking with several different groups of people that year, I realized that many people probably do not find their deer because they do not track properly. For example, there were multiple occasions while we were tracking at night and the blood trail started off well. In response, some of the hunters, and occasionally even some of the guides, got excited and started walking ahead just looking for the white belly of a dead deer with their flashlights. Their overconfidence and impatience was costly! Every step they carelessly took through the woods made it more difficult to actually track and find the deer. They'd sometimes step on the last few remaining drops of blood without even realizing it, which wiped out the blood trail. Other times they overturned leaves by the careless shuffling of their feet, which also hid crucial clues.

In other tracking situations, people simply gave up too easily and aimlessly wandered through the woods hoping to stumble upon the dead deer. For example, one of our hunters shot a buck about thirty minutes before dark. He thought he hit it either in the liver or the guts, so we waited a few hours before going to look for it. After tracking for about forty yards and not finding much blood, we left the woods and headed back to the lodge.

We waited until the next day and started tracking again around nine o'clock in the morning. There were five of us on the trail. After we had gone about sixty yards, the blood seemed to stop. Within a minute or two, everyone haphazardly continued walking down the main trail the deer had been on. Eventually, they started randomly wandering through the woods looking for the body of the deer. This really irritated me, because, as I said before, they could have been stepping on and ruining crucial clues.

Rather than mindlessly following the other trackers, I went back to the last spot of blood and crouched down. I looked for fresh deer tracks in the dirt and managed to find one. I had studied some concepts on tracking and even attended a professional tracking school two years prior to this situation, but I did not consider myself to be very good at tracking yet. Regardless, one of the things I learned through my tracking studies was that you can always predict where the next track will be by analyzing the last one you have found. In order to do this, you need to pinpoint where the pressure releases are in the track.

It took me a few minutes of analyzing, but I thought I finally figured out where the next track was going to be. I then turned my body to the right and walked up into the woods off of the main trail. After five yards, I found a spot of blood. Within a few feet, I found a much less obvious trail that the deer had taken. It had more blood on it, and I quickly yelled to the others to indicate my discovery. They all came running over to me. As soon as they got there, they ran ahead of me on the trail. Once again, their actions and impatience deeply irritated me!

Fortunately for us, the buck was only another forty yards from where I had found the new direction. Everyone celebrated! After the hunter put his tag on the deer, we moved it from that spot. It was very stiff and had been shot in the liver. It probably died before we even tried tracking it the night before. Even though the temperature was fairly cold overnight, the area where the buck's chest had been in contact with the ground steamed when we moved him. The steam was obviously a result of the buck's body heat. His body had maintained a fairly high temperature overnight, yet the meat had not gone bad. This gave me a new confidence in letting a deer sit overnight before tracking it.

OHIO GUIDING

It was particularly hard for my wife while I was in Illinois. She was home alone, while I was in my glory getting paid to scout deer and hang tree stands. Because of how the situation was impacting her, I decided to give up the week I was going to be able to hunt at the end of my time in Illinois, and I went home early. I then got to spend a few weeks with my wife before going to Ohio for my guide work there.

The outfitting job in Ohio only required me to be away for eight days. I was to learn the land for three days, and then guide for five. In addition to the fair chase hunting, which is what I was guiding, this outfitter also had a hunting preserve. It was a large fenced in area where people could come and shoot deer, elk, or other species of big game animals that were on hand. Regardless of the species, the larger the animal's rack, the higher the price you had to pay to shoot it.

The very first day I was at this outfitter's preserve in Ohio, there were skinned deer carcasses lying on the ground next to the utility shed. I asked one of the workers what was going to happen to all of the deer meat. He said, "It will be thrown in the dumpster for the trash men to take." "Why?" I furiously asked. He responded, "Because those deer were darted within the last two weeks. You can't eat the meat if they've been tranquilized that recently."

The reason why the bucks had been tranquilized was that they had been purchased as inventory from a deer farm and were drugged in order to be transported to the fenced-in preserve. Regardless, the worker's answer made me sick to my stomach!

I encountered similar problems while I was in Illinois. Many of the hunters only cared about shooting a big buck and nothing else. For instance, after one of my hunters harvested a deer, I'd skin the hide off for him and ask, "What would you like me to do with the meat?" In response, some would say, "I don't care. Throw it out if you want." This deeply hurt me, and their attitudes made me want to vomit! It made me wonder what had become of the sport of hunting, a sport that I loved so much.

When you feel sadness from killing an animal as I have, you grow in respect for the animal. However, many of the "trophy hunters" I had encountered seemed very displaced from this reality. It seemed as though their hearts had become very callous and hardened. I pray that neither you nor I will end up like that. Rather, let us focus on being the best people we can be, which includes always respecting, caring for, and making good use of the *entire* animal that we harvest.

WATER HOLE

During the following year the temperatures were unseasonably hot during the early archery season. Because the wind was not blowing in the right direction for any of my normal spots, I decided to try an area I had scouted many times the previous winter and spring but had never hunted before. The area had plenty of good buck sign the previous year, and I even saw a buck that would have scored almost 120 while hunting not far from that area a few years earlier.

Unfortunately, there were many other people who hunted in that particular area as well. This was evident by the fact that there was a ladder stand locked to one of the trees and many scent wicks hanging in other locations nearby left by other hunters.

It was a long, exhausting hike up the mountain to get to this particular spot, but I was mentally prepared to do it. What I had not anticipated was how *much* I would sweat on the way. While hiking, I realized I should bring a change of clothes in the future. I could put my sweaty T-shirt in a sealable plastic bag, spray my body with scent elimination spray, and then put a fresh T-shirt on under my camouflage.

At any rate, as I made it about three quarters of the way up the hill, I looked over to my right and saw something that seemed out of place, so I went over to investigate. What I discovered was that there was a small mountain spring coming out of the ground right there. The mud that the water created was littered with fresh deer tracks!

This was an exciting find, and I started looking around for a good tree to get up into with my climbing stand. The highest I could climb in any of the trees was about fourteen feet. Unfortunately, this would leave me eye level with the deer trails on the two adjacent hillsides. Although I preferred to be higher, I set up in that tree anyway and hoped for the best.

Just after I got into the tree, the wind started swirling and blowing in the worst possible direction. Even though I knew this may ruin my chances at getting a deer, I stayed in that spot since it would take a lot of time and energy for me to get down and find somewhere else to hunt that evening.

Within an hour, I saw movement on the hill above me. Two deer were headed my way. As they got closer, I could see that they were both doe. I immediately reminded myself that it would be extremely difficult to drag a deer all the way out of that area, so I did *not* want to shoot unless it was a really nice buck!

The two doe cautiously made their way to the spring of water. By the time they got there, they started acting very skittish. They must have caught my scent as the wind swirled. The larger doe got a drink and proceeded to walk to my left into the only shooting lane I had. She stood there for several minutes almost as if to say, "Here I am! Go ahead and shoot me!" However, I repeated in my mind, "I'm not shooting. I'm not shooting. I'm not shooting unless it is a big buck!" Time passed, and I started to get the idea that the Holy Spirit was setting the whole situation up for me to harvest this doe.

Reluctantly, I stood up and picked up my bow as I repeated, "I'm *not* shooting unless it is a big buck!" The deer continued to stand there looking the other way, but she was acting a little nervous. I worried she might start snorting. My experience with the deer in this area had been that they like to snort excessively! This would obviously ruin the rest of my hunt. As a result, I reluctantly decided it would be better to get a doe than nothing at all. I hesitantly drew back my bow and thought, "Fine, I'll shoot." I focused, took aim, and shot. The arrow went into flight and made a perfect hit. The deer ran thirty yards and fell over dead. As soon as she hit the ground, she started sliding back down the steep hillside toward me.

What did I learn from this hunt? First, I am not just a hunter for myself, but also for God and His animals. Sometimes God may need or want me to harvest a deer I may not have intended to take. Although it is difficult to put into words, I actually had an inner sense that God wanted me to harvest this deer. The very last deer I harvested on my 2010 hunting video, *The Lone Hunter*, is another example of this. Either way, God sees a much larger picture than I do. I believe this is part of what it means to be a steward of the earth. It means staying in tune with God, and making the management decisions and deer harvests that we believe He is leading us to make.

This particular hunt also taught me the importance of water when it is very hot. The mountain spring made it much easier for the deer to get a drink so that they didn't have to walk all the way down the mountain to the stream below. Going all the way down and back up would cause the deer to use a lot of energy and also significantly increase their body temperature. I realized this body temperature component during my strenuous hike up the hill that day. Regardless, finding and hunting near a water source like this mountain spring on hot days can be extremely productive!

DENNY'S DOE

My cousin Dennis had never gotten a deer by this point in his life. It was my mission to help him get one. He had come up to my house for three days the previous hunting season. Some of the footage I got from those hunts can be viewed on my *Humble Beginnings Part Two* video. However, the only deer that came within bow range the previous year when I was videoing him were doe. Dennis had not gotten an antlerless deer tag that year, so he couldn't shoot at any of them. This year, however, I pestered him all spring and summer to make sure he applied for an antlerless tag. I simply wanted him to be able to shoot a doe if the opportunity presented itself.

Our first morning hunting this year was spent in the area we had seen many doe the year before. We got into our stands an hour and a half before dawn. My hopes for him getting a deer during that morning's hunt were dashed when another hunter walked up through the woods just before daylight. The path he took completely cut off the deer movement that would have come to us from the crop fields on the neighboring property. As a result, we didn't see a single deer all morning.

Every time I had taken my cousin hunting up to this point, I brought my video camera hoping to record his first deer kill on video. However, before we left my house for the evening hunt, I realized that trying to video was stressing me out. Rather than continue to let myself feel strained, or make my cousin feel extra pressure when it came time for him to shoot, I decided to leave the video camera at home. Instead, I simply focused on enjoying the hunt.

We went to a new area that I had not hunted before but had scouted many times in the past. To get there, we had to hike to the top of a mountain. Despite the fact that we took our time and tried to not break a sweat, we were both sweating profusely by the time we reached the top of the hill. Even though I was more prepared for it this time, we still chose to get as high up in a tree as we possibly could to make sure the deer wouldn't smell us.

About two hours before dark, I spotted a doe moving through the woods. The area she came from was almost a vertical cliff. This was the last place I would have expected a deer to come from, which made me think to myself, "Deer never cease to amaze me!"

My cousin was on the opposite side of the tree, so I reached around, tapped him, and told him to get ready. For a moment, it looked as if the doe was going to cross the hilltop forty yards in front of me and then go down the other hillside. This would have put her out of range. Fortunately for us, however, she turned and walked straight in our direction instead. This caused me to think, "This is going to be good!"

I remained perfectly still as the doe walked under me. After she passed my side of the tree, I could see in my peripheral vision that my cousin was drawing back his bow. As he did this, he accidently made a noise with his foot on the tree stand. The deer immediately froze. She stood still and carefully looked around for about thirty seconds. Meanwhile, I was screaming in my mind, "SHOOT! SHOOT!" I just couldn't imagine why my cousin was not shooting. The deer became very nervous and began to step back. She then turned and quickly started walking away. Just then, the sound of Denny's bow went off. The arrow struck the doe right in the butt, and I discouragingly thought to myself, "Oh, no!"

I watched the deer run off and I carefully made mental notes as to which path she took. I tried to remain positive. I also tried to encourage my cousin by telling him about the femoral artery that runs through that area of the deer's hind quarter. If he hit that artery, the deer would not last long. Dennis appreciated my encouragement and was very happy to finally get a shot at a deer after all those years of hunting. Eventually, we both sat down and relaxed. My plan was to wait an hour and a half, and then we'd get down and look for blood.

About an hour later, we heard a tremendous amount of noise in the direction his deer had run. Both of us stood up and looked intently to see what it was. As the sound grew closer, I saw movement though the trees. We then heard clucking noises. This caused me to excitedly think, "It's a flock of turkeys! This is great! He will get to experience them. This ought to be a good education for him!"

As the sounds drew closer, I told Dennis that turkeys were coming and that he needed to remain perfectly still. The first one stepped out of the thicket about forty-five yards away from us. As soon as she did, she tilted her head to the side. I knew instantly she had spotted us by the way she tilted her head. She then chirped with a spark of fear and hopped about three feet off the ground. As soon as she hit the ground again, she took off running and chirping. The other turkeys were not sure what was going on. They hesitantly followed her, and the whole flock jogged down the steep side of the mountain. It was an awesome experience, and my cousin was amazed by how quickly and efficiently the turkey had spotted us even though we were not moving.

With thirty minutes of daylight left, we climbed down and picked up the blood trail. At first, it was better than I expected! Unfortunately, it tapered off quickly after thirty yards. We then heard a deer snort in the direction his deer had gone. Because of the fading blood trail, and the snorting deer, I told Dennis we were going to leave and come back in the morning.

I had a few tissues in my pocket to help identify blood so I left a little piece of tissue on a stick to help mark the last spot of blood. I also intensely made mental notes as to what the surrounding area looked like. Primarily, I observed the direction and layout of the blown down trees in order to help me find that exact spot in the morning.

When we returned the following day, something had eaten my tissue paper, which made it much more difficult to find our last spot of blood. I immediately decided that I would never again use something dissolvable or edible like tissues to mark the last spot on a blood trail.

There was no more blood at all beyond that point. This made me feel a little disappointed and concerned. By the look on my cousin's face, the lack of blood seemed to cause him to feel a little strained and disappointed as well.

Since there was no more blood, I began to look for tracks. After doing my best to follow the doe's hoof print compressions in the leaves for about twenty yards, I looked up and saw her white belly about twenty-five yards in front of me. She was barely a hundred yards from where he shot her and only forty-five yards from where we stopped tracking her the night before.

The moment I saw the dead deer I stood up, spun around, and screamed, "Yeah! Good shot buddy!" Dennis looked up from the ground with a depressed facial expression, because he was still worried that we were not going to find the deer. He then stood up. I immediately ran over and jumped on him. While giving him a big hug, I excitedly yelled, "Yeah, baby! Good job!" He still didn't know what was going on until I stopped, put my feet back on the ground, and pointed over at the deer. The moment he looked past me and saw her, we both went crazy and started yelling with joy! (It was Sunday, so we weren't worried about disturbing any other hunters, since hunting was not permitted on Sunday in Pennsylvania.) We immediately ran over to the doe, and I took a picture of him with the deer using my cell phone. We then tagged her, gutted her, and joy-

fully drug her down the mountain.

Being able to share that moment with my cousin was probably one of the most exciting and memorable experiences I've ever had. We had worked so hard for several years to get him a deer and finally accomplished our goal!

In addition to being exciting, this hunt reaffirmed that whether you make an excellent shot or a poor one, the choices you make regarding how and when you track the animal can play a crucial role in recovering it! If your hunting experiences are anything like mine have been, there will be times when you will need to leave and come back the next morning. There will also be times when you will need to exclusively follow the animal's tracks because there is no blood trail to follow. The more difficult the track, the more patient, dedicated, and disciplined you will need to be while tracking.

ILLINOIS AGAIN

Later that season I went to guide in Illinois again. This time I only went for three weeks and was permitted to hunt the first week while scouting. The outfitter I worked for required a buck to score at least 120 for it to be shot. Hunters were charged a fine if they shot a buck smaller than that.

Like most hunters, I would love to always shoot big bucks. However, I would still have been content with a 120 class deer at that time especially since I had never shot one that big. In my mind, I said to myself, "My day will come when God will give me a monster buck. In the mean time, I'll just continue to focus on improving my skills each year."

On the first evening I was in Illinois, I hunted in a ground blind that one of the other guides had set up. I also set my video camera up on a tripod next to me hoping to get a shot on film. Forty-five minutes before dark, a group of bucks made their way toward the clearing in front of me. The first two were nine-pointers. One's rack was high and wide yet with very little mass. The other's rack was tight but had extremely thick beams. Both would have scored around 109, so I couldn't shoot.

While those two bucks fed on the white clover that grew in the clearing in front of me, a third buck appeared. He was a ten-pointer with everything I had ever wanted in a buck. His rack was high, wide, and very massive. He probably would have scored between 140 and 150.

The ten-pointer stood still at the edge of the clearing. He was steeply quartering toward me about twenty-five yards away. Suddenly, something made the other two bucks nervous. Perhaps the wind shifted and they caught my scent, I don't know. What I do know is that the two nine-pointers started to walk over toward the ten-pointer and the ten-pointer started acting cautiously. I drew back my bow and took aim at the big ten-pointer. If he turned and offered me a broadside shot, I planned to release the arrow. Unfortunately, he instantly spun around a hundred and eighty degrees and ran back the way he came from before I could do anything about it. That was very disappointing!

The following morning I planned to go to a good stand location that I had not been to since the year before. It was a ladder stand that was left up throughout the year. It was located in a ravine, which was not my preference because it made it easier for the deer to wind me, but the area was so good that I wanted to try it anyway.

I had no idea what kind of condition the stand was going to be in when I got there. As soon as I got onto the platform that morning, I used my flashlight to intensely inspect the stand, the straps, and the surrounding tree limbs. Everything seemed fine except for a few branches that had grown in around the stand. I quietly pruned them in order to be able to shoot, and then sat down.

As daylight arrived, I reached for my rangefinder. It must have fallen out of my pocket, because it wasn't there. As I looked up to the access trail on the other side of the ridge, I estimated the center of it to be about twenty-four yards away. It was difficult to tell, because it was up higher than the stand and there were many trees between me and the trail.

Thirty minutes after daylight, I heard a buck making a scrape on the other side of the evergreen trees located on the ridge in front of me. I stood up and got ready. Suddenly, the buck's enormous rack popped out from behind the trees and began passing through my narrow shooting lane. He was gigantic! My eyes nearly popped out of my head in disbelief!

The buck was walking very quickly up the access trail, the one I had guessed to be twenty-four yards away. My shooting window was only two feet wide, so I didn't have much time to draw, aim, and shoot. On this occasion, I tried to stop the buck by grunting with my voice like I had seen many hunters do on hunting videos. I expected the buck to stop and give me plenty of time to aim, which is what always seemed to happen on the videos. Unfortunately, that didn't happen for me. Instead, the buck just kept walking at a quick speed. I grunted even louder, but he didn't respond. It seemed as if he was in a trance and on a mission to get somewhere. He wasn't paying attention to anything else around him. While all of this was happening, I didn't take time to carefully aim. Since the buck didn't stop, I panicked and rushed my shot. Unfortunately, the arrow looked a little high in flight. As it got closer to the buck, he dipped his back in reaction to the sound of my bow going off. When he did this, the arrow just barely missed over the top of him, and he took off running.

Missing that buck was painful for me. He was much bigger than the one I almost had a shot at the day before. There were lots of extra points sticking everywhere, but I'd say his main frame had ten or twelve points. I'm guessing he would have scored at least in the 160s if not the 170s.

Almost immediately after the shot, I realized I heard the sound of grunting and snort-wheezing about 80 yards above me toward the road. At first, I wasn't sure what was going on. Eventually, I realized it was a person. This made me mad. As it turned out, the person who was making the deer calls was from the outfitting service right next to the one I worked for. Since this guy had already shot a buck, he didn't have anything to do while all of his friends were out hunting. As a result, he decided to sneak down onto our property thinking that no one was going to be there. He then started calling simply to entertain himself and see if he could lure in a big buck that he could brag about to his friends.

Ultimately, the reason why that buck didn't stop when I grunted at him with my voice was that he was focused on intimidating the buck he thought he heard snort-wheezing at him 80 yards away. When bucks get into that kind of mentality, they often get tunnel vision and sometimes seem to block everything else out, which is what happened in my situation.

What that other hunter did was inconsiderate of others. I hope you never have anything like that happen to you. I also hope you never do anything like that to anyone else. Regardless, one of the biggest lessons I learned from this hunt was how to better train myself to shoot in those types of situations in the future. When practicing in my backyard, I planned to mentally picture a deer walking fast like this buck had been. I then planned to make a grunt noise with my voice but act as if the deer never stopped. I'd then lead the deer a little bit and shoot as he stepped into the spot where I was aiming. I believed that by training myself in this way I would be better prepared and more efficient in those types of situations in the future.

RATTLING

The evening after that last hunt I set up along a field on the other side of the property. After sitting there for about an hour, I saw a buck moving through a different field several hundred yards away. The very fact that I could see his white rack at that distance indicated to me that he was probably a good sized buck. I quickly took my rattle bag out and started pounding away. Unfortunately, it didn't seem to have any impact at all on the buck. A few minutes later, I lost sight of him. I decided to rattle one more time anyway. I then looked over to my right and saw another giant buck! Much to my surprise, he was even bigger than the buck I had missed the previous morning. The mass at the base of his rack seemed as big around as a soda can, which I would not have believed if I hadn't seen it with my own eyes.

The buck stood still for a long time. He was a hundred and twenty yards away. After he stood there for a few minutes looking around the field, he turned around and went back into the tree line he had come out of. I tried rattling one more time, but he didn't respond. There was about a half hour of shooting light left, so I decided to get down and try crawling through the field to the tree line. The wind was in my favor, and the weeds in the field were tall enough to make it possible.

As soon as I packed up my gear and prepared to climb down, my head turned to the left. To my surprise, there was a nice ten-pointer trotting up the edge of the field near me. The moment I saw him, I thought, "Oh no! You've got to be kidding me!" Even though I wasn't moving, the buck turned his head and looked straight at me. He then snorted and ran back in the direction he came from.

This experience reminded me to *look carefully* in all directions after rattling. If I had done this, I may have seen this buck coming and I would have gotten an easy fifteen yard shot at him. He probably would have only scored around 125, which was not nearly as big as a few of the other bucks I had seen, but I would have been happy with him at that point in time.

LAST NIGHT OF THE HUNT

On the very last night I could hunt in Illinois, I watched two bucks chase a few doe around for several hours. With only forty minutes left in the hunt, I decided to let out a few grunts. To my surprise, the larger buck left the other deer and headed in my direction. He stopped and stood perfectly broadside thirty-five yards away on the other side of my clearing. His G3 and G4 tines were broken off on the right side of his rack, but I didn't care. I just wanted to fill my tag. His remaining rack still scored around 120, so I drew back, patiently aimed, and then shot. The arrow flight looked absolutely perfect and was headed straight for his heart! However, when my arrow reached the halfway point in its flight, the buck dropped down a full body height. My arrow only ended up nipping the very top of his back by the time it reached him. Ugh!

After the buck ran away, I waited a few minutes and then climbed down to inspect the arrow. The arrow had muscle meat on it from the very top of the loin. There was no blood to be found anywhere. This made it obvious that I had not hit anything vital. Just to make sure, I came back later with three people to try tracking him. We looked for a long time but didn't find any sign of him.

When I described this buck's rack to people at the lodge, several people ridiculed me. Some said, "Why would you shoot since his rack was broken up?" My response was, "Because it is not all about the rack to me. I would have been satisfied with the deer. I didn't feel the need to be greedy about it. I'd rather go home with a buck that had a broken up rack than no buck at all. It's the stories, the memories, the joy, and the experience that matters the most, not how big or how perfect a buck's rack looks."

Although it disappointed me to not get that buck, I was very happy that I didn't terribly injure him. I was also happy that this experience taught me a very valuable lesson. Before that hunt I had never shot at a deer that was more than twenty-five yards away. However, this experience taught me that I will usually need to aim a little low when shooting at a deer thirty-five yards away or more. My arrow speed simply isn't fast enough to reach a deer at that distance before it reacts to the sound of my bow going off.

The phrase that went through my mind after this hunt was, "Know your equipment." Know how it will perform in any given situation. Know how to aim in order to compensate for the elements involved in various types of shots. I encourage you to get to know your equipment in this way as well!

BIGGEST ONE YET

There was only one week left in the Pennsylvania archery season when I came back from Illinois. Unfortunately, there were so many fall turkey hunters in the woods by my house that I was having trouble seeing any deer. As a result, my wife suggested that we go to her parents' house. They lived on two acres in a housing development located an hour west of Philadelphia. The deer in their area had been eating all of the flowers in their flower beds and were often in their yard at night.

I didn't really want to spend the last day of hunting season in a place I had never hunted before. I knew from many failed hunts in the past that it is not usually a good idea to go somewhere you have never scouted before. At any rate, I decide to give their property a try since things were looking so bleak in my area.

My wife and I drove down to her parents' house on Friday afternoon. While sitting in their living room talking with my mother-in-law, a small eight-pointer ran into their front yard from across the street. I was shocked to see the deer, especially since it was so early in the day. I immediately ran to get my bow! Unfortunately, a school bus stopped just up the road, and the deer ran away before I even got outside. I hunted that evening behind their house, but someone was riding a four-wheeler on a nearby property until it got dark. As a result, I didn't see a single deer.

It was raining pretty hard when I went out to hunt the following morning. As it started getting daylight, the rain lightened up and almost stopped. To my surprise, there was a licking branch about thirty yards in front of me. I had no idea it was there until I saw a large buck standing under it licking it. Although I could see that there was a massive blob of white on top of his head, I couldn't see my pins yet. I then looked down at my watch. It was still a few minutes before legal shooting light.

The buck turned around and went the other direction toward a thicket. I immediately begged God to bring him back. Much to my surprise, the buck actually turned around and came back a few minutes later. When he did this, I quickly pulled out my rangefinder to see how far he was. He was thirty-eight yards away. As I thought about taking a shot, I reminded myself how the buck ducked under my arrow around that distance in Illinois.

While I waited for legal shooting light, a doe walked in front of me less than ten yards away. Although I was not moving, she looked right up at me. The moment she saw me, she spun around and headed back toward the horse pasture where she came from.

I then looked back over at the buck. He was still standing by the licking branch. It was now legal shooting light. I drew back my bow but couldn't see him as clearly as I wanted through my peep sight, so I eased back down and waited. The thick cloud cover made it seem darker than it normally would have been at that time of day. A minute or two passed, and I periodically clicked the range finder to make sure I had the correct yardage.

Without warning, the buck suddenly took off running in the direction the doe had gone. When this happened, my eyes opened wide, and I panicked! I immediately began grunting with my voice in an effort to stop him. The first two grunts didn't faze him. The third one was even louder than the first two. This one finally stopped him, and he looked in my direction. I was already at full draw by that point. I took a hard look at him and deduced that he was thirty-five yards away. I aimed as if he was about thirty-three yards and then released the arrow. It looked good! When the arrow made it halfway to the buck, he began to drop just as the buck in Illinois had done. This made me nervous, and I hoped I had aimed low enough. I continued to watch the arrow as it soared at the buck, and his body continued to drop toward the ground. The arrow then made a thud noise as it penetrated the side of the buck. The hit looked a little high, but it was right behind the shoulder. The buck then took off and ran into the thicket.

The buck stopped after about sixty yards and looked back. I could barely see him through the dense fog. The next thing I knew he vanished and there were loud crashing noises in the weeds. I hoped he didn't make it all the way out of the thicket and across the road into the big block of timber. Nevertheless, I made a mental note of where I last saw him and then began to celebrate! Words could not express how excited I was at that moment! It seemed as though all of my hard work and many hours of practicing longer distance shots had finally paid off!

My wife's parents had told me they saw a big eight-pointer on their property, and I thought I had just shot him. However, I was so focused on making a good shot that I never even looked closely at his rack. I just knew it was big and massive!

The rain started again, but I didn't want to rush and begin tracking the buck yet. Instead, I tiptoed over to where he was standing to see if there was any blood. The first thing I saw was my arrow sticking in the ground. It was completely covered with bright lung blood. This made me even more excited!

Although I wanted to scream for joy, I held my breath and went back into my in-laws' house to tell my wife. She was still asleep when I entered the room. I excitedly whispered, "Babe, I just shot a monster!" She slowly woke up and realized what I just said. As she sat up, she yelled with excitement, "I'm helping you find him!" She wanted to leave and start tracking immediately, but I said, "No! We have to give him at least a half hour!"

Eventually the thirty minutes passed, and we eased our way down through her parents' back yard. I showed her where the arrow was and expected to see good blood all over the ground. To my surprise, there wasn't any. Fortunately, the ground was soft from the rain, and I was able to see where the buck's tracks went into the thicket. Upon entering the thicket, we found one small speck of blood and that was it. This began to worry me.

Once inside the thicket it became harder to decipher the buck's tracks from all of the other deer tracks. After going about forty yards, I began to feel stressed and worried. I wasn't sure which way the buck went after he stood and looked back in my direction so I sent my wife up toward the top of the thicket. I in turn continued toward the spot I last saw the deer. I frequently looked back to where I was standing when I shot in an effort to pinpoint the exact location he was standing before I lost sight of him.

Things were beginning to look bleak, and I was starting to feel sick in my stomach. I didn't know what else to do, so I started walking straight along the main trail. I intensely stared at the ground looking for tracks or any sign of blood. In the process, I looked over to my left and immediately let out an excited yell! The buck was piled up in the bushes! He must have expired right after I last saw him. I quickly jumped down into the pickers after him, and my wife ran over to see him.

It was not the big eight-pointer my in-laws saw, but he was a real nice six-pointer with good mass. He had a very large body as well, and the two of us had trouble dragging him out of the thicket. After much deliberation, we decided to get him mounted. I knew that a six-pointer like this was rare. He scored almost 100 inches which is really good for a six-pointer in Pennsylvania!

One thing I learned from this hunt was that I needed to aim even a little lower in those types of situations. My arrow ended up hitting the buck high in the lungs. As a result, the blood filled the lungs instead of coming out of the animal and leaving a trail that could be followed. Keep this in mind if you ever have a high lung shot. Remain calm. Although you may not find much or any blood, the deer should die within 120 yards or so. Sometimes they can be found near main trails because they will run along them until they expire.

Chapter 4 – The Prayerful Approach

EARLY SEASON SCOUTING

As soon as hunting season ended in Pennsylvania, I began scouting for the following year. Especially after fresh snowfalls, I'd walk for miles behind my house looking for deer tracks. I wanted to pinpoint the deer's major travel patterns after they had been pressured all season. I also wanted to learn what their primary food sources were once snow was on the ground.

In the spring, I went out looking for tree stand locations to use in the fall. After picking out a few spots, I thought of which one I liked the most. I then said the following prayer, "Lord, where am I going to get my buck this year?" As soon as I asked this question, I suddenly had an image pop into my mind of the watering hole spot where I shot the doe the season before. I was surprised that this image came into my mind because I didn't plan to hunt there during the upcoming season. It was simply too difficult to get the right wind direction to make it worth all the effort to hunt there.

After thinking about this whole topic, I asked, "Lord, when am I going to get my buck?" The thought immediately came to my mind, "During the rut." The way this happened interested me, and I looked forward to *testing it* to see if it came true. I had no intention of assuming it was God or that it was correct information until after I had put it to the test.

A major drawback to the response I received with this last question was that I had hoped to get my Pennsylvania buck within the first two weeks of the season. Obviously, the rut occurs during the last two weeks of archery season, which put a crimp into my plan.

One reason I wanted to get my Pennsylvania buck early was that I was planning several hunts in New York as well as one in Illinois. I wanted to have the comfort of knowing I filled my Pennsylvania tag before leaving to hunt in those other states. Another reason was that small game season opens in the middle of archery season in Pennsylvania. Having a bunch of small game hunters walking around the woods shooting their guns often makes it more difficult to harvest a deer in my area. At any rate, I stored all of these thoughts in the back of my mind and looked forward to the hunting season, which was still a good distance away.

GET THE CAMERA OUT

My mother-in-law and father-in-law were happy that I shot a nice buck on their property the previous season, but my father-in-law wanted me to shoot some doe. He knew that reducing the number of doe is what is needed to more significantly lower the overall deer herd. Harvesting one doe essentially removes three deer from the following year's herd, given that the doe would have had two fawns. In response to my father-in-law's request, I purchased a few antlerless deer tags to use in that area during the upcoming season.

My mother-in-law and father-in-law lived in a special regulation area where antlerless deer hunting started two weeks before the normal season opener. This area also allowed baiting that year. It was my intention to go down for the opening day of the early antlerless only season and start taking doe out of the herd.

A month before the early season started, I prayed and asked God if I was going to get a doe at my in-laws' house. I immediately had a "gut feeling" that I was meant to get one. However, just two weeks before the early season started, my wife was talking to her mother on the phone. My mother-in-law told her that I may not want to bother coming down to hunt at their house. For some reason, the deer had stopped coming around.

Despite this news, I kept my plans. It was a perfect opportunity to *test* what I thought God was telling me. If I did not get a deer, then I could analyze the "gut feeling" I had. This would help me know if I should reject those types of prayer answers in the future. If I did get a deer, however, perhaps it would help me refine my ability to discern and detect when God *is* speaking to me.

Before leaving for my in-laws' house for the doe hunt, I decided to get my video camera back out and try recording myself again. There had been many times in the past when I had not gotten a shot at a deer simply because I was too busy moving the camera around trying to get extra footage as they approached. I wasn't going to make that mistake this time. Instead, I planned to just point the video camera where I thought the deer might go. If they walked into my video screen, I'd try to shoot them on video. If they did not, I'd just shoot them where they were and not worry about getting it on video. However, since the Pennsylvania Game Commission allowed baiting in the special regulation areas that year, I also decided to put a small patch of corn on the ground where I was planning to point the video camera. My hope was that this would hold the deer in front of the camera long enough for me to get a shot on video.

There were no deer in sight as dawn broke on opening morning of the early season, but I didn't let that bother me. I just trusted my gut sense that I was going to get a deer. A short while later, one of the neighbors came out of their house and started their car. This spooked three deer down through the horse pasture next to my in-laws' house. The deer ended up running into the thicket where my six-pointer had died. Two of the deer were only first-year deer, which excited me, because my intention was simply to harvest a doe. I was actually hoping for a small one, because it would fulfill my goal of managing the deer herd numbers. At the same time, it would be easier for me to drag a small deer all the way up the hill by my-self.

Twenty minutes went by before the three deer worked their way out of the thicket and headed toward me. Although they came to within bow range fairly quickly, I didn't shoot right away. Instead, I waited so that I could get as much video footage of them as possible before shooting. I also wanted to wait for the smallest doe to give me a slightly quartering away shot, which would give me the best angle into the vitals. This footage can be viewed on my *Humble Begin-nings Part Two* video as well as my *Spirituality of Hunting* video.

When I finally decided to draw my bow, the small buck that was with the two little deer heard my arrow sliding over my new arrow rest. Unfortunately, he looked right up at me. This bothered me! He immediately started stomping his hoof, which indicated that he was trying to identify what I was. I knew that if he associated me with danger he'd run away. The other deer would follow him, and my hunt would be over.

Things were not looking good. It seemed as if the buck might snort and run at any second. At the same time, the two little deer were chasing each other around and were oblivious to my presence. Although the closest doe was angled slightly toward me, I decided to take the shot since the buck was acting so nervous. Just as I released the arrow, the doe turned a little more toward me which intensified the angle in an unfavorable way. Despite the angle, my arrow still struck the deer right behind the shoulder, which made me feel good about the shot. I carefully watched the deer run off and made mental notes as to which direction they went. Unfortunately, I couldn't see very far through the foliage on the trees so I wasn't sure which way they turned once they got near the thicket.

I got down and inspected the arrow, which is when my confidence dramatically dwindled! My arrow was covered with a green film. This indicated that it had gone through the deer's guts. To make matters even worse, there were only three specks of blood on the ground before the blood trail completely disappeared.

Allow me to interject something at this point. I eventually realized that I had a lot of difficulty finding all of the deer I ever shot directly behind the shoulder when the deer was quartering toward me at the time of the shot. For instance, the first deer I ever shot this way was the doe I harvested on video with my friend Eric in college. If you will recall, we had virtually no blood trail to follow. I also hit the doe at my house in Lamar this way that I was unable to find.

After considering these details, I concluded that I needed to think more about the angle of the arrow and how it moves through the deer once it penetrates the deer's skin. In the past, I always just aimed behind the deer's shoulder. However, I now realized that on steep quartering toward me angles, I needed to shoot in front of the deer's shoulder instead of behind it. Doing this enables the broadhead to slice all the way through both lungs of the deer, which can be a very lethal shot. If you aim behind the shoulder blade like I did with the doe in this situation, you may only hit the very back of one lung before possibly hitting a little of the liver. The arrow will then most likely exit through the guts, and the guts often plug up the hole. The end result is that very little or no blood is left for you to follow, which is what happened with this doe at my in-laws' house.

(Aside: An example of me correcting this problem and aiming in front of the shoulder blade instead of behind it on a quartering toward me shot can be seen in my 2012 hunting video titled *How to*

Hunt Whitetail Deer. That shot takes place at the 13:00 minute time mark, and the deer died within 50 yards. I actually got the idea to shoot in front of the deer's shoulder blade this way after harvesting a five pointer at my in-laws' house the year after I had trouble finding the doe I am telling you about in this situation. The video of the five-pointer can be seen on my 2010 hunting video titled *The Lone Hunter* at the 35:45 time mark. The deer was slightly quartering away, and the arrow entered directly behind the shoulder closest to me. However, it exited *in front of* the other shoulder, and the deer died within 45 yards. Seeing how the arrow exited in front of the shoulder in that situation is what made me realize I could have shot the deer from the opposite direction and still passed through it making an extremely effective kill shot.)

At any rate, getting back to the situation at hand with the doe I shot at my in-laws' house, after waiting an hour, I tried to follow the doe's hoof prints through the grass. Unfortunately, I eventually got her tracks confused with all of the other deer tracks near the bottom of the property. This caused me to feel very stressed!

I then walked over to the edge of the thicket looking for blood. I searched every major trail that entered the weeds hoping to find at least one small speck of blood, but there was none! This caused the feeling of tension to intensify within me. My concerns were amplified by the fact that I was in a suburban area. It was crucial for me to make a quick, clean kill. If I didn't, the deer could run off and die in someone else's yard, and that could end up becoming a huge mess!

Feeling somewhat desperate, I knelt down and prayed, "Dear Saint Anthony, please come around. This deer is lost and cannot be found." I listened intently within, hoping to hear him direct me as he had in the past. Unfortunately, there was silence. The feeling of dread escalated within me. I then thought of having to tell my father-in-law what happened. This made me feel even worse about the situation because I believed he expected me to be an efficient hunter.

All of the negative thoughts and emotions that were flowing through my mind and body made me want to give up. I then closed my eyes and *forced myself* to remain focused, hopeful, and calm in order to overcome all of those negative thoughts and feelings. I took a deep breath and stood up as I repeated, "Dear Saint Anthony, please come around. This deer is lost and cannot be found!" As I re-peated this prayer, and without thinking about it, I turned my head in the opposite direction. The white belly of my doe was facing me, and her body was twisted up from the way she fell when she died. She was only about forty yards from where I was standing. I imme-diately looked up at heaven and said, "Thank you, God, and thank you, Saint Anthony!"

This hunt taught me how my negative emotions can really make it difficult for me at times. They influence me to lose hope, which causes me to want to give up. This happens to me in other areas of my life too. However, this hunt helped me realize that I can over-come those kinds of negative thoughts and emotions by praying and *forcing myself to be calm* and not give up.

I encourage you to take a look at your own life and observe if anything like this has ever happened to you. If so, notice how your negative thoughts and feelings impacted you. Did they make it hard for you to continue? What will you do in the future if anything like that happens? I hope you will use my example to help you get through those types of situations.

In addition to all of that, getting this hunt on video is what in-spired me to start working on my hunting videos again. It helped me realize I could actually do it on my own without needing someone to video for me. In fact, it was precisely because of this hunt that I was able to reference all of the other hunts I referred to that took place after 2009. Before that, I had completely given up on making hunt-ing videos by myself. After this situation, however, I rededicated myself to the effort of videoing and producing my own hunts, and I haven't stopped since!

The doe I harvested in this situation also verified that the gut feeling I had while praying before the season started was correct. Upon realizing this, I thought back to exactly how that experience felt so that I could easily recognize it if it happened again in the fu-ture.

This hunt also helps to portray how our prayers can sometimes be answered differently. In some instances, I have a thought, feeling, or sense as to what the answer is just as I had a gut sense that I was going to get a deer. In other situations, the answer is simply in front of me without me feeling or sensing anything at all, just as the dead deer was right in front of me when I turned my head. In fact, God has often answered my prayers through St. Anthony in this way. There have been many times in my life when I lost something, or I was around someone who lost something. Whether or not they believed that saints can hear and help us on behalf of God, I'd say the Saint Anthony prayer out loud anyway. Many times the lost object just suddenly appeared without me sensing any kind of answer in my mind or feelings. There have also been times when the lost item mysteriously appeared later in a spot I had already looked.

When I was younger and more immature, I didn't take the time to stop and thank God and His angels and saints for helping me in circumstances like this one. At this point in time, however, I try to make sure I stop what I am doing and consciously express my gratitude and appreciation to God and my heavenly family members (angels and saints) before moving forward. I hope you do the same if you pray and are helped by them as I have been.

In addition, I am aware that asking a saint for help is traditionally a Catholic practice and not something Protestants typically do. However, I will say that we as Catholics view saints as our *family members* in Heaven. We simply ask them for help just as we ask another person or family member here on earth for help. I know for a fact that God works through His heavenly family in this way, but you are free to choose to believe whatever you want.

However, if you don't believe in asking a saint for help, be prepared for God to one day make you a believer. What I mean is, you may have lost something or are even having trouble finding a deer or other game animal you have shot. You may ask God a million times for help, but help may not seem to come. If that is the case, try asking Saint Anthony for help finding it. If the help comes, it is not because God couldn't do it for you by Himself. It is simply that God wants to show you that you have a much bigger family than you realize, and that He intends to work through His heavenly family in order to help you during your time here on earth. In that sense, God is working through that situation to help you deepen your awareness of, and appreciation for, the heavenly family He has given you.

NO SENSE

It made me happy that I was able to spiritually sense that I was going to get that deer long before it actually happened. The thing that concerned me was that I did *not* have the same kind of sense about either my New York hunt or my Illinois hunt.

On opening day of the regular archery season in Pennsylvania, I planned to take a guy out who had never gone bow hunting before. He worked with my wife and got his first bow over the summer. He was extremely excited to try bow hunting and deeply believed he was going to shoot a monster buck that year.

The farm where he had permission to hunt seemed great! We even saw a deer walking through the woods fifty yards away from us on the afternoon we went to scout it out together. On our next trip to this spot, we hung two stands in the same tree, so that I could video him on opening morning.

In the meantime, I had been looking for a new spot to take my dad. I was searching for one that wasn't overly steep so that it was easier for my dad to make it to his tree stand location. Much to my delight, I found a spot that I really liked. I had an incredibly good feeling about this place. I figured I could set my dad up at the base of this mountain and then I could hike all the way up to a spot that looked really good near the top!

Because I was so excited about this spot, I quickly abandoned the prayer response I had back in the spring about where I was going to get my buck. I then prayed, "Lord, am I going to get a buck at this new spot?" I felt so good about it that I thought the answer was, "Yes!" I then prayed, "Lord, how big is it going to be?" Since my feelings about this spot were so good, I thought I was going to get a big ten-pointer there!

The whole situation made me very excited. I thought I was going to video my friend on opening morning shooting a big buck, since he told me he had a really good feeling about it. Then I thought I was going to video myself shooting a big ten-pointer in the afternoon. Afterward, I came up with the idea that I was going to go up to New York two weeks later and video myself shooting a really nice eight-point buck. After that, John Thomas and I were going to go out to Illinois together. I'd video myself shooting a nice buck, and then I'd video him shooting one. Finally, I'd meet up with my other friend,

John Ortlieb, who was also going to be hunting in Illinois on a different piece of property during the same week John Thomas and I were going to be in Illinois. I could then video John Ortlieb shooting a nice buck. I thought that having all of these big bucks on video would make my dream come true and I'd finally have my long-awaited hunting video.

Opening day of the Pennsylvania hunting season arrived, and my wife's coworker and I headed to the woods. The weather forecast said the wind would be blowing from the east. However, once we got set up in our tree stands, the wind was actually blowing from the south and from the west. These were the absolute worst possible directions for this spot. As a result, we didn't see a single deer while we were in the stands. Although I was disappointed that we didn't get a buck on video that morning, I still believed I was going to get one in the evening.

Before I left that afternoon to hunt in my new spot, I checked the weather forecast. The wind was supposed to be coming from the south throughout the afternoon and evening. This was the best possible direction for my spot, and I felt as though God was making things work in my favor!

After I arrived and got out of my truck at the public hunting ground, I stood still to observe the wind direction. It was blowing from the west. Although not ideal, it would still work, so I proceeded to hike all the way up the side of the big mountain to my new spot. Even though I tried to take my time, I started sweating profusely about halfway there.

It took me over an hour to reach the tree I planned to hunt from. The hike was far more strenuous than I expected, and my muscles were shaking from the exertion of the climb. The worst part of the situation was that the wind shifted about twenty minutes before I reached my tree. When I got to my spot, it was blowing from the north, which was the absolute *worst* possible direction for this location. I was so tired and worn out from the climb that I set up in my originally intended tree anyway. I figured that the whole hunt would serve as an education tool if nothing else. Needless to say, I didn't see or hear a single deer that evening. All I saw was a flock of turkeys about eighty yards below me on the hill.

Both of these hunts gave me valuable information. I went back and carefully observed the thoughts and feelings I had while praying before the hunts. I also made note of how my friend had impacted me. We were both wrong. The good feeling I had about this spot was actually *different* from the "gut feeling" I had about the doe hunt two weeks earlier. The feeling I had about this most recent hunt was not coming from God. It was coming from my own wishful thinking.

Once again, I felt tremendously grateful for the gift of hunting and the opportunity it gave me to tremendously develop and grow in my prayer life! These experiences were helping me learn how to tell when a prayer response was simply coming from me and my own good feelings, and when it was coming from God. I was then able to apply this awareness and understanding throughout the rest of my everyday life. This significantly improved the quality of my life, because I was more in tune with God's will for me.

NEW YORK HUNT

Just two days before opening day of archery season in the southern zone of New York, which at that time was two weeks after Pennsylvania's opening day, there was an unusually early snow storm. The morning after the snow started falling, which was one day before I was supposed to go to New York, I decided to try hunting behind my house in Lamar for a little while.

There were still many leaves on the trees and the weight of the snow on them exerted an intense strain on the branches. Because of this, huge trees and tree limbs were cracking, splintering, and crashing to the ground all around me! It was thunderously loud. Needless to say, I was extremely afraid that a tree was going to fall on me, or that the tree I was in was going to fall!

As I waited for daylight to arrive, trees continued to crack and crash to the ground all around me. I was petrified! I decided to wait for daylight and then climb down so that I could get out of there!

I'm glad I got down when I did, because just as I made it to the ground, an oak tree crashed to the ground about fifteen yards away! It literally shook the ground I was standing on when it hit. Fifteen yards may not sound too close in some instances, but when you are talking about a giant oak tree falling to the ground in your direction, fifteen yards seems like inches. It actually looks like it is going to hit you until you realize that it missed by a few feet.

I scurried and slid down the mountain as quickly as I could, which was also a pretty intense prayer experience in itself, as I begged God to let me live! After I made it home, I began to think about my New York hunt. The thought of sitting in freezing, snowy conditions for an entire day did not appeal to me. Since I originally planned to sit in the woods all day, but the weather was now going to be unfavorable, I thought about not going. Another reason I thought about skipping the trip was that the snow cover on the ground would dramatically alter the deer's travel patterns and food sources, which I was not prepared for. The last thing that really bothered me about the New York hunt was that I still did *not* have a feeling that I was going to get a deer.

I really wished I had a good feeling about the hunt, so I prayed, "Lord, am I going to get a deer in New York?" In response, I felt as though He said, "No." Between this answer, and everything else I just explained, I thought to myself, "Why even bother going then?" So I prayed, "Lord, should I still go to New York?" I immediately got a feeling as if He was saying, "Yes." So I asked, "Why? What's the point?" "You are preparing for the future," is the idea I had. When I got this impression, I also had a sense that I was not just going to scout and learn the woods for my own sake. It was also for my children. Although I did not have children at that time, I believed I would someday. When I did have them, this trip to New York could be one of the annual trips I would take them on when they were old enough to go.

What did I learn from this experience? The main thing was that I needed to stop thinking only about myself all the time. There are plenty of things in life that I must do, or that God might ask me to do, that will not be for my own direct benefit. It will sometimes be for the good of others, the good of the animals, and/or the good of the environment.

I did go on my New York hunt. I did freeze while sitting in the tree stand, and I did *not* get a deer. However, on the first morning of the hunt, I saw two very memorable things. The first was something I will probably never see again as long as I live. It happened right as dawn started to break. There were little things moving in the branches in front of me. As the light grew stronger, I saw that the moving objects were actually large snowflakes that had gotten stuck to silky vertical threads in the branches in front of me. The silky threads were probably left behind by either caterpillars or spiders. Because they were single, stand-alone strands, they were not noticeable until a snowflake became attached to one of them. Gravity would then pull down on the flake which caused it to actually slide down the thread. The flakes then piled up at the bottom of each thread before eventually falling off due to the gravitational pull on them.

The other special observation I made dealt with the snowflakes themselves. They were all very large and dense. Growing up in Pennsylvania provided me with many opportunities to see snow, but it was not until that morning in New York that I actually cared enough to look closely at each flake. I remembered learning in elementary school that every single snowflake has no more and no less than exactly six points. On that morning, this reality struck me profoundly for the first time in my life. How is it that *every single* snowflake that ever falls from the sky yields exactly six perfect points, and every single one is completely unique? This simply blew my mind. In my opinion, it was a clear sign of the awesomeness and order of God.

This experience reminded me that there are many wonderful marvels out there in the world. Very often we just walk right past them without even caring because we are so caught up in our busy lives. We allow all the distractions and business of society to steal our connection with the wonders of nature. What will you do to recapture that connection with God's creation for yourself if you do not have it already?

TESTING THE PRAYER

Before leaving for my Illinois hunt, I had a young buck stand in front of me for twenty minutes at my in-laws' house. I included a little footage of this buck on my *Humble Beginnings Part Two* video. Although he was small, he was legal. I felt torn over the decision to shoot. Like most people, I'd still like to shoot a big buck. In fact, I often daydream of God giving me a record book buck just to help me get media attention, so that people will want to read this book or watch my hunting videos. At the same time, I'm not obsessed with the idea of getting a record book buck anymore. I'm satisfied with something average.

In addition to everything I just mentioned, it is not very often that I have a deer stand still in front of me for a long time allowing me to get good video footage of it by myself. Because this buck didn't move from his spot, I zoomed in on him and could easily have drawn back my bow and shot. The deciding factor for me to not shoot him was the prayer experience I had back in the spring regarding where and when I would get my buck. I wanted to test it out. This meant I had to pass on this little buck, so that I could hunt the watering hole spot near my house during the rut.

ILLINOIS 2009

This was the first year I went to Illinois simply to hunt and not to work as a guide. A gentleman by the name of Brian, whom I met while working for the outfitter, invited me to hunt on his farm in Illinois. Since I had never been to his property before, my wife and I drove out for a weekend during August so that I could scout the land.

After I scouted and picked out a few places for tree stands, I prayed, "Lord, where am I going to get my buck?" An image of the worst place of all the ones I had picked came into my mind. Then I prayed, "Lord, when am I going to get my buck?" "The second morning," is the idea I had. Although I didn't want to hunt that spot, I decided I was going to try it for the first two mornings to *test* out the response I *perceived* in my prayers. Were the thoughts coming from me or from God? If from me, what factors caused me to think that way? This insight would help me recognize and dismiss similar experiences if or when they happened again in the future. If the ideas came from God, what details about the experience could I pinpoint to help me recognize God's way of communicating with me again in the future?

John Thomas was particularly excited for our hunting trip to Illinois. He frequently called me and told me he had a really good feeling about it. He believed he was going to shoot a big buck. I also had a good feeling about the trip. I thought we were both going to shoot big bucks.

Although I felt very positive throughout the months leading up to our trip, my feelings dramatically changed the moment I got into John's truck to leave for Illinois. At that moment, I suddenly had a very strong inner feeling that I was *not* going to get a buck. This was disappointing!

It was pouring rain the day we got to Illinois. The rain was so intense that we couldn't even hunt the first evening. In the morning, I hunted at the spot that came to my mind when I made my prayer back in the summer. However, I didn't see a single deer. Although I didn't have any confidence in that spot, I went back the next morning in order to *test* my perceived prayer response. The only thing I saw was a doe moving through a thicket about sixty yards away.

After that morning, I realized that the prayer experience simply came from me. In addition, I looked back over the entire season and realized that something seemed to go wrong almost every time I went out hunting. Usually the wind was blowing in the exact opposite direction the forecast had predicted. It seemed as if the forces of nature were working against me. I was also getting tired of making these prayers only to have things not work out for me.

It finally dawned on me that God may have been teaching me a lesson through all of these challenging experiences. Maybe He was actually trying to motivate me to take my hunting skills to an even more advanced level rather than expect Him to make everything easy. I was also learning how to recognize when my perceived prayer responses were just coming from me and not from God. Having this knowledge enabled me to more easily dismiss similar experiences I had in my everyday life.

The intense rain in Illinois did not let up until the afternoon of the second day. It was at this time that we set up our practice target and took some shots. Even though my bow had been in a hard case during the trip, something must have happened to it. My arrows were hitting about ten inches from where I was aiming. This surprised me. It also made me glad I did not get a shot at a deer during the first two mornings of the hunt. Once again, I could see God's wisdom in not answering my prayers the way I expected.

This whole situation also helped me begin to realize that I need to carry a greater level of flexibility in my life. What I mean is, I can't expect to always know everything that is going to happen in advance, because I won't always know all of the factors I will be dealing with until that time comes.

At any rate, it was extremely difficult for me to sight my bow in because the wind was blowing hard throughout the day. We even took the target into the barn out of the wind, but I was still having problems. My field points and fixed-blade broadheads were hitting a few inches apart from each other. This was the first time they had ever done that with the bow and broadheads I was using. Even after I made some adjusts, my broadheads still hit a different spot from my field points. It was clear that the tuning of my bow had gone out. To be perfectly honest, I was beginning to wonder if there was some kind of evil force at work against me in this situation.

The only thing I could do was simply sight my bow in with my broadheads and focus on trying to get a shot at a deer 20 yards or less. I would then deal with all of the tuning issues later when I was home. I knew that as long as my broadheads hit where I was aiming up to 20 yards, I could effectively hunt.

After many hours of hard work sighting my bow in with broadheads, I was finally ready to go! Unfortunately, as I climbed into my tree stand that night, my foot slipped off of the first step. I then inadvertently fell back to the ground and stepped directly on my bow. As a result, two arrows snapped in half, two others cracked, and my bow got pushed down into the dirt. Things were just not working in my favor! With each passing day, my feeling intensified that I was *not* meant to get a deer on this hunt.

The next day I used all of the hunting knowledge I had gained throughout the years. Rather than ask God where I should go, I chose the absolute best spot I could think of on the farm based on habitat, feeding, bedding, wind direction, and travel patterns. Afterward, I asked God to bless me with a deer *if* it was according to His will. If it was not, I would simply accept it. I then went to the area I selected and hung a tree stand.

I saw twelve deer that evening, but they all crossed on a trail below me about fifty-five yards away. I sat in the same stand the following morning and watched a young buck and several doe walk along the same trail the other deer had traveled the evening before. Later that day, I set up a stand where all the deer had been crossing. My plan was to leave that area alone for the rest of the day and try sitting there the following morning.

Partially because I felt very confident about my new spot, and that I'd get my buck the following morning, I decided to sit with John Thomas that evening in order to video him shooting a buck. John felt sure he was going to get a buck that night. After we got set up, he predicted the exact time he was going to shoot his deer. I then said, "Okay, we'll test it out and see if your prayers and instincts are correct." I then turned on the camera and videoed him making his prediction. The footage from this hunt can be found on my *Humble Beginnings Part Two* video at 47:45.

As John's predicted time approached, we both looked extra intently in the woods. However, nothing came our way. It was funny to see the faint look of embarrassment on John's face when no deer ended up coming. I didn't harass him about it though, because I was having the same problem of confusing my own good feelings with the inspirations I thought God was giving me.

I thought about John's thoughts and feelings leading up to this hunt as well as the ones I had before getting into his truck to come to Illinois. We both had the same kinds of thoughts and feelings that my wife's coworker and I had leading up to the opening day of the Pennsylvania hunting season. In all of those situations, my friends and I had great *feelings* that we were going to get big bucks. However, those feelings were coming from us and were actually *different* from the "gut feeling" I had before getting my doe in the early season at my in-laws' house. This comparison helped me better recognize the difference between my own good feelings and the inspirations that come from the Holy Spirit.

I mention this to help people who are new to this concept. Hopefully these ideas will help them know what to look for as they develop their own ability to comprehend when and how God is speaking to them through their prayers and how that differs from their own wishful thinking. If you are working on this type of discernment, I encourage you to look through your past experiences and determine if there are any that compare to the hunting situation I just shared with you. Hopefully, getting to read about what happened in my situation will give you insight into your own experiences, which will help your ability to determine when an idea is coming from your own wishful thinking and when it is actually coming from God.

THE LESSONS CONTINUE

The following morning I went to my new stand location where I had seen all of the deer. I thought for sure I was going to have deer filing past me. Instead, my cell phone kept vibrating every few minutes with a text message from John. He had passed on two ten-pointers, a few smaller bucks, and several doe. Meanwhile, I hadn't seen a single deer. This caused me to feel frustrated and discouraged. I even began to complain in my mind saying, "This isn't fair! I'm the one who arranged this hunt. I'm the one who drove all the way out here during the summer to do all the scouting. I should be the one seeing all the deer, not him."

In addition to dealing with my negative emotions, I was thinking about going home empty-handed from Illinois for a third year in a row. Although I originally wanted to wait for a buck that would score in the 160s, my desperation motivated me to settle for the first buck that came by me in at least the 120s. In a certain sense, I was being humbled by the situation.

About an hour later, I turned my head to see a beautiful eight-pointer making a scrape directly underneath the tree where my other tree stand was located. He probably would have scored around 130, which was good enough for me! I immediately stood up and got ready.

The deer never came my way, so I tried bleating at him. This didn't even make him look in my direction, so I snort-wheezed at him a few times. He stopped and looked, but didn't come. I then did a long drawn-out tending grunt. Eventually, the buck turned and started walking in my direction to investigate the deer noises.

The video camera was rolling. All I needed was for the buck to walk on the trail I had the camera pointed at. As he drew closer, it looked as if he was going to pass behind my stand. Even though I would not be able to get the shot on video on that side of the tree, I planned to shoot him anyway. Just as I thought this, he turned and walked toward the perfect spot for me to get the hit on video.

As the buck got close, I began to draw my bow. While I was halfway back, the arrow started to make an awful, loud, squeaking, scraping noise on the rest. This had never happened before. In a mental state of panic, I tried to slow down my draw in an effort to reduce the amount of noise it was making, but it didn't help very much. While feeling very disturbed by the noise, I thought back to how nervous the buck had acted earlier in the season at my in-laws' house when he heard the arrow sliding across my rest moments before I shot the doe on video. Considering that experience, I thought this big eight-pointer was going to hear the noise and run away before I even got a shot at him.

Fortunately, the buck must not have heard the noise for some reason, because he didn't stop or look up at me. I then tried to refocus, hold steady, and make a good shot. I felt as though my muscles were fairly relaxed and that I was holding steady. Much to my surprise and disappointment, however, the shot went four inches lower than where I was aiming. Instead of hitting the buck in the heart, the arrow nipped the very bottom of him. He then trotted about twenty yards into the thicket and stopped. He didn't act hurt at all. After standing still snorting for a while, he slowly walked away and continued to snort as he left the area. Some of this footage can be seen on my *Humble Beginnings Part Two* video starting at 51:40.

After the buck was out of sight, I sent a text message to John telling him I just hit a nice eight-pointer. He was incredibly excited for me and said he was on his way over. Although he wanted to get right on the blood trail, I said we had to wait at least four hours because the hit looked very low. At best, it may have only nipped the very bottom of a lung or the liver.

When I got back to camp, I shot my bow. Sure enough, the shots were hitting four inches low. It turned out that my peep site had gotten moved in the string the night I slipped while getting into the stand and stepped on my bow. This was my first year hunting with a peep sight, so I didn't even realize that it had not been tied in properly in the first place. As a result, it needed to be readjusted and tied in tighter, which I did later that afternoon.

After working on my bow and finishing lunch, John and I went to look for the buck. There was decent blood for about twenty yards. When John saw the blood trail, he yelled, "Yeah, baby! You smoked him! We are definitely going to find him!" I hoped he was right. However, after taking a few more steps, we quickly learned that there was absolutely no more blood at all. It was as if someone had turned off a switch and the blood shut off completely. I then tried to find the buck's tracks in order to follow them but was unable to do so in the terrain.

We eventually headed toward the area where I last saw the buck. When we got close to that spot, a deer jumped up that was bedded down in the thicket. I didn't get a good look at the deer, but it seemed too small to be the one I shot. Regardless, I walked over and studied the bed as thoroughly as I could. It was small and didn't have any blood in it, so I concluded that it was not my buck. An hour passed, and we still had not found a single speck of blood or sign of the deer.

Throughout the search, I prayed, "Dear Saint Anthony, please come around. This deer is lost and cannot be found." The only thought that came to me was, "You are not going to find him if he is not dead." Even though we gave up looking that day, I went back and searched for him again the following day to do my due diligence. I never found him. It is my heartfelt hope that I did not kill that buck.

The biggest lesson I learned from this hunt was that I seriously needed to change as a person. When John was texting me all morning telling me about his deer sightings, I was jealous. I wanted to be the one to get a big buck, and I didn't care if he got one or not. In fact, part of me felt it wasn't fair that he was getting all the action when I was the one who did all the work scouting and scheduling the trip.

John's reaction to my shot made me realize just how greedy and selfish I had been. It also helped me realize I was looking for all of my enjoyment to come from shooting a big buck so that I could feel proud of myself and have other people respect me. John on the other hand simply rejoiced with all his friends. He found his enjoyment in celebrating with people when they had a successful hunt. He didn't put all of his focus on just getting a buck for himself like I did. Realizing this helped me see that I would be much happier as a person if I *learned* how to be more like John. From that day forward, I resolved to let go of my greed and selfishness to the best of my ability. I have also sought to celebrate with others whenever they get a deer, even if it is a buck I wanted to shoot. I have also sought to apply this same lesson to many other aspects of my life in addition to just hunting situations.

I encourage you to look within yourself and determine if you are anything like me. Do you rejoice with others like John, or do you get a little bothered like I did when someone else gets what you want, such as getting a job promotion you wanted? I truly believe we can be happier more of the time, and enjoy life more, if we train ourselves to celebrate the positive experiences of others rather than just look for all of our enjoyment to come from getting what we want.

STOP CALLING

There was one other thing that happened while I was in Illinois that I want to tell you about before moving on to the next hunt. The second day I was in Illinois my grunt call fell out of my pocket. Despite strenuously searching for it, I couldn't find it. I purchased a new one the following day and immediately put the lanyard around my neck so that I wouldn't lose it.

When John and I returned to the farm from the store, Brian asked us to help him hang a few tree stands. We quickly and excitedly agreed. At one location, Brian and John stood on the ground while I climbed up and down the tree hanging the ladder sticks and then the tree stand. It was not until we got back to camp that I realized the lower half of my brand new grunt call was missing. I thought it must have fallen off while I was climbing up and down the tree, so we went back looking for it. Unfortunately, we never found it.

This caused me to ask myself, "Is God trying to tell me to stop calling?" This idea had already been on my mind from my Pennsylvania hunts. It had been my most unsuccessful season of calling deer ever. The same held true when I used deer scents during that season. There were times in the past when it seemed as though a deer showed up every single time I blew into a grunt call or put deer scent out. The opposite was true for this season, which made me think it was time for me to improve my skills to hunt effectively without needing scents or calls.

After thinking about this topic, I began to observe my reason for using deer calls while I was in the woods hunting. Most of the time I reached for a grunt call simply because I was bored. However, this is not being a good hunter. As a result, for the remainder of the season, I wanted to try only grunting when I had a specific reason to do so. It would either be when I saw a deer that was not coming my way, or when I had a spiritual sense within me that I should start calling. Other than that, I wanted to push my skill level to be able to pick hunting spots that would keep me within twenty yards of where the deer would be without needing any additional help drawing them closer. I would also work on being disciplined enough to remain still and silent even when I was unbearably bored. I encourage you to push yourself to enhance your skill level in a similar way if you haven't been doing so already.

THE BROW TINE BUCK

John Thomas and I left Illinois without either of us getting a buck, so my focus returned to Pennsylvania. We pulled into John's driveway at two in the morning after driving the entire day. I told him I was going to wake up early and shoot "The Beast." John said, "Do it, dude! Just don't shoot my Brow Tine Buck!"

The Beast was the nickname I gave to one of the big bucks John had gotten trail camera pictures of on his property over the previous two years. This is a picture of The Beast from the previous season.

 His body was large and fat compared to most of the bucks in that area.

The "Brow Tine Buck" was a buck John had been waiting to shoot. He had many trail camera pictures of him and even had a chance to shoot him the year before in 2008. However, John let him live because he had several tines broken off by the time he had the opportunity to shoot him. There are two pictures of the Brow Tine Buck below from 2008 just before his tines got broken off. John was looking forward to getting a chance at him this year (2009) before he broke off any points.

The moment John said the words, "Just don't shoot my Brow Tine Buck," I spiritually sensed and believed two things. The first was that I was not getting a buck the following day because I

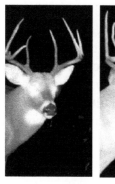

thought I was supposed to get my buck at home in Lamar. The second thing was that the only buck I was going to see the following morning was going to be the Brow Tine Buck.

John was so excited to check his trail cameras when we got back from Illinois that we literally ran into the woods with our flashlights as soon as we got out of the truck. It must have been three in the morning before we finally got the truck unpacked and the trail camera pictures uploaded to the computer.

Virtually all of the pictures were of doe and one straggly little buck. Near the end of the pictures, however, John screamed, "No! Oh man, I can't believe that!" "What?" I exclaimed. He said, "Look at this picture. See that deer?" The picture contained the very edge of a buck's body. Most of the buck's rack was out of the picture because of the way his head was turned. The only thing I could see was the very back of the main beam. I then said, "Yeah, what about it? It looks like a pretty good buck judging by his body size. It's hard to tell though because you can't really see his rack." John then said in a very disappointed tone of voice, "That's my Brow Tine Buck. See that right there? He's already busted off his tines." This meant John was going to have to wait another year before shooting him because he wanted to get him while his rack was still perfect.

The following morning started slowly. Forty minutes after light, a group of doe walked past me about 40 yards away and then went through a horse pasture. Another half hour passed, and I was getting bored. Since I knew I was not getting a buck anyway, I decided to grunt a few times even though I told myself I wasn't going to call unless I saw a deer first or felt inspired to do so.

As you may recall, my grunt tube was missing the bottom half, so it didn't even sound very authentic. However, to my surprise, I heard a noise to my right about three minutes after I grunted. I looked over to see an enormous deer with a huge rack coming out of the thicket! I immediately thought to myself, "I can't believe it! I'm going to shoot 'The Beast!'" He seemed even bigger in person than in the pictures!

When I first spotted him, he was twenty-five yards away walking on a broadside angle heading toward the horse pasture. He then stopped and looked right at me. As he turned his head, I had two distinct thoughts. The first was, "I can't believe it! It's the Brow Tine Buck!" The size of his body and how big his rack looked in person  really impressed me! His spread was several inches wider than it was the year before. The second thought I had was, "It's confirmed! He's all busted up!" His G2 and G3 tines were broken off of the left-hand side of his rack. If you look carefully at the picture of him here, you can see his incredibly long brow tines and the fact that his tines are missing on the left side of his rack.

Eventually, the Brow Tine Buck turned and walked down through the neighbor's horse pasture. He was looking for the deer that had been grunting and he seemed ready for a fight! After he was far enough away that he wouldn't see my movement, I reached around and grabbed my video camera. I had to take it off of the camera arm in order to get the footage, which is why the footage is so shaky in my *Humble Beginnings Part Two* video.

After videoing for a while, I put the camera down and sent a text messaged to John that stated, "It's confirmed. Your Brow Tine Buck is all busted up." He texted back saying how disappointed he was. Needless to say that news ruined his day!

I will also say that the Brow Tine Buck was four and a half years old the year I encountered him. That was four years ago. At least at this point, as far as we know, no one ever harvested him. In addition, John never got another trail camera picture of the Brow Tine Buck. Essentially, no one knows what happened to him although John's neighbor thinks she saw him in a field last year.

IN THE SUBURBS

My wife stayed at her parents' house while I was in Illinois. I went there for two days before my wife and I drove back to Lamar. Right before I went on my Illinois hunt, however, I met my in-laws' neighbor. In our conversation, I purposefully mentioned that I was going hunting in the Midwest. I did this so that I could work my way into asking him for permission to hunt on his property. Virtually all the deer I had ever seen while hunting at my in-laws' came from his land.

Immediately after I told the neighbor I was going on a hunting trip, he yelled, "Why are you going all the way out there? Stay here and shoot the deer! In fact, just last week I was on my back deck and had a real big one standing in my back yard looking at me." "How big are we talking?" I quickly asked. He replied, "Oh, I don't know how you count them, but there were a lot of points on the thing. I've been looking at the deer in my yard for many years now, and this was the biggest one I've ever seen!" Without hesitating, I asked, "So do you mind if I try hunting here some time?" He said, "No, not at all! You can put up a tree stand anywhere you want. Shoot those annoying things. Shoot them all for all I care. The more the better! We can't even have a garden around here because the deer eat everything. The only thing I ask is that you call and let me know before you come here hunting." I promised I'd call beforehand and gave him my business card. He in turn gave me his.

Although I was really excited to try hunting the neighbor's property, I stayed on my in-laws' land the evening I got there from John's because I didn't have a chance to call the neighbor beforehand. As I stood there in my normal spot, I watched the deer pass through the same little funnel on the neighbor's property that I had always seen them walk through in the past.

It was particularly windy that night as I looked down in the direction the deer had gone. As I studied the area, I brainstormed as to how I could possibly set up on them. There were no trees big enough to put up a tree stand where the deer liked to cross through the bottleneck in the neighbor's yard. As I tried to figure out how to hunt the neighbor's land, the willow tree to the side of the bottleneck caught my attention. The wind blew the branches in such a way that made it look as if there was an outline of a person in the branches.

This gave me an idea. Although I could not get a tree stand in that tree, I could simply stand under the branches at the base of it. The slightest breeze moved the branches in a way that could mask any motion I might make while drawing my bow. This observation excited me! I couldn't wait to try hunting under the willow tree and I thanked God for the idea.

I rose early the following morning, got my bow and video camera out, and then headed down to the willow tree. It was probably one of the most efficient setups I had ever been in. In addition to the willow tree branches, there was a very thick bush between me and the funnel where the deer liked to walk through. The bush created an excellent barrier which helped to conceal me from the deer.

Not long after daylight broke through the darkness, my conscience started to bother me. I had promised the landowner that I would call him before hunting on his property but I had not kept my word. It wasn't the easiest decision to make, but I quickly packed up my things and headed back to my spot on my in-laws' property.

Only thirty minutes after I moved and got set up again, I saw a big deer walk right past the willow tree. He was only fifteen yards from where I had been set up. After passing that spot, he made a scrape about twenty-five yards from the willow tree. He was a very big eight-pointer. My guess is that he was a three and a half year old that would have scored around 115, which is a good sized buck for

that area! There is a picture of him here that I pulled from the video footage I got of him.

There wasn't much I could do, so I tried bleating at him. He didn't respond, so I snort-wheezed at him a few times. This turned him around, and he started to circle around to the downwind side of me. As he did this, he walked right over my tracks that were imprinted in the frozen grass where I had walked down to the willow tree and back. The buck immediately stopped and started sniffing where I walked. "This is not good," I thought to myself. Even though I had rubber boots on that I had sprayed with scent killer, I knew deer still smell them anyway. The buck looked around for a minute, but then turned and went back to where he had made his scrape. I watched as he then went through the thicket where my big six-pointer died. The buck then trotted across the horse pasture and out of sight.

Instead of letting myself get overly upset about not getting a shot at this buck, I chose to look forward to testing my prayer experience regarding the watering hole spot on the public hunting ground near my house. However, I will say that it is experiences like this one that have helped me grow and mature as a person in life. I use these types of events as reminders to always do what is right. I firmly believe that I could have gotten a shot at that buck had I not gone against my word and walked down to the neighbor's property that morning. The next time I feel tempted to go against my word, I can recall this event and use it to motivate me to be honest and honorable. You can do the same. If you ever feel tempted to go against your word, just think of how I missed out on an opportunity at this nice buck. Use that thought as motivation to do the right thing so that you don't end up missing out on a good opportunity like I did.

BACK HOME

The following day my wife and I drove home. On Monday afternoon, I walked the trail toward my spot at the mountain spring that I refer to as "the watering hole." Along the way, I noticed a tremendous amount of deer hair all over the ground. Someone had obviously drug a dead deer out of the woods very recently. This started to really bother me, and my first reaction was to wonder if someone shot my buck. I then reminded myself that God is in control, and hopefully no one else would shoot the buck He had planned for me to get.

After turning off the main trail to go up to my stand location, a wounded doe jumped up from her bed and took off through the woods. Judging by the way she ran it looked as if she had been shot in the front left shoulder. This bothered me, and I thought to myself, "Man, someone has been in here shooting up all the deer!"

No deer moved near me that day. I returned and hunted the same stand the following morning. All I saw was a broken off half-rack two pointer. He came partially up the trail toward me, but stopped about twenty-five yards away before heading off in a different direction.

On my way out of the woods, I came across another hunter who was sitting down next to a dead doe he had just shot that morning. The guy was about my age. After introducing myself, I sat down to talk with him. In our conversation, I learned that he was the one who had drug a deer out of the woods earlier in the week. It was a six-pointer. I told him about the wounded doe I saw, and he said that his friend had shot her the previous week. They tracked her for two days before giving up. He was glad to know that she was still alive. Although he was glad, I was not. Her chances of surviving the winter with that kind of injury were not good.

After I got home from work the next day, I checked the wind direction. It was blowing the worst possible way for the watering hole spot, so I decided to go where my cousin Dennis shot his doe the year before.

The hunter I talked with the previous day said he laid out a scent trail and his little six-pointer came right to him grunting the whole way. Since I wasn't hunting the spot I thought I was supposed to shoot my deer, I didn't take the hunt very seriously. As a result, I decided to drag a doe-in-heat scent rag all the way up the mountain to see what would happen. I planned to use the experience as an education tool and nothing more.

Much to my surprise, there were scrapes all over the top of the mountain when I got there. This excited me! It made me change my mind about the hunt. Suddenly, I abandoned the idea of waiting until I could hunt by the watering hole to shoot my buck.

After sitting in the tree stand for a while, my excitement and enthusiasm began to settle down. I then looked across the valley to the mountain where the watering hole was located. I then started to have a change of heart. I had wanted to get a buck off of the mountains directly behind my house for five years but still had not. If I shot one at Denny's doe spot, I would not fulfill my true desire for at least another year. I also wouldn't be able to test my prayer experience from the spring. As a result, I put my bow down and decided to simply observe what happened throughout the rest of the hunt.

As the sunlight began to fade, a group of doe happened across the scent trail I had laid out. They didn't like it at all! After running in circles all over the place, they began snorting. Eventually, they worked their way up through the woods about fifty yards away from me. They were extremely cautious the whole time. After it was too dark to see them anymore, I packed up my things and began climbing down. Before I made it to the ground, I heard them snorting in the distance indicating to me that they heard my movement.

Over my five years of hunting the cautious deer in Lamar, I had grown to be very hesitant to use doe-in-heat scent for the exact same reason I observed that evening. It can often spook the doe. Although it can sometimes help to harvest a buck, I now prefer to keep the entire deer herd calm and on their natural routines as opposed to spooking them with deer scent. As I mentioned before, I also wanted to push my skill level to be able to choose the right hunting location in advance instead of needing to depend on artificial scents to get a deer to come close.

This hunt also clearly showed me how quickly I can change my mind about things when I become excited by something. In this case, seeing all the scrapes all over the top of the hill excited me, and it immediately influenced me to change my mind about where I'd shoot my buck. It was the feeling of excitement that distracted me from the choices I had previously made. After thinking about this, I realized I should be watchful of this same kind of influence and reaction in my everyday life. I must be mindful to keep my previous commitments and stay true to the decisions I have made while being in the right frame of mind and not under the influence of excited emotions.

Have you ever had and experience where you got excited or attracted to something or someone and changed your mind about your previous decision concerning that topic? If so, what was the outcome of it? If applicable, what will you do to avoid making the wrong decision in those kinds of situations in the future?

TESTING MY ETHICS

After realizing that I only wanted to shoot a buck on one of the mountains directly behind my house, I decided to spend the rest of the season hunting there even if I couldn't go to the watering hole. The following morning was a perfect example of that. Since the wind was not blowing in the right direction for the water hole spot, I hiked way up behind my house to a different area. My plan was to simply harvest a doe if the opportunity presented itself, so that I could at least fill my antlerless deer tag.

On this particular hunt, I heard a deer coming toward me just as daylight arrived. The deer walked straight to the tree I was in. Even though I had gone through extreme measures to eliminate the odor from my rubber boots, the deer began sniffing the ground where I had walked. "These deer are utterly amazing," I thought to myself. Fortunately, the deer did not seem concerned and eventually began to walk away in the direction it had initially been traveling. Because of the angle the deer was walking, I couldn't tell if it was a big doe or a spike buck. Sometimes short spikes can hide behind a buck's ears, which makes him appear to be a doe.

It had been almost two months since I shot the small doe during the early season at my in-laws' house, and I was anxious to get another deer. As this deer moved out to where I could see it more clearly, I looked down at my watch. It was technically legal shooting time, but because the cloud cover was so dense, it was darker than usual. Next, I looked at my sight pins. I could see them, but they were still fairly dull and I knew it would be difficult to see them through my peep sight.

Although I wanted to shoot very badly, I repeatedly thought to myself, "Be ethical. Be ethical. Be ethical." Since spikes are no longer legal to shoot in Pennsylvania, and I could not positively identify if this was a spike or a doe, and because it also wasn't light enough for me to see my sight pins well, I knew the most ethical decision was for me to let the deer pass. Although it was painfully difficult for me to do, I chose to let the deer walk away. At that moment, I thought of people who shoot first and then check later to see if the deer is legal. I didn't want to be like them.

A half hour after the deer left the area, I heard something coming. As I listened intently, I could tell it was a bear by the sound of its soft paws on the leaves. Deer hooves are hard and make a sharper, crisper sound when they come in contact with the ground.

The sound of a walking bear grew closer, and I watched the pine trees looking for movement. Eventually, I saw a glimmer of black through the branches, and then a small bear lumbered out into the open. It stopped to smell a branch on a tree before it walked past me at twenty-five yards. I quickly pulled my cell phone out of my pocket and took a few pictures as it passed. The bear liked to jog as it made its way up the hill. As a result, it was out of sight in less than a minute.

Three minutes passed, and I heard the sound of another bear coming. This greatly surprised me! The second bear came up the same exact trail as the first. It even stopped and sniffed the same spot that the other bear had smelled. I knew I had not touched that tree or walked past it. My conclusion was that the bears must have some kind of scent marker there. The second bear then came to within seventeen yards of the tree I was in before heading up over the top of the mountain. This bear was the exact same size as the first one. Both were just over a hundred pounds.

About seventeen minutes passed, and I heard something coming. To my amazement, it sounded as if it was another bear! Sure enough, a third bear eventually lumbering up through the woods just as the first two had. It also was the same size as the others.

All three bears seemed to have their own unique personality. The first one seemed happy and had a hop in its step. It was more energetic than the other two and ran more frequently in the direction it wanted to go. The second bear was more evenly tempered, whereas the last one was much more lethargic. It actually seemed lazy compared to the first two and stopped more frequently. That is probably why it was so much farther behind them.

The last bear had a black snout, whereas the first two had a gold snout. The last one also had a patch of hair missing on top of its right shoulder. I imagined that it lost that patch of hair while crawling under a fence or something like that. Since all of the bears weighed around a hundred pounds and were basically hanging out together, I concluded that they must have been the same ones the other hunter told me he saw together on the backside of the mountain near where he shot his six-pointer and doe. I also imagined that they came from the same mother.

At any rate, after all of the bears were out of sight, I began to ponder what had happened that morning. I never would have seen any of those bears if I had shot the deer that came by me at first light. I would have gotten down and started tracking the deer before the bears came by. As a result, I would not have discovered this great location to hunt for black bear. It seemed as though God was rewarding me for being ethical. I say this because the two day archery bear season in Pennsylvania was only a week away. I now knew exactly where I was going to go in an attempt to get one!

Finding this trail on the mountain where the bears crossed over the top brought a whole new sense of meaning to my hunting. There was a reason I had not gotten my buck earlier in the year like I originally wanted to. If I had, I would not have kept going out deer hunting. In turn, I would not have found this great new spot to hunt black bear. All of these details gave me a strong sense that I was meant to get a bear the following week.

At any rate, it came down to the last two days of archery season for deer. My wife had been working out of town during the week and was going to be home Friday night. She had to leave again on Sunday afternoon, which added to my strain of getting a deer. I had to make time for her yet also find some time to hunt. This was particularly difficult because the spot I thought I was supposed to get my buck took over an hour to walk to from our house and was an extremely exhausting hike. Doing it several times a day would be very strenuous.

On Friday afternoon, I got unexpectedly delayed at work. This put me an hour behind schedule for getting to my tree stand. When I got to within a hundred yards of the tree I planned to set up in, a group of deer took off running. They were literally standing directly under my tree. This deeply bothered me at first, but I got over it quickly and calmed down.

With just ten minutes left in the hunt that evening, I heard a deer coming up the hill the way I had walked in to get to my location. The deer stopped when it got to within thirty yards of me. It was a small buck. Unfortunately, the branches on the evergreen trees behind me were so thick that I couldn't see through them very well. As a result, I couldn't tell how many points the buck had, but it seemed to be a four-pointer.

Although this deer was not far from me, I started to feel very impatient because time was running out. Just then, I heard another deer coming from over the top of the hill. At first, I could barely see it moving through the trees, so I couldn't tell if it was a buck or a doe. However, the sound of the way it walked gave me the impression it was a very large-bodied buck. As it got closer, I begged inside my mind, "Come on! Don't stop! Keep coming!" Unfortunately, this deer frequently stopped to eat acorns as it made its way toward me. When it got to within thirty-five yards of me, I looked down at my sight pins. They were looking dull. Although I didn't want to, I looked at my watch. Sadly, it was already a minute past the close of legal shooting hours.

While this was happening, I began to notice subtle, tempting thoughts in my mind, and how they were impacting my decision-making process. Part of me wanted to change the time on my watch so that it would seem like it was still legal shooting hours. I also started to rationalize the end of shooting hours by thinking, "Shooting hours are only in place so that you don't shoot someone. In that sense, it is a safety issue. Since I know this is a deer and not a person, and I can clearly see my target, it should be fine for me to shoot."

About three minutes later, the buck finally stepped out into my shooting lane. He was only fifteen yards away, and I could see the glimmer of his big white antlers in the dim light. I could also see his big brown body. At that moment, I began to overcome all of the tempting thoughts as I repeated to myself, "Be ethical. Be ethical. You have to let him go." Although it was incredibly painful for me to do, I let the deer pass.

One of the things I thought about when this hunt was over was how tempted I felt to shoot this buck even though shooting hours were over. I then realized that we can learn how to notice these types of tempting thoughts through our hunting experiences and in turn watch for them to occur in our everyday life. Since we are learning how to recognize them through our hunting, and also are training ourselves to respond righteously and ethically in spite of them, we will be better equipped to recognize and handle them in our everyday experiences.

I am very grateful to God for giving us the sport of hunting. Through it, I believe we can learn many things about how to live ethically and also how to pray. In that sense, I believe we have amazing potential as hunters, because hunting provides us with an incredible training ground that we can carry into every aspect of our lives. To a certain extent, I believe we can lead the rest of society with the lessons we learn through hunting and in turn share with others.

THE FINAL HOUR

The first thing I did when I woke up the following morning was check the wind direction. It was *not* blowing very favorably for the watering hole spot, but I went there anyway. My hope was that a buck would simply come from the opposite direction I expected him to, which would mean the current wind direction would actually work in my favor.

As I sat in the stand that morning, I thought through the whole situation. I needed to make time for my wife. I also needed to get into my stand very early in the afternoon because the deer were there at three o'clock the day before. In addition, I knew I should focus more on my afternoon hunt as opposed to this morning hunt because this was primarily an evening setup. After considering all of these details, I got down around nine in the morning so that I could spend a few hours with my wife.

At noon, I left our house and headed back to my tree stand location. This was it. It was the final night of the regular season, which meant it was also my final night to hunt during the rut. Although I really hoped for a nice buck that year, I was now willing to shoot a small one in order to fill my tag. I just wanted to break the curse of never getting a buck from the woods behind my house after all those years of hunting there.

Time passed slowly, and I felt incredibly bored! No matter what happened, I devoted myself to sitting perfectly still and not using any deer calls. I believed that if God planned to give me a deer, I didn't need to do any calling.

Throughout the hunt, I closely observed my behavior and tendencies while feeling bored. My purpose in doing this was to become more familiar with these tendencies, so that I could more clearly recognize them when they happen in other situations in my life. Rather than let them compel me to do something I was not supposed to do, I would recall how it felt to overcome them in this hunting situation. I could then apply the same approach in overcoming them in other situations in my life.

As I sat there, I thought about how much I had given up that year in order to discern my prayer experience from the spring. If I didn't get a deer, then I would at least know I should not listen to that type of impression in the future. If I did get a buck, then the experience *might* have come from God. However, I would not make any definitive decisions until I had more experiences like it to compare it to.

Legal shooting hours ended a little after five o'clock. It was now approaching four, and I had been sitting perfectly still for three hours waiting on God. Let me tell you, it can be quite difficult to wait for God to act in your life at times!

At four o'clock, I heard something moving in the woods. I could tell it was not a squirrel, so I stood up and got ready. As I looked over the hilltop, I saw a buck cresting the hill. He was headed straight toward me. I immediately turned on the video camera, which was pointed at the opening where the big buck had walked the night before.

As the deer got closer, I twisted all around in the tree leaning back and forth trying to see if he had brow tines. I could see that he had forks on both sides, but I needed at least one more point for him to be legal. It turned out that he had two brow tines, which meant he was legal.

Eventually, I was able to draw back my bow. However, I wanted to wait until I knew he was in my camera angle before actually taking the shot. Before he went all the way into the middle of my shooting lane, he stopped and put his nose to the ground. His body was slightly quartering toward me, which is not my preferred angle.

I quickly began deliberating as to what I should do. If he continued on the path he was already headed, my shot options would only get worse. Although he was not standing in a preferable angle, I decided to take a shot so that it would definitely be on video. I then focused hard, calmed my muscles, aimed, and pulled the trigger on my mechanical release. The arrow soared through the air and clipped the buck's spine as it entered his body. This knocked him over. As you can see if you watch either of my videos, *Humble Beginnings Part Two* or *The Spirituality of Hunting*, the buck initially didn't move at all after he hit the ground. At that moment, I thought to myself, "Wow! That worked out well!" Unfortunately, the buck then started to flop around as he fought to get up. This surprised me.

The hill was so steep that the buck began to slide down the mountainside. After sliding ten yards, he landed in an erosion ditch and continued to flop around. It made me sad to see him suffer that way. Still, there was nothing I could do at that moment because he was behind a huge tree, and I couldn't shoot him again.

I waited until the buck stopped moving before focusing the video camera on him again because I didn't want to record his suffering. To my surprise, as soon as I began videoing him, he started flailing and struggling again. As the deer kicked, he continued to slide downhill. He was now about twenty-five yards from where I shot him. I had hoped that he was going to die quickly, but that obviously wasn't happening. When I realized this, I rapidly packed up my gear and climbed down the tree. Immediately upon reaching the ground, I grabbed my bow and went over to the buck.

The deer was lying perfectly still with his head down on the ground when I got to within fifteen yards of him. This caused me to think he had already passed away. However, when I made it to within ten yards of him, he picked his head up and looked straight at me. He had the same somber look of death on his face that the second seven-pointer had that I shot on Eric's farm. Without hesitating, I quickly drew my bow. The deer continued to look straight into my eyes. Sorrow filled my heart, and I said out loud, "I'm sorry!" I then pulled the trigger on my release and shot him through the heart.

The situation made me extremely sad. I couldn't stand there and watch the deer any longer so I walked back over to take my tree stand off of the tree. As I stood at my tree stand, I recorded a little commentary footage for my hunting video and then went back over to the deer.

Experiences like this one are very valuable. It keeps me humble and in touch with reality. Seeing an animal die a few feet away that I have killed can make me extremely sad, which reminds me to be very respectful of life. It also inspires me to not be wasteful of the deer's meat, or any animal that has been slaughtered so that I can continue to live.

I hope every hunter has at least one experience like this one. It is an important reminder that killing an animal should not be taken lightly. We also should not view hunting animals as just a game, entertainment, sport, or trophy. A deer is a living creature that dies for our sakes, and we should be respectful and grateful for that. I believe that letting these kinds of experiences positively transform our mindsets and attitudes is a necessary component of becoming a world-class hunter.

ALWAYS KNOW THE RULES

Even though Pennsylvania's bow hunting season for deer was now over, southern New York's season was open for another week. I decided to go up after church on Sunday afternoon to try harvesting another buck on video. I also planned to take the day off from work on Tuesday so that I could hunt all day in New York if I didn't get a buck on Sunday.

That Sunday afternoon was my first time back in New York since before I went to Illinois. I had no idea how hard the area had been pressured by other hunters while I was away but I was hoping it had not been overly bad. After arriving in New York, I went straight to the best spot I knew of. I had seen more deer in this one area than any of the others I had tried earlier in the season.

Near the end of the hunt I looked to my left and saw a buck slamming his head into some bushes. After standing and getting ready to shoot, I turned the video camera on and started videoing him. It disappointed me when he raised his head and I saw that he only had one spike. It was about seven inches long while the other one had been broken off.

The small buck thrashed the bushes for about five minutes and then began to limp toward me. The thoughts I had were, "What should I do? Should I shoot him? He looks injured. He may not make it through the winter if his injury is bad. Would the ethical decision be to use my tag on this deer even though he is much smaller than I was hoping for? My primary goals are to get hunting footage and fill my tag. I could accomplish both if I shoot him."

There were many thoughts that contested these. To start, I couldn't remember if it was permissible to shoot a spike in that area of New York. I had taken the New York's archery education course earlier that summer and remembered the instructor saying that some counties in New York started requiring a buck to have at least three points on one side of his rack before it could be harvested. I couldn't remember if that rule included the county I was in. I also didn't remember reading anything about it in the rule book. This was never a concern for me before, because I didn't plan on shooting anything less than an eight-pointer.

Aside from my concern with the antler restriction, it was getting late. I had forgotten to check the exact time shooting hours closed that day and I knew New York's hunting hours were different from Pennsylvania's. This meant that it could possibly be past legal shooting hours already even though I could still see well enough to video and shoot.

As this battle raged in my mind, the buck limped toward me and stood broadside in front of me just fifteen yards away. I had trouble making my decision until I recalled something a lady from church once told me. She said, "If you ever find yourself struggling to make a decision, the answer is almost always NO." Since I was struggling with this decision, I quickly said to myself, "No. I'm not doing it." I then put my bow down and videoed the buck for a little while until I decided to climb down.

On Tuesday, I drove back to New York and set up closer to where I had first spotted the spike on the previous hunt. As I sat in my tree stand thinking, I came to terms with something I had been in denial of. The truth was that I was really stretching myself thin. Even if I hit a deer and everything went smoothly that evening, I'd still have very little energy left for my Pennsylvania bear hunt the following morning. Taking on both hunts, and harvesting animals on both, would be too much for me to handle by myself. It simply would not be enjoyable for me to have to deal with all of that. While I sat there realizing this, my cell phone vibrated from an incoming text message. It was from my friend, John Ortlieb. The message said, "Tomorrow is your bear hunt. Get some practice in today and get a lot of rest."

The moment I read the message, I had an inner feeling that God was communicating to me through my friend's words. I simply knew I was getting a bear the next day. This helped me know that I should not have come on this hunt in New York. It was my good desire to make a hunting video, influenced by my greed for more footage, that motivated me to go to New York that day. As I sat in the tree thinking about this, I realized that if I trained myself to recognize these types of influences and behaviors quicker, I could save myself from wasting a lot of time and energy in the future. As with many of the other lessons I learned through hunting, I knew this one also applied to my everyday life situations. I finished the hunt that evening, but no deer came near me. As I left, I said, "Thank You, Lord for making my lesson clear."

THE BEAR HUNT

At 4:40 the following morning, I pulled the door closed behind me as I left my house for the first morning of the Pennsylvania archery bear season. It bothered me a little that I was already ten minutes behind my anticipated schedule. I quietly grabbed my climbing tree stand and walked through my back yard. The moment I stepped into the woods I heard a big animal run in the other direction. It was definitely a bear. I could tell by the sound of its soft pads on the leaves.

I quickly freed my right hand and switched my head lamp to the brightest setting. The bear was about sixty yards away before it stopped and looked back at me. As I watched it, I disappointingly thought to myself, "Oh man! I can't believe that!" This was the first time in my five years of hunting near my house that a bear was right behind my yard when I stepped into the woods. In my opinion, it was the absolute worst possible time for this to happen.

After looking in my direction for a few seconds, the bear started running away again. It stopped one more time and looked back before continuing up the hill. One of the biggest problems with this situation was that the bear was between me and where I was planning to go. This caused me to feel very distraught and discouraged. I then thought to myself, "What am I going to do now? If I keep going the way I was planning, I'll push the bear up and over the mountain. It may even scare all of the other bears off of the hill as it goes."

The wind was blowing from the south, which meant it was coming straight down the hill in my face. As I stood still paying attention to the wind, it shifted a little bit and blew from the southeast. This caused me to think to myself, "This is not good. The bear will wind me if I get up above him on the east side."

I stood there quickly deliberating in my mind what would be the best course of action. My final conclusion was to go through the woods toward the east along the base of the hill in the opposite direction from the crop fields where the other bears might be. My hope was that if any of the bears were still in the fields, they would not hear me climbing up the mountain if I was far enough away from them. I also hoped that they wouldn't smell me if I got up high enough in a tree even though the wind was blowing downhill. (Realistically, though, they still would have winded me anyway.)

Immediately after formulating this plan, I turned and went east along the base of the mountain. As I walked through the woods, I complained vigorously in my mind, thinking, "There is no way I will get that bear I saw. This is just not good. The wind is blowing the wrong way. I just can't believe that happened."

The above thoughts made me feel very negative, and I began to lose hope. After walking about a hundred and fifty yards, I turned and started climbing at an angle up the mountain toward the spot I had originally intended to go. The wind was still blowing in my face from the southeast. This detail continued to bother me, because it would take my scent straight down to the crop fields once I was in position.

The mountain is so steep where I was climbing that I could only walk about ten yards before having to stop and catch my breath. The difficult climb was even more challenging because of all the layers of clothing I had tied around my waist, the camera equipment over my shoulder, the tree stand strapped to my back, and the bow in my hand.

After hiking up the mountain a few hundred yards, I heard an extremely loud commotion about ten feet away from me. It was clearly a bear, and it sounded as if it was about to run me over! In a state of panic, I frantically reached up and turned my headlamp back to the brightest setting. This enabled me to see that it was in fact a bear! It was standing about twenty-five yards away from me at this point. I immediately thought to myself, "Man, I can't believe this! I can't even get to my spot and I keep jumping bears. There's no way I am ever going to get one if this keeps happening. I wonder if all of the bears are in the woods this morning rather than in the crop fields."

As these thoughts went through my mind, I realized that the bear had its front paws on a tree. With a spark of realization, I thought, "Wait a minute! It looks as if that bear is ready to go up that tree." Without thinking or hesitating, I ran at the bear as fast as I could. As soon as I did this, the bear hopped off the ground and climbed up the tree about five feet. Amazed, I immediately thought to myself, "Oh man, I can't believe it! I've got this bear treed!"

The bear climbed a little higher and hung onto the side of the tree about eight feet off of the ground. I was now standing about ten feet from the base of the tree. The bear probably only weighed about a hundred and fifty pounds at the most, which dramatically frightened me! In a panic-stricken state of mind, I thought, "This could be a second year cub, which means an angry mother could charge at me in the dark at any second!" (For those of you who may not already know, black bear cubs stay with their mother for two years before dispersing.)

The bear then started hissing and snorting at me. It would make three quick snorts, and then a groaning noise that sounded as if it was getting punched in the guts. While it made this groaning type noise, it simultaneously licked its lips. I assumed this behavior was an intimidation tactic, and it was working! I was very scared at that moment in time! In addition to this possibly being an intimidation noise, I also worried that it might be some way of alerting its overprotective mother.

After about three minutes of the bear hissing and making noises, it started to climb back down the tree toward me. I knew that my only chance of getting a bear at that point was to keep this one in the tree until daylight. As a result, I lunged at the base of the tree and waved my arms. The bear then paused and stopped climbing down. It was only around 5:15 in the morning and still totally dark. I realized that waving my arms was useless in the dark so I started to yell,

"Get up the tree! Get up that tree there!" The bear climbed back up to about eight feet off of the ground and continued to snort at me and make noises.

I was terrified. For a second, I thought of shooting the bear just to protect myself, but then I immediately thought, "No. Be ethical, Sean! Be ethical." Then another thought went through my mind, "Think about the video. If I wait until daylight, I may actually get this hunt on video." (Aside: I later thought that I could possibly even become the *first person in history* to ever video himself shooting a black bear with archery equipment in the State of Pennsylvania!)

While all of this was going on, I heard the soft padded steps of another bear up above me on the hill. It was only about fifty yards away. A feeling of terror immediately throttled my body. I reached for my hand-held flashlight and nocked an arrow on my string in case things got ugly. I kept one flashlight shining on the bear in the tree to see if he was coming down and I continuously shined the other light around the woods looking for the eyes of another bear coming at me.

There I was. It was the great faceoff. Who would win? Would I be able to last until daylight? Would I end up getting run off the mountain or mauled by a big mother bear? Or would this small bear simply force his way down off of the tree and run away before daylight arrived? What would happen?

Several more times the bear started to climb down the tree, but I made a bunch of noise by kicking the leaves and yelling, which kept him from coming all the way to the ground. As I looked up at the bear during this part of the hunt, I noticed that there was an extraordinary meteor shower occurring above us. Everywhere I could see across the sky was filled with shooting stars. Just as there was a unique star to accompany the birth of Jesus, I thought God was performing this cosmic sign as the birth of my hunting video and religious ministry were about to take place. In response, I said, "Thank You, Lord, but I can't exactly enjoy looking at that right now. I'm a little too busy being nervous about the bear situations here."

Twenty minutes had now passed. The bear continued to snort at me the entire time. Although I was afraid, I refused to give up my ground. At the same time, I was starting to get very cold. It was still about an hour before legal shooting light, and there was no way I was going to make it until daybreak if I didn't do something to keep warm. In response, I quickly put a few of the extra layers of clothes on that I had tied around my waist.

Meanwhile, the bear must have gotten tired of hanging onto the side of the tree because he finally climbed all the way up to the top and got comfortable in the branches. I quickly turned on my video camera at this point and videoed myself in the dark. I gave a brief commentary as to what was taking place and then turned the camera back off. Afterward, I hastily looked around for a place I could mount the video camera arm. I then strapped it to a nearby tree, attached the camera, and pointed it up toward the bear. All that was left for me to do was wait until daylight.

The whole experience was incredibly intense this far, and I couldn't keep it to myself any longer. As a result, I quickly took out my cell phone and sent a text message to my wife and hunting buddies.

Time seemed to move slowly. Even though it was an exciting opportunity, I was still afraid of another bear coming at me in the dark. For this reason, I started to sing church songs out loud to try to frighten them away as well as keep myself calm.

As I waited for daylight, a different feeling started to pervade within me. It was a somber feeling. My heart knew that the bear and I were in the process of waiting for its death, which made me sad. Instead of thinking about this feeling and letting it bother me, I did my best to ignore it. I knew this was not the most mature way to deal with my emotions, but that is how I chose to handle them in this situation. I knew that if I thought too much about killing the bear, I would not be able to do it. This would also mean I would not fulfill my hopes of getting a bear for my hunting video.

Periodically, I shined my light up into the tree to see what the bear was doing. His back legs were hanging over the side of the branch he was sitting on. Admittedly, the bottoms of his paws looked extremely adorable. The cuteness of the bear made the whole hunt all the more difficult.

My high school hunting buddy, John Ortlieb, then called me on the phone. It was now about fifteen minutes before daylight. He yelled, "Yo dude! What's going on? I got your text message!" I quickly told him the news. He was utterly shocked. He also told me to get ready, because once it became daylight the bear would probably get very nervous. I thanked him for his input and then got off the phone. I also felt it was fitting for him to call and be part of the hunt since he was the one who sent me the text message the day before when I was in New York.

After the sky turned blue from the rising sun, I turned the video camera on and gave a quick commentary as to what was happening. To my dismay, the camera battery was about to die, and I was almost at the end of the videotape that was in the camera. (It was an old camera that recorded onto film tape as opposed to a digital storage device.) Being almost out of video tape motivated me to talk very quickly and then turn the camera back off to wait for better daylight. At the same time, I was bothered with myself for not checking those details before leaving for the hunt.

John was exactly right. As soon as the bear could see me, he started to panic. I no longer looked like a bright light in the woods, but a human being wearing fluorescent orange. As a result, the bear was constantly moving and swaying in the branches. It also started snorting profusely again. I looked down at my watch to see what time it was. It was five minutes past the opening of legal shooting hours. I was trying to wait as long as I could to make sure I had adequate light for the video camera and to make it perfectly clear that the bear was harvested during legal shooting light.

The intensity of the bear's movements continued to escalate, and I knew I needed to act soon. In my mind, I thought, "It's time to shoot! This bear is getting ready to do something!" The base of the tree was a few yards in front of me. My arms and body suddenly began to shake from the adrenaline that began to pulsate through my veins as I thought about taking a shot. I drew back my bow and slowly started to raise my left arm in order to take aim. My arm wasn't even half way up in the air when it began to get difficult to raise the bow any farther. "This is going to be more difficult than I expected," I thought to myself. When my arm was finally pointing straight up at the bear, I became even more concerned about the shot. It never occurred to me that while holding the bow vertically upward at full draw I would not be able to use my normal anchor point. Instead, my release hand was about an inch beyond its normal anchor location because of the angle of my arms. I then asked myself, "What am I going to do?"

The bear continued to move around snorting and making noises. His position did not offer me a clear shot at the vitals at first. Fortunately, he pivoted and faced straight down the tree at me. The next set of words that went through my mind were, "It's now or never." To the best of my ability, I lined up my pins through my peep sight and hoped for the best. The sound of the shot went off, and my arrow crashed into the bear. Before I even knew what was happening, the bear yelled and practically fell half way down the tree before grabbing on and stopping itself. "He didn't like that! Here he comes," I frantically thought to myself. I quickly yanked another arrow from my quiver and nocked it on the string.

The bear held onto the tree for a moment and then started climbing down with his tail-end first. I sized up his speed, drew back, and held steady about six feet above the ground. At that moment, the image of the four-point buck I shot prematurely along the fence row in college flashed through my mind. If you will recall, I got so excited in that hunt that I released the arrow before the deer's vitals were all the way out from behind the tree. I never found the deer as a result of my premature shot.

With that experience in my mind, I forcefully repeated in my thoughts, "Patience... Patience... Be patient!" As I watched the bear's body travel through my peep sight, I repeated the word, "Patience... Patience... Patience." I did this to encourage myself to overcome my excitement and compulsion to shoot early. The intensity of the moment escalated. I needed to refrain from pulling the release trigger until his lungs had reached my sight pin. It seemed like an eternity was passing as I waited for the perfect moment to shoot, yet in reality it was only a matter of seconds.

Eventually, my time arrived, and my *second shot* rattled through the air. It made a thunder clap as it smashed into the side of the bear. The bear then let out a slight roar, crashed to the ground, and took off running. He definitely looked injured by the labored appearance of his run. I quickly reached down and yanked up on the video camera handle to get footage of the bear running away. However, by the time I got the camera focused on the bear, he had already fallen over onto his back.

The bear then began to let out a death moan. This is exactly what the bear in Canada did after I shot it with the rifle back when I was seventeen. At any rate, as the Pennsylvania bear moaned, an intense sadness consumed my soul. This feeling of sadness was even worse than how I felt the week before when I shot the six-pointer in the spine and then had to shoot him again at close range.

It took all my strength to keep from crying as the bear continued to let out the sad moan of helplessness and death. At that point in time, blood began to fill his lungs, and the moans became gurgled from the fluid. When this happened, I said out loud on video, "That is sad right there, folks. That is not exciting at all." The emotional sadness and pain I felt at that moment was so great that I didn't think I would ever be able to hunt for black bear again.

AFTER THE SHOT

After shooting the bear, I filmed a commentary of what happened. When my sadness finally started to pass, I called John Ortlieb. His voice mail picked up, so I left him a message. While I walked over to the tree the bear had been in, John Thomas called me. I figured he had just gotten the text message I sent earlier. As soon as I answered the phone, John said, "Tell me what's going on!" At that moment, a burst of excitement exploded from within me. In response, I yelled, "I just shot a Pennsylvania black bear with my bow!"

Telling John about the hunt over the phone ranked as one of the most exciting moments of my hunting career, and the excitement did not come from killing the animal. It came from getting to share the experience with someone who cares about hunting, someone who knows how incredibly difficult it is to get a Pennsylvania black bear with a bow, and who also is a close friend of mine. This helped me understand that my enjoyment in hunting doesn't necessarily come from killing. It comes from *sharing the experience* with others. It comes from the closeness it creates between me and my family members and friends. I also realized that when there is no one to share my hunts with, although I may feel somewhat happy when I am successful, I typically don't feel the intense joy I've experienced when sharing the hunt with someone I know and care about.

After getting off the phone with John Thomas, I started looking around on the ground for the first arrow that hit the bear. I knew it was on the ground in that area because I saw it drop out of the tree shortly after it hit the bear. You can actually see this arrow come out of the bear on the video if you know where to look at the time of the shot.

It didn't take much searching for me to find the arrow. However, I was surprised to see that it was broken off at the fletching and that

there was virtually no blood on the shaft.

Upon walking around to the other side of the tree, I saw part of the second arrow lying on the ground. This surprised me because I expected the second shot to have passed completely through the bear in one piece and I thought I was going to have trouble finding that arrow. Instead, it was broken completely in half, and I imagined that the other half was still inside the bear's chest cavity.

Blood covered the forest floor from where I was standing all the way over to the bear. It only ran twenty-two yards. While videoing the whole event, I slowly walked over to the bear. I then touched the bears head with the edge of my bow to make sure he was dead. Then I videoed his body.

After setting the camera on the ground, I turned the bear over. The first thing I did was look at the front of his chest to see where the first shot hit him. The fur was thick, and I couldn't see the point of entry, so I just started videoing some commentary, explaining the background to the hunt. I told the whole story of how I saw this bear the week before and really wanted to get him for two reasons. One was because I loved his personality. The other reason was that he only weighed about a hundred and thirty pounds which was a manageable weight for me to handle on my own.

It was not until after I finished my long commentary that I realized this was not the same bear I had seen the week before. Although it was the same body size and it had a black snout, it was not missing the two inch patch of hair over its right shoulder. I made this discovery just as I finished telling the lengthy story of how this was the bear I had seen before. As a result, I later had to edit the whole story out of that segment, which makes me laugh when I think about it now.

There is also something else that I think is funny about that video commentary segment. Just as I finished talking, I looked down at the bear's head. What I saw took me completely by surprise. There was a three-blade broadhead cut on the side of the bear's head next to his eye, yet it was completely clean. There was no sign of any blood, which gave me the impression that the cut was a few days old. At first, I thought, "Wow, someone recently shot this bear with an arrow!" I then realized the cut was from *my* broadhead. This meant that I hit him almost a foot away from where I was aiming with my first shot. This also meant that I was very blessed and fortunate to have hit the bear at all! In the video, you can actually see me do a double take of the bear's head when I initially notice the broadhead cut. It happens at the very end of the commentary just before I put his head down on the ground at the end the segment.

There is still something else that I found interesting to note about this hunt. My first shot had hit the side of the bear's head. It barely made it under his skin and didn't penetrate his skull. The arrow proceeded to go through his neck muscle and then between his shoulder and ribcage without entering the chest cavity. It then exited out the top of his shoulder. The arrow never hit anything vital at all. As a result, the first shot did nothing more than stun the bear. If I wouldn't have gotten the *second shot*, I never would have gotten the bear. As a result, I had to thank God for *second chances*!

Dragging the bear out of the woods went even better than I expected. It was truly a blessing from God. There were so many leaves on the forest floor, and the hill was so steep where the bear died, that I was able to slide him all the way down the mountain with tremendous ease. In fact, I was even able to carry all of my hunting and video equipment with me as I drug him down the mountainside. I appreciated being able to do this so that I didn't have to hike up and down the steep slope multiple times in order to get everything out of the woods.

When I got to within thirty yards of the bottom of the hill, I left the bear and went to my house. After putting all the video and hunting equipment down, I got my game cart and went back to the bear. I set the cart up on the other side of a blown down tree trunk that I had to hoist the bear over. This was the hardest part of the entire drag, yet it still was not that difficult. The bear went easily onto the cart. I strapped him down, and then wheeled him back to my house. The ease of this retrieval reminded me of all the times I had harvested deer and felt as if God's providence was there helping me and making it easy for me.

What did I learn from this hunt? One of the most significant lessons was actually just a reminder of something God had taught me in the past. The lesson had to do with my *attitude* and my faith in God and what I believed He was going to do for me. So many times in my life I have complained and grumbled because things were not working out the way I wanted or expected. Instead of complaining, I should have simply trusted that God had a plan and that it was all going to work out for the best.

This hunt was a perfect example of that. I believed God wanted me to get a bear but I thought He wanted me to get it where I had seen them the week before. What I didn't realize while the hunt was unfolding was that God was only using the original bear sightings from the previous week to start me *in the right direction*. If I hadn't seen those bears, I never would have chosen to hunt right behind my house in the first place.

On the morning of the hunt, when I entered the woods behind my house, I actually pushed a bear. This caused me to walk way off course from my originally intended travel pattern. In actuality, this was God's way of making sure I went to the right area. However, as I headed in that direction, I stopped trusting God and started complaining vigorously. I thought my entire plan had been ruined and that there was no chance I was going to get a bear. As you can see, I was wrong. This realization has inspired me to not let seemingly adverse situations, or my own negative thoughts or feelings, influence me to doubt or lose hope.

This whole hunt was a reminder that sometimes things simply don't happen the way I want or expect in life. However, from situations like this one, I know I can view seemingly negative situations as the possible work of God getting me to the right place at just the right time. Essentially, I know I can always remain calm and *trust* that things are going to work out for the best, because I know God has a plan for me. He is simply leading me to the place I need to be in order to fulfill that plan. All it takes is for me to remain calm and trust in Him, and I know things will all work out for the best! I encourage you to maintain the same mindset and to use this hunt as a helpful reminder when challenging situations come your way.

CONCLUSION

There have been many things I have learned through my years of hunting. Some of the lessons have been on a practical level and others on a spiritual level. Practically speaking, the hunt begins with your preparation. If you do not prepare properly, your chances of harvesting an animal will majorly decrease. In fact, lack of preparation leaves too much of the hunt to chance or luck, and a world-class hunter focuses much more on developing and mastering his or her own skills as opposed to just relying on getting lucky.

Pre-hunt preparations begin with practice. Your equipment should be well tuned, and you should have a great level of confidence that your shot will hit where you aim. Even after the season starts, you should continue to practice at least a few shots a day if possible. This is important, because your equipment can get damaged in the field as you have observed from some of my hunts. If you do not practice, you are also susceptible to forgetting important aspects of your shot. The end result may be decreased accuracy, which can lead to a loss of confidence in your own abilities. This can also lead to missing or injuring an animal instead of harvesting it. With that in mind, you don't just owe it to yourself to be as prepared as possible, you also owe it to the animals you hunt.

The next important phase of preparation is controlling your human scent. I prefer to utilize scent elimination soaps and deodorants for my body and clothing. In addition, I store my hunting clothes in a scent free environment such as an odorless plastic bag. I also sometimes utilize scent eliminating sprays to help cut down on odor. Although I have at times used clothing that claims to hold in human scent, I do not rely on them to totally conceal me from a game animal's nose. Instead, I focus my attention on monitoring the wind direction.

Using the wind to your advantage is one of the absolute most important components of hunting most big game animals. The reason is that the greatest defense against predators that most big game animals have is their sense of smell. Even if you have taken every precaution possible to eliminate or control your human odor, I encourage you to hunt as though every big game animal will smell you anyway. Allow this to motivate you to always use the wind to your utmost advantage. Do everything you can to enter your hunting area from the downwind side of where you think the animals will be. Also, try to position yourself on the downwind side of their food sources and primary travel trails.

When hunting over a scrape, always be mindful that a buck is most likely to approach from the downwind side. In addition, wise animals will circle downwind of your location when you call to them. The only time I have seen bucks not follow this protocol is when they have been snort-wheezed at. The snort-wheeze sometimes gets them so mad and territorial that they will come straight to you looking for a fight regardless of the wind direction.

Keep in mind that if you are blindly calling to deer without seeing or hearing them first, they may circle downwind of you without you even knowing it. You may not see anything at all during that hunt, and could also be ruining your spot without even knowing it, if you blind call when the wind is blowing in the wrong direction. For this reason, I prefer to wait until I see a deer that is not downwind of me before I try calling.

Be very careful about leaving human scent behind after hunting an area. This involves every single tree or object you touch and every time your foot comes in contact with the ground. Even if you are like me, and make every effort to eliminate human odor on your clothes and footwear prior to entering the woods, try to walk in and out of your hunting area from a direction that the deer will not travel frequently or at least will not cross until after you have had a chance to shoot. Even if you are not there when they pass through your hunting area, if they smell that you've been there, they may not come back, which is why I suggest walking in and out of the woods through a place where they may not step over.

Also, pay close attention to the topography and obstacles in your area. Not only should you try to determine the exact yardage to potential shot opportunities *before* an animal comes to within range, you also need to be mindful of how the animals will react to obstructions in their travel patterns. Expect deer to stop and look around before hopping over a fence, a blown down tree, or going through a ditch. Try to position your stand on the side of the obstacle that will give you a shot opportunity *before* the animal crosses.

Now that I have touched on some of the practical aspects of hunting, I'd like to transition and address some of the spiritual and ethical components of hunting. First of all, it is my experience that hunting provides us with an amazing opportunity to develop our prayer life. In fact, it has been easier for me to *test* my prayer experiences and enhance my ability to notice God's activity in my life through hunting than through any other format I have tried.

When I first started praying while hunting, I wasn't exactly sure what to do, so I applied a concept I had heard from various Christian sources. The concept was to ask God for something and then believe in "faith" that He will grant it. Every time I did that, I applied my whole heart, mind, soul, and strength to perfectly performing my prayer of faith. You may recall that it always left me feeling mentally and emotionally exhausted. One example of this is recorded in the section titled, "Keep Working on It." In that situation, I begged God for two straight hours to give me a deer. Initially, I didn't understand why God hadn't granted my request. Later that day, I discovered that my arrow rest had been moved without me realizing it. This meant that my arrows no longer hit where I was aiming. For this reason, it was wise for God to not give me what I asked for, because I would have only injured or missed the animal.

A very similar thing happened to me during the hunt I recorded in the section titled, "Don't Lie." You may recall that I begged God to give me a big buck the whole time I was in the woods hunting. I also believed in faith that He would answer my prayer. After exiting the woods, I discovered I was unknowingly hunting in an illegal area. If I had gotten a deer, I could have also gotten in serious trouble! As a result, I was very grateful I did not receive what I asked for in prayer!

These types of experiences have helped me see that God always has a good reason for what He does. He may not grant my prayer request because of important factors I am not aware of. As a result, I stopped allowing myself to get upset if I didn't immediately get the things I asked God for. Instead, I simply trusted that there was a very good reason for it, and that God had my best interest in mind. I also applied this same exact concept in my everyday life experiences and found that it brought me a tremendous amount of peace in situations that previously left me feeling annoyed or frustrated when I didn't get what I wanted.

As a result of these lessons, I realized that the "prayer of faith" approach that I learned from various Christian preachers is simply incorrect. I may never have discovered this had it not been for hunting. In fact, there are many people in the world today who have not figured this out, which is why they still use and teach this approach to prayer. However, since I realized that it was not the right way to pray—because it did not take all of the unseen factors into consideration—I also realized I needed to search for a more effective way to pray. Once again, I turned to my hunting experiences in order to help me figure out how to do that.

Rather than only ask God to give me what I thought I wanted, I started asking Him questions like, "Lord, am I going to get a deer (or whatever animal I am hunting)? Where am I going to get a deer? When am I going to get a deer? What do You want to say to me through this hunt? What do you want me to learn through this hunt?" Immediately after I'd say these types of prayers, I'd listen and observe the thoughts and images that came into my mind. I also paid attention to the emotions, feelings, and inspirations I experienced in my soul. When I thought God was directly saying something in response to one of my prayers, *I tested it* against the outcome of the hunt. Doing this time and time again has helped me see when it was just my own wishful thinking (or perhaps even negative thoughts and feelings) that prompted my perceived responses. I have also been able to see more clearly when in fact it has been God who inspired the message. Developing my familiarity with these differences has enabled me to apply the same concepts in my everyday life, which has made a positive difference for me.

Turning to Scripture, I pulled from the example of Jesus to learn how to pray in situations when I did in fact want to make a direct request for a deer. If you will recall, when Jesus was in the garden the night he was betrayed, He prayed, "Father, take this cup from Me, yet not My will but Your will be done" (Luke22:42). With that in mind, I now sometimes pray, "Lord, please let me get a deer, yet not my will but Your will be done." In this way, I express my desire, but also leave room for God to do what is best for me in my life. In that respect, although things may sometimes seem bleak, as it did for Jesus during His passion and death, I know that there will ultimately be good things ahead, just as Jesus rose from the dead on the third day.

Unfortunately, when I was younger, I missed all of the wonderful messages and lessons God was giving me though my hunts, because my focus was strictly on getting a big buck and on making a hunting video. Thankfully, I am now paying closer attention to what God is teaching me. For example, in the situation I recounted in the section titled, "Don't Lie," I didn't intend to lie. I didn't want to do the wrong thing, but I did. After it was over, I was able to look at myself and ask, "Why did I do that?" Asking this question enabled me to realize that my sinful response was not a premeditated choice. It was an insecure reaction. My fear of getting in trouble compelled me to react, and I lied without thinking. After seeing this weakness in my personality, I was able to consciously work on it. I then spent every moment of every single day for a month consciously watching and waiting for situations like that to happen. Every time something happened that made me feel afraid in that way, I intentionally kept my mouth shut until I overcame the feeling of fear. I then forced myself to tell the truth.

Once again, I am grateful I had that hunting experience because it helped me realize I needed to actively and intentionally train myself to change that aspect of my personality. I believe that this type of growth and maturation can only come from intense, conscious effort. Individuals who never become aware of these types of shortcomings within themselves may never apply themselves to grow the way you and I are able to as a result of the insights we gain through our hunting experiences.

Another important realization I made as I matured as a hunter is that none of us can take our trophy animals with us when we die. Ultimately, the only things we take with us are our personality and our relationships with God and other people. This awareness changed my focus while hunting. I no longer obsess over getting a record-book animal, because I could die tomorrow. Instead, I focus on making ethical choices and watching for God to speak to me through my hunts. If I happen to be blessed with a large buck while I am out there then I consider it to be a delightful bonus.

That being said, I admit that I used to wish that all of my hunting videos had many big bucks on them. My reason for desiring this was partly that I wanted to impress other people. Eventually, I let go of that desire and embraced the fact that it is the messages in those videos that are important and not the size of the animals harvested.

Aside from the educational and spiritual messages I've given in my hunting videos, I've also given the unspoken message of persevering in working toward your dreams, goals, and the things you believe God is calling you to do. We must never give up. This detail is revealed by the fact that it took me *fourteen years* to make my very first video. It finally came together because I didn't give up even though it didn't come easily and I had to do a lot of it on my own. In addition, I gave that video to the world even though it wasn't what I was originally hoping it would be.

Another important message that I've been able to give is that we should focus on the joy we share with others through hunting as opposed to just the size of the animals we shoot. This was especially evident in the very first deer I ever harvested on video, which was a little spike. It took John and me weeks of hardship and hard work to capture that hunt. By no means was it a big buck, but it made us incredibly *happy*. Remembering the feeling of joy that John and I shared that day is far more powerful than the feeling I get when I sit on my couch and look at my biggest buck hanging lifelessly on the wall. If you remove the components of sharing the experience with other people, as well as achieving a hard sought after goal, the whole event seems almost pointless. For this reason, I encourage you to not look down on others if they do not shoot a deer that meets up to your standards. Instead, focus on enjoying the experience with them!

When it comes to the ethical component of hunting, we should make sure to focus on caring about the animals we hunt as a top priority. Unfortunately, there were times when I cared more about money than the animals. As a result, I caused some of them to suffer simply because I didn't want to spend money on more arrows and broadheads. I'm glad I now put the animals first, and I don't hesitate to take extra shots if and when I need to! I hope you do the same.

We also need to realize that ethics involves much more than just caring about the animals we hunt. Ultimately, we should expect God to *test us* and give us opportunities to learn how our thoughts and emotions can influence us to make unethical choices. These tests are fairly easy to detect if we are paying attention, because there is a clear set of rules in hunting, just as there is a clear set of commandments that God calls us to live by. It is typically other people's bad influences and/or our own fallen thoughts and emotions that compel us to willingly sin and disobey God's commands or go against the rules in hunting. Thankfully, we can use our experiences in hunting to help us learn how to detect and overcome these shortcomings and temptations. We can then take that training with us into our everyday life and grow in righteousness and ethical living!

With these ideas in mind, I think you and I have an unbelievable opportunity to become extremely holy people by applying the lessons God teaches us through hunting in all of our other life experiences. I don't know about you, but that thought alone really excites me! As part of this, I think we need to lead other people by our good examples. I think we should seek to teach them how to recognize these kinds of behaviors in their own lives just as we have learned to notice them in our own.

When I look at my life and my hunting in this way, I am amazed and edified by the incredible growth potential it gives me along with the positive impact I can have on the world around me as a result of it. It is my hope that every hunter will someday view world-class hunters as people who do much more than just harvest record-book animals. I think world-class hunters grow and mature as individuals through their hunting experiences. I believe world-class hunters are also constantly striving to develop their prayer life through hunting experiences. In addition, the lessons they learn in the woods help them deepen their care and respect for other people, for the animals they hunt, the environment they live in, and for God Himself.

When our lives come to an end, I hope you and I will be able to look our God in the eyes and know with sincere hearts that we truly lived as world-class hunters, because I believe a world-class hunter and an ethically righteous and wholesome person are one in the same!

ABOUT THE AUTHOR

Sean McVeigh is an author and educator who currently offers guest speaking services throughout the country at hunting clubs, sportsmen dinners, fund raisers, trade shows, churches, schools, and other organizations. He also provides educational videos on his websites. Wherever Sean speaks or teaches, he strives to be realistic, down to earth, helpful, and inspiring. For more information regarding Sean's endeavors, visit his Internet websites at, SeansOutdoorAdventures.com, McVeighMinistries.com, or CatholicGuestSpeaker.com. He also welcomes your support through sharing his books and videos with others. May God bless you and your loved ones throughout this life on earth.

NOTES – These blank pages are for you to make notes if you like.

Lightning Source UK Ltd.
Milton Keynes UK
UKHW021954030120
356334UK00007B/1738/P